THE WORKS OF SHAKESPEARE

EDITED FOR THE SYNDICS OF THE
CAMBRIDGE UNIVERSITY PRESS

BY

JOHN DOVER WILSON

OTHELLO

EDITED BY

ALICE WALKER

AND

JOHN DOVER WILSON

Richard Burbage

OTHELLO

CAMBRIDGE
AT THE UNIVERSITY PRESS
1957

PUBLISHED BY
THE SYNDICS OF THE CAMBRIDGE UNIVERSITY PRESS

London Office: Bentley House, N.W. 1
American Branch: New York

Agents for Canada, India, and Pakistan: Macmillan

Printed in Great Britain at the University Press, Cambridge
(Brooke Crutchley, University Printer)

CONTENTS

THE FRONTISPIECE IS REPRODUCED BY PERMISSION OF
DULWICH COLLEGE FROM A PAINTING OF RICHARD
BURBAGE BY AN UNKNOWN ARTIST HANGING IN THE
DULWICH GALLERY, AND PROBABLY ONCE THE PROPERTY
OF EDWARD ALLEYN, FOUNDER OF THE COLLEGE, AND
BURBAGE'S RIVAL AS A TRAGIC ACTOR.

PREFATORY NOTE

Though this edition of *Othello* is the joint-product of Dr Alice Walker and myself, she has generously shouldered a good three-quarters of the burden by making herself responsible for the preparation of the text together with everything in the volume that comes after the text, leaving the introduction to me. Once we had made our drafts, however, they were exchanged and criticized freely. The Notes and Glossary, indeed, passed to and fro between us more than once, and readers will observe that we were not always able to find agreement even then. Textual scholars will also remark that the conclusions of the Note on the Copy, which is by right Dr Walker's alone, do not entirely tally with those reached by Sir Walter Greg in his recently published *The Shakespeare First Folio*. Such differences of opinion are in fact inevitable in the existing state of textual research, especially when dealing with a play like *Othello* where the origin and character of one of the two substantive texts can only be guessed at. Nevertheless, I believe Dr Walker has here succeeded in giving us a far cleaner text than that printed by any previous editor. And for myself it has been an exhilarating and encouraging experience to collaborate, after thirty-five years of editorial endeavour, with one whose masterly handling of textual problems is matched by so sensitive an appreciation of the aesthetic issues involved. Her next undertaking for 'The New Shakespeare' will be an even more difficult one—*Troilus and Cressida*.

Finally, the thanks of us both are due to Mr J. C. Maxwell for unfailing helpfulness.

J.D.W.

INTRODUCTION

I. *The Moor*

Shakespeare wrote two plays about Venice, the comedy or tragi-comedy of *The Merchant of Venice* and *The Tragedy of Othello, the Moor of Venice*, the most conspicuous figure in both being an alien. Shylock is a despised outcast from the ghetto; Othello a distinguished general of the republic, honoured by the council of state, and trusted by the senators; yet isolation from the society of Venice is insisted upon in both cases. With Othello, indeed, it is kept constantly before our eyes on the stage from first to last by the mere fact that he is black. And whatever facial characteristics the actor who plays him may possess or assume, Bradley was undoubtedly correct in his belief that Shakespeare intended us to think of him as a Negro.[1] That is what 'Moor' meant to Englishmen in the Middle Ages and at the time of Elizabeth and James. Roderigo's contemptuous reference to 'the thick-lips' may be prejudiced evidence, but it should at least have warned nineteenth-century producers and their successors that to present the Moor of Venice as a bronzed and semitic-featured Arabian prince might seriously disfeature the play. We are not told how Othello's hair grows but we learn that Aaron 'the Moor' in *Titus Andronicus* is not only 'coal-black' and 'thick-lipped' but has a 'fleece of woolly hair', while in *The Merchant of Venice* (3. 5. 35–6) Negro and Moor are treated as identical terms. For me, however, the crowning proof of Othello's race is that I once had the good fortune to see him played by a Negro—that great African gentle-

---

[1] A. C. Bradley, *Shakespearean Tragedy*, pp. 198–202.

man with the golden voice, Paul Robeson;[1] and I felt I was seeing the tragedy for the first time, not merely because of Robeson's acting, which despite a few petty faults of technique was magnificent,[2] but because the fact that he was a true Negro seemed to floodlight the whole drama. Everything was slightly different from what I had previously imagined; new points, fresh nuances, were constantly emerging; and all had, I felt, been clearly intended by the author. The performance convinced me in short that a Negro Othello is essential to the full understanding of the play.

The marriage between an African with a 'sooty bosom' and an Italian girl with 'whiter skin than snow' sets the racial problem in its extremest form, and most of Act I is given to bringing this out. We see it reflected first in the foul mind and disgusting language of Iago, next in the despairing horror of Desdemona's father who feels that such an unnatural union can only be explained by depravity in the girl or witchcraft on the part of her black seducer. Othello's colour was no bar to promotion, otherwise he could not have commanded the armies; and not all his officers shared Iago's contempt for it, since Cassio was even prepared to further his courtship with 'the divine Desdemona'.[3] Yet when Emilia, at a later stage, speaks her mind and calls

---

[1] At the Savoy on 19 May 1930, the first night; Maurice Browne, who played Iago, being an old friend of Cambridge days.

[2] See A. C. Sprague (*Shakespearian Players and Performances*, 1954, p. 1) for the impression Robeson made upon American audiences in New York and elsewhere with his performances in 1943. See also R. Withington ('Shakespeare and Race Prejudice' in *Elizabethan Studies in honour of G. F. Reynolds*, Colorado, 1945); who cites other evidence to the same effect, though not himself believing that Shakespeare had a Negro in mind.   [3] 3. 3. 94–100.

Othello a 'black devil' and Desdemona's 'most filthy bargain'[1] we cannot doubt that she speaks the mind of many an Englishwoman in the seventeenth-century audience. If anyone imagines that England at that date was unconscious of the 'colour-bar' they cannot have read *Othello* with any care.[2] And only those who have not read the play at all could suppose that Shakespeare shared the prejudice, inasmuch as Othello is his noblest soldier and he obviously exerted himself to represent him as a spirit of the rarest quality. How significant too is the entry he gives him! After listening for 180 lines of the opening scene to the obscene suggestions of Roderigo and Iago and the cries of the outraged Brabantio we find ourselves in the presence of one, not only rich in honours won in the service of Venice, and fetching his 'life and being from men of royal siege',[3] but personally a prince among men. Before such dignity, self-possession and serene sense of power, racial prejudice dwindles to a petty stupidity; and when Othello has told the lovely story of his courtship, and Desdemona has in the Duke's Council-chamber, simply and without a moment's hesitation, preferred her black husband to her white father, we have to admit that the union of these two grand persons,

---

[1] 5. 2. 134, 160. The Devil, now for some reason become red, was black in the medieval and post-medieval world. Thus 'Moors' had 'the complexion of a devil' (*Merchant of Venice*, 1. 2. 125).

[2] Withington, *op. cit.* disputes this but ignores the sentiments of Iago, Roderigo and Emilia. See also E. E. Stoll, *Othello* (1915), pp. 45–6, and K. L. Little, *Negroes in Britain* (1947), pp. 195–6.

[3] An important point, when considering the play in the light of modern opinion, which is apt to think of Negroes as either the descendants of slaves or members of illiterate and poverty-stricken African tribes.

so far from being unnatural, is that rare human event, the marriage of true minds and a real love-match.

Yet the difference in their complexions, and the atmosphere of colour-prejudice that attaches itself to it, cause both the shipwreck of the marriage and the tragedy that follows. How absurd, one often hears it said or reads it written, is the jealousy of Othello! Surely he might have trusted Desdemona a little? Shakespeare, as we shall see, moulded his plot in order to meet this very criticism. The point here, however, is that the trustfulness and simplicity, which Bradley among others notes[1] as Othello's, seem his by nature, when he is played by a Negro gifted with all the winning integrity of that race. As Iago contemptuously boasts,

> The Moor is of a free and open nature
> That thinks men honest that but seem to be so,
> And will as tenderly be led by th'nose
> As asses are—   (1. 3. 397–400)

lines which may be said to sum up the relations between African and European for the past three and a half centuries.

Finally, the primitive yet dignified spirit which a Negro Othello brings to the play accounts at once for the mingled tenderness and ferocity of the murder-scene and the priest-like attitude in which he addresses himself to the sacrifice. Never too shall I forget the radiant bliss of Robeson's face as Othello first greeted Desdemona at Cyprus or its dreadful deformation when he became possessed with the 'green-eyed monster'.

[1] Bradley, *op. cit.* p. 190.

II. *Date and Source*

Most students now agree that *Othello* follows *Hamlet* in the chronological order of Shakespeare's plays. Bradley stresses their 'similarities of style, diction and versification', and even detects 'a certain resemblance in the subjects'. 'The heroes of the two plays', he remarks, 'are doubtless extremely unlike, so unlike that each could have dealt without much difficulty with the situation which proved fatal to the other; but still each is a man exceptionally noble and trustful, and each endures the shock of a terrible disillusionment.'[1] Furthermore, though *Hamlet* is the most discursive and leisurely of Shakespeare's tragedies, and *Othello* the tensest and swiftest, they have much the same atmosphere. That of *Hamlet*, as Caroline Spurgeon first pointed out, is one of corruption, which Wolfgang Clemen later showed may be traced to the leperous disease that invades the body of Hamlet's father after his poisoning in the orchard. For, he says,

this now becomes the *leit-motiv* of the imagery: the individual occurrence is expanded into a symbol for the central problem of the play. The corruption of land and people throughout Denmark is understood as an imperceptible and irresistible process of poisoning.[2]

It seems possible that what primarily attracted Shakespeare's attention to the Othello story was that he saw it as a particular example of such 'an imperceptible and irresistible process of poisoning' at work upon a character of exceptional nobility, corrupting his very soul and dragging him down from the height of human happiness to the gates of Hell itself. The 'dram of evil',

---

[1] Bradley, *op. cit.* p. 175.
[2] Wolfgang Clemen, *The Development of Shakespeare's Imagery*, p. 113.

administered by Iago, douts for a while 'all the noble substance' in his victim; Iago himself pictures the operation as a process of poisoning; and when he says

> I'll pour this pestilence into his ear,
>
> (2. 3. 349)

he seems to carry us back to the garden at Elsinore and Claudius pouring his leperous distilment into the ears of a sleeping brother.

These symptoms of affinity are borne out by external evidence of a close proximity, evidence mostly discovered or established within recent years. The earliest reference, for example, we have to *Othello* is an entry in one of the annual accounts of the Office of Revels which records the performance on Hallowmas Day (i.e. 1 November) 1604 by the King's Majesty's players (i.e. Shakespeare's company) 'in the Banketinge house att Whit Hall' of a play 'called The Moor of Venis', written by a poet whose name the official, evidently no theatre-goer, writes as 'Shaxberd'.[1] But this performance is the first of a number recorded in the Accounts between 1 November 1604 and Lent, 1605, including early plays by Shakespeare such as *The Comedy of Errors*, *Love's Labour's Lost*, and *The Merchant of Venice* which King James and Queen Anne, newly arrived in England, had not yet seen. It by no means follows, therefore, that *Othello* was a new play at this time. Indeed, the 'bad quarto' of *Hamlet*, published in 1603, sometime after 19 May,[2] contains four or five echoes from it, which suggest that the pirate-

---

[1] Though probably known to Malone and printed as long ago as 1842 these Revels' Accounts were suspected of being a forgery until their final authentication in 1930 by A. E. Stamp. See his *Disputed Revels Accounts reproduced in collotype facsimile*.

[2] Greg, *Bibliography of the English Drama*, i. 197.

player or players, responsible for this memorial recon-
struction, had been acting in *Othello* not long before.
Further, in Part 1 of Dekker and Middleton's *Honest
Whore*, published in 1604 and certainly written before
14 March, Hippolito, accused of murdering Infelice,
is described as 'more sauage than a barbarous Moore',
which sounds very like a reference to Othello.[1] The
play, then, can hardly be later than early 1603, and
may even belong to 1602; and that would bring it
close to *Hamlet* which Edmund Chambers places in
the summer or autumn of 1601 in his final review of
the matter.[2] This dating accords, moreover, with
passages in the play which some have explained
as echoes of books published in 1601 and read by
Shakespeare.

What he read for the plot itself, however, was the
seventh *novella* of the third *deca* or decade of stories in
the *Hecatommithi* by Giraldi Cinthio; and this he seems
to have read in the original since there is no English
translation known at this date;[3] and indeed the play
seems to suggest that he could read Italian with ease.
In the first place Othello's account of the magical
origin of the handkerchief given to Desdemona,[4] not
found in Cinthio, who merely relates that it was 'finely
embroidered in the Moorish fashion', may well be

[1] See 1. 1. 37–8; A. Hart, letter in *The Times Literary
Supplement*, 10 October 1935.
[2] E. K. Chambers, *Shakespearean Gleanings* (1944),
pp. 68–70.
[3] There have been three since: (i) in Mrs Lennox's
Shakespeare Illustrated (1753); (ii) by W. Parr in a little
volume entitled *The Story of the Moor of Venice...with
two essays on Shakespeare*, 1795 (reprinted in J. P. Collier's
Shakespeare Library, 1844; 2nd ed. by W. C. Hazlitt,
1875); (iii) by J. E. Taylor (1855) (reprinted in Furness's
Variorum ed. of *Othello*). None of these is satisfactory.
[4] See 3. 4. 73–8.

derived from the description in Ariosto's *Orlando Furioso* of Hector's magical tent which his sister the 'damsel' Cassandra, inspired by 'prophetic fury', had worked with her needle. If so, Shakespeare would, it appears, have had it from Ariosto direct, not from Sir John Harington's translation printed by Richard Field in 1591, because the English version has nothing corresponding to the words 'furor profetico' which Shakespeare echoes. Again, the passage in question comes from stanza 80, canto 46, which suggests an easy familiarity with the language on the part of one who not only knew *Orlando Furioso* well enough to remember an incident in it and adapt it to another purpose, but had presumably perused the earlier forty-five cantos before he reached it.[1] And there is a further point.

[1] This parallel with Ariosto was first pointed out in 1898 by G. Brandes (v. p. 445 of his *William Shakespeare*, 1916 ed.) The original stanza and Harington's translation run as follows:

Ariosto

Eran degli anni appresso che duo milia,
Che fu quel ricco padiglion trapunto.
Una donzella della terra d'Ilia,
Ch' avea il furor profetico congiunto,
Con studio di gran tempo, e con vigilia
Lo fece di sua man di tutto punto.
Cassandra fu nomata, ed al fratello
Inclito Ettor fece un bel don di quello.

Harington

Two thousand yeare before, or not much lesse,
This rich pavilion had in Troy bene wrought,
By fair Cassandra, that same Prophetesse
That had (but all in vaine) in youth bene taught
Of future things to giue most certaine guesse
For her true speech was neuer set at naught:
She wrought the same with help of many others,
And gaue it Hector, her beloued brother.

Shakespeare speaks of a sibyl; Ariosto of the damsel Cassandra. But Boiardo in a similar connexion, which Ariosto obviously had in mind, also speaks of a sibyl. Had Shakespeare read Boiardo's *Orlando Innamorato* as well as its sequel *Orlando Furioso*? The possibility cannot be ruled out.[1] A French translation, which we have not seen, of Cinthio's story appeared, it is true, in 1584,[2] and Professor Charlton tells us 'it follows the original with a literal fidelity' so close 'that it provides not the slightest clue as to whether Shakespeare had the tale from the Italian or the French'.[3] Since, however, what Othello says at 3. 3. 361–6 ('give me the ocular proof.... Make me to see't') corresponds with Cinthio's 'se non mi fai...vedere cogl'occhi...', whereas the French gives us only 'si tu ne me fais voir', we seem to have here a pretty definite clue pointing to the Italian, especially if we remember that the word 'ocular' is not found elsewhere in Shakespeare.[4] There are other passages in the play also which may well echo the Italian of Cinthio,[5] while a familiarity on Shakespeare's part with Italian proverbs would go some way towards clearing up the vexed problem of the line,

> A fellow almost damned in a fair wife.[6]

Observe finally that the only character to whom Cinthio

[1] The Boiardo parallel (*Orlando Innamorato*, Bk. II, xxvii, st. 51) was pointed out by Professor Alexander in *R.E.S.* (1932), p. 100. See Brandes, *loc. cit.*, for another.

[2] Gabriel Chappuys, *Premier Volume des Cent Excellentes Nouvelles de M. Jean Baptiste Giraldy Cynthien* (Paris, 1584), pp. 323–33.

[3] Charlton, *Shakespearian Tragedy* (1948), pp. 114–15 n.

[4] W. Wollatsch, *Archiv*, CLXII (1932), pp. 118–19. We owe this reference to Mr Maxwell.

[5] See notes 1. 3. 330; 3. 3. 186.

[6] See note 1. 1. 21.

gives a name is Desdemona, or Disdemona as he spells it; all the other names in the play appear to be of Shakespeare's invention and are Italian in formation. One has only to compare them with the names in *Hamlet* to see what shifts he is put to when dealing with a country whose language is unknown to him: the rag-bag, Claudius, Horatio, Polonius, Laertes, Ophelia, Marcellus, Barnardo, Francisco, Reynaldo, suggest anything but Denmark.

Cinthio (1504–73) was a professor of philosophy at Ferrara and a dramatist who both by theory and practice exercised a considerable influence upon the development of drama in Italy and Europe generally from the middle of the sixteenth century onwards. Tragedy had until his time been almost wholly Senecan in form and spirit. He now made tragi-comedy fashionable, that is to say a type of drama which, though still compounded for the most part of the Senecan ingredients of blood and horror, took a new turn shortly before the end so as to close on a happy note. And he also started a new fashion in dramatic themes by taking his plots from stories of modern life, especially love-stories borrowed from Boccaccio and other writers of *novelle*, instead of following his predecessors by drawing upon the plots of Seneca and other classical dramatists. It is, in fact, difficult to avoid the suspicion that Shakespeare owed more to him than the plots of *Othello* and *Measure for Measure*. Professor Charlton, who speaks with authority on these matters, has for instance pointed out that after trying his hand on two thoroughly Senecan tragedies, *Titus Andronicus* and *Richard III*, Shakespeare gives us in *Romeo and Juliet* one founded on a fictitious tale of a romantic love derived from a volume of Italian *novelle*, in a word one that follows Cinthio's prescription. And if Shakespeare read Italian, it is more than likely that he was familiar

with the *Discorso* in which Cinthio expounded his theory of tragedy.[1]

Cinthio had himself written seven plays before 1565, when his *Hecatommithi* appeared, and this volume was, as it were, a present to his countrymen of a hundred new plots suitable for the type of drama he advocated, some of them being dramatized by himself later. Moreover, as a professor he was inclined to emphasize the moral or at least the educational function of drama though every dramatist at that period professed to do so more or less. Like the *Decameron*, his collection of stories opens with a Proem and Introduction explaining the circumstances of the persons who are to relate them. But whereas Boccaccio's is a group of seven girls and three men, the group in Cinthio's Introduction is of men only, one of them a senior who guides the discussion and in the end directs it towards a definite problem, that of success in married life, for all the world like a professor with his seminar. The secret of such success, the leader insists, must be looked for in a spiritual union of the partners, though he suggests that this kind of union is difficult to maintain if husband and wife, owing to the circumstances of their birth or upbringing, have a different outlook on life or have been accustomed to different modes of living. After this, the Introduction ends with a proposal by one of the young men that the thesis should be illustrated by tales, since 'examples' may do more than discussion to show where the truth lies. Though, as Dr Walker suggests, little more than a tissue of late medieval commonplaces,[2] the foregoing

---

[1] Charlton, *op. cit.* pp. 49 ff., the best and fullest account of Shakespeare's handling of Cinthio's tale. Cf. also Charlton's *Senecan Tradition in Renaissance Tragedy* (1946), pp. lxxii–lxxv, and his lecture on *Othello* in the *Bulletin of the John Rylands Library*, vol. XXXI, no. 1 (January, 1948).

[2] For which reason perhaps ignored by Charlton.

discussion may well have been before Shakespeare's
mind when he set about the writing of his play sometime in 1601 or 1602.

III. *Cinthio's Moor and Shakespeare's Othello*

Certainly one theme, if not the central theme, both
of *Othello* and of Cinthio's tale of the Moorish Captain,
his Venetian lady and the wicked Ensign, is that of
a marriage which begins as a spiritual union but is
brought to disaster through differences of race and
social tradition. Disdemona, Cinthio tells us, is attracted
to the Moor not by physical desire but by his great and
valorous spirit (dalla virtù del Moro), while he on his
side falls in love with her beauty and the nobility of her
mind (dal nobile pensiero). And Disdemona points
the moral of the story when she declares to the Ensign's
wife [Emilia] that her fate is a warning to Italian girls
not to marry a man divided from them by race (la
Natura), religion (il Cielo) and manner of life (il modo
della vita).

Shakespeare turns Cinthio's hint of a spiritual union
to great account. It is implicit in Othello's description
of the courtship, and in everything they say to or of
each other before Iago's poison begins to take effect.
Moreover, if we forget it we miss, as some critics seem
to have missed, the whole meaning of Othello's speech
and action in the last scene. Perhaps, indeed, the difference between Shakespeare's Othello and Cinthio's
Moor is seen most glaringly in the different manner of
the wife's murder. Shakespeare shows us the pitiful yet
stern minister of justice offering her up as a sacrifice to
outraged Chastity. In Cinthio, Moor and Ensign
combine to batter her skull to pieces and then, loosening
a beam above the bed, give out that the ceiling has
fallen and crushed her, thus escaping all suspicion for
the deed. No 'honourable murder' this! Yet though

Cinthio has nothing corresponding with Othello's final speeches, their burden—an agonized realization of the spiritual divorce from her which faces him for eternity —is a development of the hint in Cinthio above mentioned. Again, although Cinthio's heroine possesses something of Desdemona's courage, gentleness and humility, his Moor altogether lacks the dignity and nobility of Shakespeare's Othello. The latter retains sufficient resemblance nevertheless to show it to be a transfiguration of the other.

But this transfiguration gave rise to a difficulty with the plot. The fundamental cause of the catastrophe in both story and play is, of course, the husband's lack of confidence in the wife, which the Ensign merely awakens and then plays upon. In the story this required little motivation: husbands in Cinthio's world, as in Emilia's, are distrustful of wives by nature:

> They are not ever jealous for the cause,
> But jealous for they're jealous.   (3. 4. 164–5)

Coleridge and Bradley have been taken to task for maintaining that jealousy is not the main point in Othello's character:[1] 'I take it to be', Coleridge is reported to have said,

rather an agony that the creature, whom he had believed angelic, with whom he had garnered up his heart and whom he could not help still loving, should be proved impure and worthless. It was the struggle *not* to love her. It was a moral indignation and regret that virtue should so fall: 'But yet the *pity* of it, Iago! O Iago! the *pity* of it, Iago!'[2]

And many other readers and spectators reach the same conclusion. *Othello*, the most popular of Shakespeare's

---

[1] See e.g. F. R. Leavis, in *Scrutiny* VI, pp. 262 ff.

[2] *Table-Talk*, cited in Raysor's *Coleridge's Shakespearean Criticism*, ii. 350.

plays in Soviet Russia where it is played in sixteen
different languages in different countries of the Union,
is apparently always produced there according to
Pushkin's prescription: 'Othello was not jealous by
nature, he was trustful.'[1]

The point is not that Othello never becomes jealous—
his jealousy, 'being wrought', is terrible—but that he is
not 'jealous by nature'. On the contrary, he is one of
the great lovers in the literature of the world, the
greatest lover in Shakespeare.[2] Not only is physical
passion a trifling thing compared with the delight he
takes in his lady's conversation[3], but association with her
becomes the meaning of life, so that the mere sight of
her after a brief parting fills him with ecstasy.

> It gives me wonder great as my content
> To see you here before me. O my soul's joy!
> If it were now to die,
> 'Twere now to be most happy; for I fear,
> My soul hath her content so absolute
> That not another comfort like to this
> Succeeds in unknown fate.[4]

It confirms his faith in the harmony and stability of the
universe, as he implies at 3. 3. 91–3:

> Perdition catch my soul
> But I do love thee; and when I love thee not
> Chaos is come again.

---

[1] Pushkin was killed in a duel in the same year that
Coleridge's *Literary Remains* were published, and could
therefore have known nothing of his views.

[2] Bradley, *op. cit.* p. 189.   [3] Cp. 1. 3. 261–65.

[4] 2. 1. 180–90. Granville-Barker's comment (*Prefaces to
Shakespeare*, 4th Series (1945) p. 20) on these lines that
they give us 'the already ageing, disillusioned man', I find
incredible. True, they are spoken before the wedding night,
but by this placing of them Shakespeare surely meant to
emphasize what Othello has said already at 1. 3. 260 ff.

And it gives a deeper significance to his religion. So at least I interpret Iago's sneer that for her sake he would be prepared to

> renounce his baptism,
> All seals and symbols of redeeméd sin;
>
> (2. 3. 336–7)

and so I interpret also the terrible lines envisaging an eternity of separation at 5. 2. 276–84. When, therefore, he is brought to think her false, everything else becomes false, meaningless, empty, even the profession he had served from 'boyish days' with ever-increasing fame and ever-increasing devotion to the state, the profession which had won him the heart of Desdemona herself.[1] 'Chaos is come.'

How could such a lover descend to the vulgar and degrading depths of sexual jealousy? How could Shakespeare in other words so arrange matters as to convince his audience that in truth the thing happens? Not a few critics feel that he fails to convince, but only, I think, because they read *Othello* like a novel, or take memories of such reading to the theatre with them.[2] Bradley at any rate, though often accused of this kind of mis-reading, is not here guilty of it. The tragedy of Othello, he writes,

lies in this—that his whole nature was indisposed to jealousy, and yet was such that he was unusually open to

---

[1] 3. 3. 349–59.

[2] Robert Bridges (see *The Influence of the audience on Shakespeare's drama*, Collected Essays, Papers, etc. I, pp. 23–5) is an eminent example of recent times. But Thomas Rymer's *Short View of Tragedy* (1693) raised much the same objections though from the neo-classical standpoint, and T. S. Eliot considers that 'Rymer makes out a very good case' (*Selected Essays*, p. 116 n.) of which he has 'never seen a cogent refutation' (*ibid.* p. 141 n.; cf. also p. 126).

deception, and, if once wrought to passion, likely to act with little reflection, with no delay, and in the most decisive manner conceivable.[1]

This, like the next quotation, owes something to Coleridge. Yet it is a brilliant summary: as ever with Bradley every word is weighed and, as usual, every stroke is just. Equally unanswerable are his observations on the other arm of the tragic balance, Iago's 'honesty'. That Othello puts entire confidence in Iago implies, he asserts, no stupidity on Othello's part:

For his opinion of Iago was the opinion of practically everyone who knew him:[2] and that opinion was that Iago was before all things 'honest', his very faults being those of excess in honesty. This being so, even if Othello had not been trustful and simple, it would have been quite unnatural in him to be unmoved by the warnings of so honest a friend, warnings offered with extreme reluctance and manifestly from a sense of a friend's duty. *Any* husband would have been troubled by them.[3]

His use of the past tense shows, it is true, that Bradley writes as if *Othello* were history or a piece of real life. But what he says is nevertheless relevant to the verisimilitude of the stage, provided Iago is played as Shakespeare intended.

IV. *Iago*

This proviso is essential; and there can, I think, be little doubt that the main cause why we are often dissatisfied with *Othello* in the theatre is that the tragic balance just alluded to is upset by the pitiful ambition of the actor impersonating Iago. 'The tragedy of

[1] Bradley, *op. cit.* p. 186.
[2] i.e. Shakespeare showed it to be their opinion.
[3] Bradley, *op. cit.* p. 192.

Othello', Robert Bridges roundly declared, 'is intolerably painful; and that not merely because we see Othello grossly deceived, but because we are ourselves constrained to submit to palpable deception.'[1] Yet that the deception should be neither gross nor palpable is evident from the account of Bensley's Iago given by Lamb, who, despite his oft-quoted and often condemned remarks on *King Lear* as a stage-play, is one of our most interesting dramatic critics. Robert Bensley, he tells us,

betrayed none of that *cleverness* which is the bane of serious acting. For this reason, his Iago was the only endurable one which I remember to have seen. No spectator from his action could divine more of his artifice than Othello was supposed to do. His confessions in soliloquy alone put you in possession of the mystery. There were no by-intimations to make the audience fancy their own discernment so much greater than that of the Moor—who commonly stands like a great helpless mark set up for mine Ancient, and a quantity of barren spectators, to shoot their bolts at. The Iago of Bensley did not go to work so grossly. There was a triumphant tone about the character, natural to a general consciousness of power; but none of that petty vanity which chuckles and cannot contain itself upon any little successful stroke of its knavery—as is common with your small villains and green probationers in mischief. It did not clap or crow before its time. It was not a man setting his wits at a child, and winking all the while at other children who are mightily pleased at being let into the secret; but a consummate villain entrapping a noble nature into toils, against which no discernment was available, where the manner was as fathomless as the purpose seemed dark, and without motive.[2]

This appears to me the best criticism we have of Iago's character because it tells us not why he behaves as he

[1] Bridges, *op. cit.* I, p. 23.
[2] On Some of the old Actors, *Elia*, 1823.

does but how he should behave, or rather how the actor who plays him should. The question 'Why' which Othello bids them demand of Iago in the last moments of the play, Bradley remarks 'is *the* question about Iago, just as the question Why did Hamlet delay? is *the* question about Hamlet'. And he asserts that, though neither character could solve his own problem, 'Shakespeare knew the answer, and if these characters are great creations and not blunders we ought to be able to find it too'.[1] Shakespeare no doubt put that question into Othello's mouth in order that Bradley and the rest of us should ask it, or because he expected us to ask it. But the only answer he gives us and the only one we shall ever get is Iago's own—

> Demand me nothing: what you know, you know;
> From this time forth I never will speak word.

And this answer is Shakespeare's crowning stroke, his final touch to the portrait of a consummate villain, with a manner as fathomless as his purpose seems dark and without motive. For 'Demand me nothing' shuts the door firmly and finally. That critics try to force it open, and will continue to try, is of course a tribute to Iago's overwhelming verisimilitude and fascinating inscrutability, which put him in a class above Goethe's Mephistopheles.[2] None succeed, however; or can ever succeed in convincing the rest of the world. In Iago, as in Hamlet, Shakespeare created a character which, while intensely lifelike both on the stage and in the book, defies and will always defy all attempts to analyse or explain it.[3]

Yet to leave the matter there would be to leave

---

[1] Bradley, *op. cit.* p. 222.

[2] As Bradley, *op. cit.* (p. 208) remarks, Mephistopheles 'has Iago for his father', though he is less human.

[3] Cf. *What happens in Hamlet*, pp. 217–29.

unsaid one of the most significant things about Iago,
and about the play as a whole. Iago has the devil's
own cunning, but he is a human being nevertheless and
on one point a stupid human being at that, while it is
this stupidity which brings his nemesis upon him. For,
as R. G. Moulton puts it,

> The principle underlying this nemesis is one of the
> profoundest of Shakespeare's moral ideas—that evil not
> only corrupts the heart, but equally undermines the
> judgement....It is because he knows himself unfettered
> by scruples that Iago feels himself infallible, and considers
> honest men fools; he never sees how his foul thoughts have
> blinded his perceptive power and made him blunder where
> simple men would have gone straight. He thought he had
> foreseen everything: it never occurred to him that his wife
> might betray him with nothing to gain by such betrayal,
> simply from affection and horror.[1]

In our reaction against the rather crude moralising of
eighteenth and early nineteenth-century criticism, we
are apt to forget that Shakespeare is one of the great
moral forces of the world. This does not of course mean
that he had any ethical purpose in writing *Othello*.
'The Poetical Character', Keats tells us,

> has no character—it enjoys light and shade; it lives in gusto,
> be it foul or fair, high or low, rich or poor, mean or
> elevated—It has as much delight in conceiving an Iago as
> an Imogen. What shocks the virtuous philosopher, delights
> the camelion Poet.[2]

But when the chameleon poet who has penetrated
deeper into the mysteries of human nature than any
other finds that a certain obtuseness is a necessary

---

[1] R. G. Moulton, *Shakespeare as a Dramatic Artist*, 3rd
ed. (1892), pp. 238–9.
[2] Letter to Richard Woodhouse, 27 October 1818.

ingredient in the composition of a moral anarchist, we simple wayfaring men may take courage.

Iago, then, like most of the characters in the canon, exists dramatically in his own right, and he is so great a figure that he seems to stand right out of the framework of his play. Yet he is made to fit into the frame and is not even the most important character within it, his primary function being to render the development of Othello's character more credible. He bears in fact the same sort of relation to Othello as Falstaff does to Prince Hal in *Henry IV*. Shakespeare had to make Falstaff so fascinating a tempter in order to provide his Elizabethan audience with a satisfactory reason why Henry of Monmouth, the most august of English Kings, stooped to folly in his youth,[1] and he made Iago a 'demi-devil' to help us understand why the noblest of his lovers falls a prey to jealousy. As Raleigh notes:

Everything,...up to the crisis of the play, helps to raise Othello to the top of admiration, and to fix him in the affections of the reader. Scene follows scene, and in every one of them, it might be said, Shakespeare is making his task more hopeless. How is he to fill out the story, and yet save our sympathies for Othello? The effort must be heroic: and it is. He invents Iago. The greatness of Iago may be measured by this, that Othello never loses our sympathy.[2]

And the process of this invention is best explained in relation to the source, as was brilliantly expounded by Lytton Strachey, who writes:

The Ancient in Cinthio's story concealed his wickedness under a heroic guise; he wore the semblance of a Hector or an Achilles. Now it is obvious that, in Shakespeare's

---

[1] Cf. *The Fortunes of Falstaff*, p. 23. See also Swinburne, *Study of Shakespeare* (1880), p. 182, and Middleton Murry, *Shakespeare*, (1935), pp. 320–1.

[2] *Shakespeare* (1907), p. 141.

scheme, this would not do. . . . The cloak of Iago's villainy must be of an altogether different stuff; clearly it must be the very contrary of heroic—the downrightness, the out-spokenness of bluff integrity. This conception needed no great genius to come by . . . but Shakespeare's next readjustment is of quite another class. In Cinthio's story, the Ancient's motive for his villainy is—just what we should expect it to be: he was in love with the lady. She paid no heed to him; his love turned to hatred; he imagined in his fury that she loved the Captain; and he determined to be avenged upon them both. Now this is the obvious, the regulation plot, which would have been followed by any ordinary competent writer. And Shakespeare rejected it. Why? . . . Othello is to be deluded into believing that Desdemona is faithless; he is to kill her; and then he is to discover that his belief was false. This is the situation, the horror of which is to be intensified in every possible way: the tragedy must be enormous, and unrelieved. But there is one eventuality that might, in some degree at any rate, mitigate the atrocity of the story. If Iago had been led to cause the disaster by his love for Desdemona, in that very fact would lie some sort of comfort; the tragedy would have been brought about by a motive not only comprehensible, but in a sense sympathetic; the hero's passion and the villain's would be the same. Let it be granted, then, that the completeness of the tragedy would suffer if its origin lay in Iago's love for Desdemona; therefore let that motive be excluded from Iago's mind. The question immediately presents itself—in that case, for what reason are we to suppose that Iago acted as he did? The whole story depends upon his plot, which forms the machinery of the action; yet, if the Desdemona impulsion is eliminated, what motive for his plot can there be? Shakespeare supplied the answer to this question with one of the very greatest strokes of his genius. By an overwhelming effort of creation he summoned up out of the darkness a psychological portent that was exactly fitted to the requirements of the tragic situation with which he was dealing, and endowed it with reality. He determined that Iago should have no motive at all. He conceived of a monster whose

wickedness should lie far deeper than anything that could
be explained by a motive—the very essence of whose being
should express itself in the machinations of malignity. This
creature might well explain his purposes both to himself
and his confederate; but his explanations should contradict
each other; he should put forward first one motive, and
then another still; so that while he himself would be only
half-aware of the falsity of his self-analysis, to the audience
it would be clear; the underlying demonic impulse would
be manifest as the play developed. It would be seen to be
no common affair of love and jealousy, but a tragedy
conditioned by something purposeless, profound, and
terrible; and when the moment of revelation came, the
horror that burst upon the hero would be as inexplicably
awful as evil itself.[1]

But even this was not all. Shakespeare not only
seizes every opportunity up to the moment of temptation, of raising the hero 'to the top of admiration';
not only transforms Cinthio's crude villain into a
tempter of devilish malignity; he renders the temptation
virtually irresistible by drastic though imperceptible
manipulation of the time-scheme of the original plot.

V. *Time in 'Othello'*

In its simplest terms, then, the tragedy of *Othello*
represents the destruction of a sublime love between
two noble spirits through the intrigues of a villain
devilish in his cunning and unscrupulousness. And the
chief excitement of the play is provided by those scenes
in which we see this destruction taking place. To
increase their plausibility, however, Shakespeare so
moulded the plot that Othello is completely ignorant of
the ways of civilized women in general and of Desdemona's private life in particular, neither point being
made by Cinthio; and so arranged his scenes themselves
that Othello is never given any opportunity of either

[1] Lytton Strachey, *Literary Essays*, pp. 29–30.

checking Iago's insinuations or even of reflecting upon them until they have done their work. This double purpose involved, however, not only adapting the plot but resorting to yet another piece of dramatic legerdemain, the most audacious in the whole canon, which has come to be known as Double Time.

Cinthio's Moor had evidently been resident long in Venice before the expedition to Cyprus; Shakespeare's Othello tells us that he had never been in Venice until nine months before the opening of the play, having spent his whole life until then in the field. Iago's later hints that he is completely ignorant of the ways of Italian women are therefore well grounded. Cinthio, again, it will be recollected, relates that the Moor and Disdemona had lived in perfect harmony together in Venice for an unspecified period, during which, one might suppose, persons so deeply in love would have had plenty of opportunity of getting to know each other and of resolving such temperamental discords as their differences of race and upbringing might give rise to. Shakespeare's couple have no married life together at all. He deliberately leaves the sequence of events in his opening scenes a little vague, but we are evidently intended to assume that the marriage knot has only just been tied by some priest at the Sagittary when Iago arrives to warn the bridegroom that Brabantio has been informed and is about to cause trouble, while as they are talking Cassio arrives in turn with the summons to the Duke 'haste-post-haste'. The scene before the Council follows, immediately at the end of which, upon the command 'you must away tonight', Othello goes out saying to Desdemona

> I have but an hour
> Of love, of worldly matter and direction,
> To spend with thee: we must obey the time.

In a word, they obey Shakespeare's time to such
purpose that their first night in Cyprus is their wedding
night,[1] and even that is disturbed by Cassio's brawl.
Thus they have had no intimacy of any kind, and Iago's
trump card is his reminder that Othello actually knows
very little either about Italian women in general or of
the true character of Desdemona in particular.[2] Clearly,
by ridding Cinthio's plot of the married life in Venice
Shakespeare at once tightened it up and greatly increased its dramatic cogency.

Yet this change gave rise to further difficulties which
might well have seemed insuperable to any ordinary
dramatist. For, if Othello and Desdemona consummated their marriage during the first night at Cyprus,
when could she have committed the adultery that Iago
charges her with? An accusation of premarital in-
continence would not have served either his purpose
or Shakespeare's, since adultery was required to make
Othello a cuckold, and it is the dishonourable stigma
of cuckoldry that maddens Othello once his confidence
has gone and, we may add, greatly increased the excitement for a Jacobean audience. From this dilemma
Shakespeare escaped by means of a contrivance which
not only successfully imposes on us in the theatre but
paradoxically enough has been mainly instrumental in
earning the play its reputation for perfection of form.
'There is not another of Shakespeare's plays', Raleigh
has well said, 'which is so white-hot with imagination,
so free from doubtful or extraneous matter, and so
perfectly welded, as *Othello*.'[3]

The contrivance in question, which is technically
the mainspring of the play, was labelled 'Double Time,

[1] In 2. 2. Cyprus is bidden to celebrate not only the
victory over the Turks but Othello's 'nuptial'. Cf. too
2. 3. 8–10, 15–16.   [2] Cf. Bradley, *op. cit.* pp. 190, 193.
[3] *Shakespeare*, p. 142.

Short and Long' by 'Christopher North' who first expounded it in detail.[1] During the last four acts, Shakespeare keeps two clocks going, one registering short or dramatic time, the other registering long or historical time. Short Time concerns the sequence of events on the stage, which follow each other without pause or any suggestion of intervening interval; and Shakespeare, as Granville-Barker notes, takes pains to make this immediacy clear 'by the devices of the morning music, dinner-time, supper-time and the midnight dark, and their linking together by the action itself and reference after reference in the dialogue'. And he points out that Shakespeare was obliged to do this because Othello must be left no time 'for reflection or the questioning of anyone but Iago', otherwise 'the whole flimsy fraud that is practised on him' would palpably collapse,[2] as indeed it does in the eyes of critics like Bridges[3] who have leisure, denied to an audience, to pore over the play in a book. Yet, as often in Shakespeare, dramatic necessity is turned to dramatic gain; for the precipitancy of the action greatly heightens our sense both of the torrential passion that rages through the hero's soul and of the fertility and alacrity of the villain's invention. When, however, critics begin to compute the length of this short time and reckon it as twenty-four hours from the first night in Cyprus, when the marriage is consummated, to the murder of Desdemona they are emphasizing something which Shakespeare is equally at pains to keep carefully out of sight. Indeed, what his short-time clock registers is never duration but speed, the rush of events rather than the flight of hours. There is but one reference

---

[1] i.e. Professor John Wilson of Edinburgh, in articles contributed to *Blackwood's Magazine*, November 1849 to May 1850.   [2] Barker, *op. cit.* p. 32.

[3] Bridges, *op. cit.* pp. 23 ff.

to this last, and it occurs when the short-time clock
has only just got going.

Pleasure and action make the hours seem short,

says Iago at the end of Act ii, and so prepares spectators
for the speed at which subsequent events will move.
For Iago is the Jack of this clock.

Though there has been much discussion of Double
Time in *Othello*, in particular by Bradley and Granville-Barker, while for the contradictions and incon-
sistencies arising from it various explanations have
been offered, such as textual revision, the loss of a scene
or scenes, change of plan in the course of composition,[1]
etc., no one seems to have observed that Shakespeare
adopted it for the same reason that he adopted Short
Time, because he was compelled. He used Short Time
to prevent the audience realizing that Othello's acceptance of Iago's tissue of falsehood was in reality absurd.
He used Long Time to persuade the audience that the
adultery, which was rendered impossible by his cutting
out the period of married life in Cinthio's tale, had
nevertheless taken place. 'Long Time', therefore,
consists in effect of a series of references to the duration
of time, during which the married life could have
occurred, and, we are led to suppose, actually did occur.
Where it had been spent Shakespeare is careful not to
say: sometimes he seems to suggest that Desdemona
might have begun her intrigue with Cassio in Venice,
at others we are given the impression that weeks or
more may have elapsed since the arrival in Cyprus.
He is of course careful too that the hints of Long Time
should never clash in any obvious way[2] with those of

[1] K. Muir, 'Double-time in Othello', *Notes and Queries*,
16 February 1952.

[2] Barker, *op. cit.* p. 36. He speaks on p. 33 of Shakespeare's 'confident, reckless, dexterous way'. Dexterous
and confident, no doubt; but I feel sure not reckless.

Short Time. Indeed, as Barker again notes, he only begins to introduce plain hints of Long Time when the excitement of the jealousy scenes is reaching its height, since as every conjurer knows it is when the attention of an audience is deeply engaged that a sleight of hand has its best chance of success. An early and the most striking hint of the kind is Othello's cry,

> What sense had I of her stolen hours of lust?
> I saw't not, thought it not, it harmed not me:
> I slept the next night well, fed well, was merry;
> I found not Cassio's kisses on her lips (3. 3. 340–3)

which clearly implies that her infidelity to him had been of long duration, while by 5. 2. 214 Iago has persuaded him that she had gratified Cassio 'a thousand times'. But there are a dozen or more such indications of Long Time and they are to be found in speeches by Roderigo and Bianca, as well as those of Othello and Iago.[1]

The foregoing notes on technique deal with a few points only in a large field; for *Othello* is a miracle of

---

[1] The main passages are as follows:

2. 3. 357: Roderigo tires of the chase; his money is almost spent.

3. 3. 269: 'She's gone' implies at least some lapse of time.

3. 3. 294: Iago has asked Emilia 'a hundred times' to steal the handkerchief.

3. 3. 311: 'That which so often you did bid me steal'.

3. 3. 340: 'Her stolen hours of lust' (v. supra).

3. 3. 411: 'She's disloyal' like 'she's gone' implies a lapse of time.

3. 3. 415–28: Iago relates Cassio's talk in his sleep: this *could* not have taken place in Cyprus.

3. 4. 177: Bianca has not seen Cassio for a week.

3. 4. 181: Cassio excuses himself: 'I have this while with leaden thoughts been pressed' clearly refers to his degradation (a week ago!).

construction.[1] But we must now, however, pass on to some consideration of the play in action, and since selection is necessary, section VI will be devoted to the poisoning of Othello's mind, and section VIII to the question, much debated by twentieth-century critics, how Shakespeare intended us to interpret Othello's words and actions in the last scene.

VI. *The temptation and fall of Othello*

One of the most brilliant and subtle passages in Shakespeare is the dialogue in which Othello succumbs to Iago's devilish machinations. Even Bradley has not, I think, appreciated its beauty to the full, but he has at least noticed an essential point about it which many later critics have missed, namely that

It takes a long time for Iago to excite surprise, curiosity, and then grave concern—by no means yet jealousy—even about Cassio....In fact it is not until Iago hints that Othello, as a foreigner, might easily be deceived, that he is seriously disturbed about Desdemona. Salvini played this passage, as might be expected, with entire understanding. Nor have I ever seen it seriously misinterpreted on the stage.[2]

---

4. 1. 1–9: Iago hints at many acts of adultery.
4. 1. 35–43: And Othello believes him.
4. 1. 51: Othello had had a fit 'yesterday' (not yet in Cyprus).
4. 1. 85–6: 'Where, how, *how oft, how long ago* and when He hath and is again to cope *your wife.*'

[1] Instructive discussion on this matter may be found in R. G. Moulton's old-fashioned, but by no means out of date, monograph on *Shakespeare as a Dramatic Artist*, 3rd ed. (1892).
[2] Bradley, *op. cit.* pp. 434–5; anticipated by Hazlitt who writes 'Othello's confidence, at first only staggered by

That it is, nevertheless, quite often misinterpreted by critics is in a measure due, as Miss Walker points out on p. 132, to the vulgarizing of his dialogue in this scene. In the Folio, she notes, he is persistent, but controlled for some time. He does not indeed see what Iago is getting at until 3. 3. 178, when for the first time he speaks with some passion, yet still with great confidence. The Quarto, on the other hand, makes a hash of lines 109–11 and coarsens Othello's character by oaths from this point on.

All this acquires additional significance when it is linked up, as it should be by students of the play, with the source. Cinthio, I pointed out above, tells us, rather casually through the mouth of Disdemona that her marriage has come to grief because she and her husband differed in race (natura), religion and social tradition. Beyond this single reference he makes nothing of the religious difference, and had Shakespeare, following him, represented Othello as a Mohammedan, he might have lost the sympathy of a large section of his audience and we should have lost the Christian background which adds so much to the terror and sublimity of the final scene. Nor does Cinthio, in point of fact, make much of the other two differences either. We learn, however, what he means by 'natura' when his Ensign tells the Moor that Disdemona is consoling herself with the Captain [Cassio] 'because of the aversion she has taken to his [the Moor's] blackness', whereat, Cinthio adds, the Moor is pierced to the heart. This is the sole reference to the colour of the Moor's skin and it is only introduced when the Moor is already mad with

---

broken hints and insinuations, recovers itself at sight of Desdemona' viz. at 3. 3. 279 (*Characters of Shakespeare's Plays*). E. E. Stoll overlooks this important point and so misinterprets both Shakespeare and Bradley.

jealousy. In Shakespeare, on the other hand, Iago finds in it his most potent poison.

The temptation scene proper begins with Othello's last utterance of untroubled love as Desdemona goes out at 3. 3. 90:

> Excellent wretch! Perdition catch my soul
> But I do love thee; and when I love thee not
> Chaos is come again.

The lines are pregnant with irony. Perdition in the person of Iago is at his elbow, burning to catch his soul; chaos and black night are about to descend upon him. But the tempter moves warily. Starting with the fact he has just gathered from Desdemona that Cassio had been in the lovers' confidence during their court-ship, he throws out vague hints, e.g. that Othello's honour is somehow threatened; and while refusing to say what they point to, in order to excite Othello's curiosity the more, excuses this reticence as due to anxiety for his friend's peace of mind; more than half disclosing at the same time what he pretends to hide by telling him he wishes to save him from the tortures of jealousy. Yet so far he has not even come within striking distance. For, though Othello exclaims 'O misery!' as he contemplates the vivid picture of a jealous husband on the rack which Iago sets before him, he is unconscious of any application to himself.[1] Indeed, when a moment later he begins to catch a glimpse of Iago's drift, as his 'Why, why is this?' shows, he indignantly repu-diates the very idea that he is capable of jealousy. He is a general, a man to whom rapid decision is a rule of life, for whom

> to be once in doubt
> Is once[2] resolved.

[1] Cf. Bradley, *op. cit.* p. 434.
[2] i.e. at once.

And so he declares

> I'll see before I doubt; when I doubt, prove;
> And on the proof, there is no more but this,
> Away at once with love or jealousy!

It is a just self-estimate, we shall agree, having watched his encounter with Brabantio and a band of armed retainers in the street and the way he deals with the brawl for which Cassio is responsible. Yet Othello the married lover is now advancing into territory to which a life-time of soldiering offers no guide, as his talk of 'proof' testifies. For the assurance of love is unquestioning: evidence one way or another belongs to the divorce-court.[1] And Iago takes immediate advantage of this misguided self-confidence to include Desdemona for the first time in his innuendos. Not that even now he accuses her directly.

> I speak not yet of proof.
> Look to your wife; observe her well with Cassio;
> Wear your eye thus not jealous nor secure:[2]
> I would not have your free and noble nature
> Out of self-bounty be abused. Look to't.

The lines, of course, suggest as usual with Iago a good deal more than they say: 'not yet' implies that proof can be supplied at need; 'abused' is an ugly word, meaning at once deceived and dishonoured, specially applicable then, and often applied, to cuckolds; while the flattering if well-grounded tribute to Othello's 'free and noble nature' and to his 'self-bounty' (i.e. a native generosity which finds it hard to think ill of others), skilfully leads up to what follows. For the man of the world now draws aside the curtain of civilization and gives this ignorant barbarian a glimpse of the 'pranks'

---

[1] The point is suggested by J. C. Maxwell. See *The Age of Shakespeare*, ed. Boris Ford (Penguin Books), p. 225.
[2] i.e. over-confident.

that the ladies of Venice 'dare not show their husbands';
and, when Othello's startled and revolted cry 'Dost
thou say *so*?' tells him he has at last found the right
point of attack he injects charge after charge of the
poison into the life-blood of his quivering victim.

Yet he still keeps himself out of sight as much as
possible; and nearly all he now says is either fact within
Othello's memory or made to appear as if derived from
Brabantio. He opens with

> She did deceive her father, marrying you,

which recalls the old man's parting shot—

> Look to her, Moor, if thou hast eyes to see:
> She has deceived her father, and may thee;
> (1. 3. 292–3)

and what he next says,

> And when she seemed to shake and fear your looks,
> She loved them most,

reminds Othello of his own experience and of something else his father-in-law had said, while a deadly
venom lurks in both memories as we shall see in a
moment. Iago's immediate purpose, however, is to
suggest that if she managed to impose upon Othello
during their courtship she must be an accomplished
actress like other Venetian women. Othello admits as
much; and, as his now visible perturbation indicates
that he is at last beginning to perceive in what direction
the conversation tends, Iago, after rubbing it in a little
with

> Why then,
> She that so young could give out such a seeming,
> To seel her father's eyes up close as oak,
> He thought 'twas witchcraft—

breaks off in mid-sentence to let it sink in, at the same
time asking pardon, a humble pardon 'for too much
loving' the poor wronged husband, while he assures

him at the same time that the suspect party is his own 'worthy friend'. Such pauses belong to the tormentor's technique, as we have relearnt in our own day. To relax and intensify the excitement of an audience turn and turn about is also good theatre. Meanwhile the poison is at work. For when Othello lamely affirms a dozen lines later,

> I do not think but Desdemona's honest,

he is virtually admitting that he doubts her. And when in reply to Iago's fervent exclamation,

> Long live she so! and long live you to think so!

he mutters broodingly

> And yet, how nature erring from itself—

he gives us a glimpse of the monstrous thought that has now taken possession of his mind. Nature! The word Shakespeare took from Cinthio here means natural affection or desire, and Othello's use of it tells us that he is calling in mind what Brabantio said about the marriage of white and black and how Desdemona had shrunk from him when they first came to know each other. Was that shrinking a tacit acknowledgement of something fundamentally repulsive in their relationship? Her father thought so. Witchcraft alone, he had protested, could account

> For nature so preposterously to err,   (1. 3. 62)

or for the fact that

> she—in spite of nature,
> Of years, of country, credit, everything—

should 'fall in love with what she feared to look on!' (1. 3. 96–8). Witchcraft was nonsense, as he had shown the Duke; but was it not after all 'against all rules of nature' (1. 3. 101) for a white girl to mate with a black

man? one, too, older than herself,[1] and unversed in the ways of Italian suitors? His reception of Iago's next speech and his own soliloquy a little later show that these are his thoughts and his use of the word 'nature' enables Iago to divine them. For, seizing upon it as a gift from Hell, he is upon him like lightning with a viler suggestion than ever. What, he says, could have led her to encourage him, instead of lovers

> Of her own clime, complexion, and degree,
> Whereto we see in all things nature tends?

What but
> a will most rank,
> Foul disproportion, thoughts unnatural,

$$(3. \ 3. \ 232-5)$$

or, in modern terms, abnormal and disgusting desires for sexual experience with a black man,[2] desires of which she is bound to repent when she returns to her senses? This is too outspoken to be endured and Othello dismisses Iago. Not, however, in anger or indignation. The insinuation comes too near his own growing suspicions for that. He even bids him, as he goes out, set on Emilia to spy, and remarks to himself

> This honest creature doubtless
> Sees and knows more, much more, than he unfolds—

an expression of confidence which he repeats in other words a dozen lines further on.

Othello is still calm: 'Fear not my government' he assures Iago when the latter returns to suggest, under

---

[1] Othello's age is difficult to fix. Iago's 'old black ram' (1. 1. 89) is suspect evidence, but Brabantio's 'in spite of . . . years' points to a considerable difference between the ages of the couple as does Othello's admission at 3. 3. 267–8.

[2] Bradley, *op. cit.* pp. 193, 201, also interprets Iago in this sense.

cover of a friendly request to think no more of the
matter, that he may learn something perhaps by
watching Desdemona pleading for Cassio's reinstatement. But the poison is gaining its hold. Desdemona
is already condemned. Yet he can meditate with
seeming tranquility on the causes of her infidelity and
the prevalence of cuckoldry in general, while when
she enters with Emilia at 3. 3. 279 to remind him that
his guests are awaiting him at the dinner-table, the
sight of such radiant purity almost banishes doubt for
a moment. But her tender solicitude for his headache
can only be hypocrisy, since she knows the cause of it.
And when she lays her hand on the brow from which
he can feel the cuckold's horn beginning to grow and
offers to bind it with her handkerchief, the thing
becomes an outrage and he thrusts her away in fury
crying 'Let it alone!'—it is too big for your napkin!
Amazed at this sudden and inexplicable outburst she
lets the handkerchief fall, and though it is one of her
dearest possessions, so dear, as Emilia tells us immediately after,

> That she reserves it evermore about her
> To kiss and talk to,

she leaves it forgotten on the ground as she follows him
in to dinner.[1]

---

[1] Despite Booth, Salvini, and other actors (see A. C.
Sprague, *Shakespeare and the Actors* (1944), p. 196) I feel
sure this is how the incident should be played. If Othello
be not angry, why does he exclaim 'Let it alone', where 'it'
is surely his forehead, not the handkerchief? Actors and
critics seem to have forgotten the cuckold's horns there.
And how comes *she* to forget the precious handkerchief if
his astonishing conduct does not drive it out of her mind?
It seems clear to me too that she returns to the garden
after dinner to look for it. Directly she has Emilia alone
she asks 'where should I lose [i.e. Where can I have lost]

Meanwhile Iago enters, snatches the handkerchief from Emilia, and, dismissing her, delivers a soliloquy which, after announcing how he intends to use his new-won prize, prepares us for our next sight of Othello by describing the condition of his patient in this brief bulletin, which recalls his earlier prescription at 2. 3. 349–50:

> The Moor already changes with my poison:
> Dangerous conceits are in their natures poisons
> Which at the first are scarce found to distaste
> But, with a little act upon the blood,
> Burn like the mines of sulphur.

He pauses, for Othello enters at this point; and then at sight of his face now 'eaten up with passion', he points in triumph; and cries

> I did say so:
> Look where he comes! Not poppy, nor mandragora,
> Nor all the drowsy syrups of the world,
> Shall ever medicine thee to that sweet sleep
> Which thou owedst yesterday.

The poison has in Cinthio's words 'pierced the Moor to his very heart': the man is transformed and become a raging animal with blood-shot eyes.

Writing upon the terrible scenes that follow Bradley declares that their 'whole force...can be felt only by a reader. The Othello of our stage can never be Shakespeare's.'[1] He had not seen Robeson who conveyed the 'whole force' overwhelmingly.

---

that handkerchief?' as she looks for it in vain. And when Othello enters immediately after, his manner is again so strange that, knowing what store he sets upon it, she dare not tell him it is lost. I take pleasure in finding myself here in general agreement with an old opponent (see S. A. Tannenbaum in *Studies in Phil.* (Ap. 1916), pp. 73–81).

[1] Bradley, *op. cit.* p. 178.

VII. *A digression on Imagery*

Iago is so fired with his success that he borrows for a moment the highly metaphorical language of Othello; and it is now a commonplace of criticism that in his spiritual downfall Othello speaks like Iago.[1] This is most clearly seen in the matter of imagery. Each when himself has his own peculiar imagery. Othello's is lofty, poetic, solemn; opulent and sensuous; spontaneous and highly personal; so personal that what would be metaphor with other men he takes for concrete fact. When moved, indeed, there is in his mind no frontier between reality and imagination. 'My heart is turned to stone: I strike it, and it hurts my hand' he cries in agony; and, as just noted, he *feels* the brow Desdemona tries to bind swelling with the cuckold's horn. Moreover, his imagery is generally drawn from the larger and grander phenomena of the universe: the sun, the moon, the stars, the sea, the irresistible current of the Hellespont, tempest, Heaven, Hell, Chaos. Iago, on the other hand, speaks much in prose as befits a cynic. His attitude towards natural phenomena is rational and objective. He uses imagery occasionally only and then not to express personal feelings but in order to influence the feelings of others, as is shown by the absence of imagery from his soliloquies.

He measures his words with calculating guile, attuning them to the person he has to deal with. Consider, for instance, the images which he employs with Roderigo and Cassio in 1. 3 or 2. 1....They are devised to kindle in the brain of the other man a notion that will further his own plans; they

---

[1] Wilson Knight, *Wheel of Fire* (1930), ch. 6; M. M. Morozov in *Shakespeare Survey*, 2 (1949); Clemen, *Development of Shakespeare's Imagery*, ch. 13.

are a means of influencing, or they may also be a means of dissimulation.[1]

I quote from Wolfgang Clemen, our best authority on Shakespeare's imagery. But, as he also points out, the most striking thing about Iago's imagery is its repulsive quality. He is particularly fond of referring to animals of a low order, e.g. asses, cats, spiders, flies, dogs, goats, monkeys, wolves; creatures which he generally represents as engaged in activity obscene, cruel, or otherwise ugly and repellent.[2] And Caroline Spurgeon had noted earlier that while 'the main image in *Othello* is that of animals in action, preying upon one another, mischievous, lascivious, cruel or suffering...' more than half of these animal images belong to Iago.[3] Furthermore it has been since realized that Othello's allusions to foul toads breeding in a cistern, summer flies in the shambles, aspic's tongues, the raven o'er the infected house, throwing Cassio's nose to the dogs, goats and monkeys, crocodile tears, and so on all belong to the period of his overthrow, i.e. they occur between 3. 3. 331 when he enters 'eaten up with passion' and the beginning of 5. 2 when he has recovered his balance. In other words, to quote a Russian critic, 'Iago gains the ascendency over Othello's soul, so that he begins to think in Iago's images, to see the world with Iago's eyes'.[4] His exclamation 'Goats and monkeys!' is for example an echo of what Iago had said earlier. He is possessed of the devil who has 'ensnared his soul' (5. 2. 304).

[1] Clemen, *op. cit.* pp. 121–2.
[2] *Ibid.* p. 125.
[3] Spurgeon, *Shakespeare's Imagery* (1935), p. 335.
[4] M. M. Morozov, *op. cit.* p. 86.

VIII. *The last scene*

Shakespeare is one of the few great writers in modern English literature whom there has been no attempt to 'debunk' during the past forty years, though Lytton Strachey who started the fashion did his best with the last plays. This escape is due in part to the fact that his nineteenth-century expounders have acted as whipping-boys for their royal master; and none of them more often than Andrew Bradley, whose *Shakespearean Tragedy* represents the culmination of the romantic or psychologizing tradition which began with Coleridge. Nor has any part of that work attracted more attention from his depreciators than the two chapters on *Othello*. It will be evident to readers of this Introduction that in my opinion we still have a great deal to learn from Bradley and that it is, at least, never safe to ignore what he has said about any particular point in the play. But he and modern critics differ most markedly over the meaning of the last scene; and as their conflicting interpretations illustrate in striking fashion the confused state of present-day Shakespearian criticism, a few words may be given to them.

Shakespeare loves to surprise us and he sometimes elects to do so by taking a principal character off the stage and bringing him back after an interval in a mood quite unexpected by the audience. Hamlet's entry in the Nunnery scene for the astonishing 'To be or not to be' soliloquy is a case in point, and we have already noted another in Othello's change of mood between the exit comparatively calm at 3. 3. 291 and the return forty lines later frenzied with jealousy. A still more unlooked-for transformation is that which greets us at the beginning of 5. 2. Early in the previous scene, persuaded that Iago has killed Cassio, he rushes out to complete his 'great revenge' by himself killing Desde-

mona, and killing her at once, for he cries 'Strumpet,
I come!' No critic denies, or can deny, that when we
next see him uttering the solemn opening words of 5. 2,
a profound change has come over him, though if we
ask them to explain the change or to tell us what kind
of man he has now become, we hear in reply a chorus
of discordant voices. And we are in much the same
plight as regards the meaning of Othello's last speech,
which is in a way a more serious matter, since from
what he then is and says our minds receive the final
impression both of his character and of the play as
a whole.

Bradley accounts for the change of mood by telling
us that 'the supposed death of Cassio' had in the mean-
time satiated Othello's 'thirst for vengeance'. There is
no evidence for this in the text, but it is at least a
possible explanation and one consistent with the rest of
Othello's character, as understood by Bradley, who
continues as follows:

The Othello who enters the bed-chamber with the words,

> It is the cause, it is the cause, my soul,[1]

is not the man of the Fourth Act. The deed he is bound
to do is no murder, but a sacrifice (ll. 68, 1–3, 16–17). He is
to save Desdemona from herself (l. 6), not in hate but in
honour (ll. 296–7), and also in love (ll. 16–22). His anger
has passed; a boundless sorrow has taken its place; and

> this sorrow's heavenly:
> It strikes where it doth love.

Even when, at the sight of her apparent obduracy, and at
the hearing of words which by a crowning fatality can only
reconvince him of her guilt, these feelings give way to others,
it is to righteous indignation they give way, not to rage;
and terribly painful as this scene is, there is almost nothing
here to diminish the admiration and love which heighten

---

[1] See note at 5. 2. 1. on 'cause'.

pity. And pity itself vanishes, and love and admiration alone remain, in the majestic dignity and sovereign ascendancy of the close.[1]

The passages I have referred to in the notes below show that Bradley here follows the text closely. It should be observed also that while he is of course telling us what emotions the last scene evokes in himself and he believes Shakespeare intended to evoke in every spectator, they are emotions which, following Aristotle, he considers the normal and approved response of the sensitive human spirit to the catastrophe of any great tragedy. In the chapter on 'The Substance of Tragedy', he says, for example:

A Shakespearean tragedy is never, like some miscalled tragedies, depressing. No one ever closes the book with the

[1] Bradley, *op. cit.* pp. 197–8. The 'almost' refers to Othello's outburst,

> She's like a liar gone to burning hell:
> 'Twas I that killed her,

commenting upon Desdemona's last words in reply to Emilia's cry, 'O, who hath done this deed.'

> Nobody: I myself. Farewell;
> Commend me to my kind lord: O, farewell!

'One is astonished', says Bradley (note O), 'that Othello should not be startled, nay thunder-struck, when he hears such dying words coming from the lips of an obdurate adulteress.' But that, as Professor Alexander has persuaded me, is exactly what this savagery betokens. His heart acknowledges the sublime falsehood as conclusive evidence of her truth and fidelity, which the whole of the rest of his being violently repudiates. As the writer of another type of murder story has observed: 'It is odd how when you have a secret belief of your own which you do not wish to acknowledge, the voicing of it by someone else will rouse you to a fury of denial' (Agatha Christie, *The Murder of Roger Ackroyd*).

feeling that man is a poor mean creature. He may be wretched and he may be awful, but he is not small. His lot may be heart-rending and mysterious, but it is not contemptible. The most confirmed of cynics ceases to be a cynic while he reads these plays.[1]

Since Bradley wrote, historical events have encouraged cynicism and made it more difficult to accept the assumptions upon which his interpretation of tragedy rested. For after two World Wars and the intervening period of Nazi despotism in Europe it is not easy to think nobly of Man, while the advent of the new psychology associated with the name of Freud also makes it less easy to entertain the simple and unified conception of human personality which Bradley finds exemplified in Shakespeare's tragic heroes. It is not surprising therefore that by 1945 Granville-Barker had reached a very different conception of the last scene. When Othello enters the bed-room, we are now told,

He is calm as water is when near to boiling, or the sea with a surge of storm underneath. Exalted in his persuasion that it is justice he deals and not vengeance, he regains a Satanic semblance of the nobility that was his.

Hence

> Be thus when thou art dead, and I will kill thee,
> And love thee after

implies ghoulish perversion, and

>   this sorrow's heavenly:
> It strikes where it doth love

becomes blasphemy.[2] In short, Othello for most of 5. 2. is a madman; and though 'he speaks his own epitaph before he dies, a last echo of the noble Moor that was'[3] (since Shakespeare had 'to restore him as

---

[1] Bradley *op. cit.* pp. 22–3.
[2] Barker, *op. cit.* pp. 117–18.   [3] *Ibid.* p. 184.

much to himself, and to such a consciousness of himself, as will give significance to his end'[1]), the whole scene before that

is a terrible, shameful spectacle, of which Shakespeare spares us nothing, which, indeed, he elaborates and prolongs until the man's death comes as a veritable relief, a happy restoring of him to dignity.[2]

In one point alone do the critics seem to be agreed: both find Othello restored to his true nobility in the final speech. A third critic, Dr T. S. Eliot, will hardly allow this. On the contrary, what, so far from depressing Bradley 'excites his love and admiration', not only depresses Eliot but appears to him the most 'terrible exposure of human weakness' he knows of in literature. It is in fact, he says, an extreme instance of that 'attitude of self-dramatisation', ultimately derived from Seneca, which some of Shakespeare's other characters, as well as those of other Elizabethan dramatists, are apt to assume 'at moments of tragic intensity'. He then goes on:

What Othello seems to me to be doing in making this speech is *cheering himself up*. He is endeavouring to escape reality, he has ceased to think about Desdemona and is thinking about himself. Humility is the most difficult of all virtues to achieve; nothing dies harder than the desire to think well of oneself. Othello succeeds in turning himself into a pathetic figure by adopting an *aesthetic* rather than a moral attitude, dramatizing himself against his environment. He takes in the spectator, but the human motive is primarily to take in himself.[3]

Without questioning the influence of Seneca which is evident in other parts of the scene also, I find this

---

[1] *Ibid.* p. 128.   [2] *Ibid.* p. 116.
[3] Eliot, *Selected Essays*, pp. 129–31. The italics are Eliot's.

strange criticism for a stage-play, and when the critic
says 'He takes in the spectator' he seems to give the
whole case away. For what 'takes in' spectators is
a dramatic fact and there is no getting behind it, even
by a Freudian psychologist. It is of course incontestable
that Shakespeare's plays, and in particular his characters,
are full of subtleties and nuances which spectators
cannot be aware of in the rapid and complicated traffic
of the stage, whatever may be the unconscious effect
upon their minds; for his is 'a largesse universal like
the sun'. It is true also that when it suited his purpose,
he might set himself to 'take them in': we have just
been watching him doing so. But such deception is
a very different thing from what Dr Eliot posits,
namely that of a dramatist who presents his hero as one
man in the theatre while he himself thinks of him as
quite another kind of man and reveals this private
conception in a passage here and there which only an
initiated reader is likely to notice. Criticism or ap-
praisal of a Shakespearian character, however subtle or
refined, must start from the general impression the
character makes in the theatre. Critics who call this
in question are left with no guide but their own notions,
fads, or guesses. When, for example, Dr Leavis develops
Dr Eliot's point by informing us that Othello's 'habit
of approving self-dramatisation' is often a 'disguise'
for the man's 'obtuse and brutal egotism',[1] we are left
asking whether this Othello does not come from some
poem (it can hardly be a play) unknown to us, written
by another author. I would even dare to suggest that
the criticism by Granville-Barker, actor, producer and
dramatist as he was, is open to the same objection as

[1] *Scrutiny* VI, p. 270. The burden of this article by an
academic journalist like the present writer is that Bradley,
academic bookman, was incapable of understanding
Shakespeare's portrait of a man of action.

Eliot's. For though I have no doubt that, impersonating Othello himself, he could have acted the suppressed passion or leashed insanity he writes of, he would surely have been hard put to it to *act the acting* of a regained nobility, satanic or otherwise.

Readers and spectators may take their choice of these Othellos. Bradley's, with minor qualifications, is unhesitatingly mine. For I agree with him that human integrity is still possible and that Shakespeare, whether he knew his Aristotle or not, wrote this final scene, as he wrote those of most of his other tragedies, with the double purpose of first harrowing his audience with the terror and pity of the catastrophe and then sending them home with the feeling of redemption, reconciliation and even exultation which the great tragedians of all ages have aroused. The hero's last speech reminds us that he *is* a hero, the most heroic of all Shakespeare's characters. And that Shakespeare intended us to think of him as heroic throughout the scene is confirmed by what is to me very strong evidence, that of style. As Wilson Knight truly says of the opening speech,

This is the noble Othello music: highly coloured, rich in sound and phrase, stately...the most Miltonic thing in Shakespeare.[1]

Miltonic too is most of the verse he speaks until the end. Indeed, the stoical tone, marmoreal phrasing and calm dignity of the concluding speech, a calmness the more noticeable in contrast with the tumultuous violence of the lines that preface the blow that ends all, are not found combined again in such simple majesty before the conclusion of *Samson Agonistes*. Is this style put on, a 'disguise', a means of 'self-dramatisation', a 'satanic semblance of nobility'? Is it not simpler and far more plausible to suppose it was given Othello to show us

[1] *The Wheel of Fire* (1930), pp. 114-15.

not only that his mind is no longer defiled by Iago's imagery but that he is in fact a great spirit? And what spectators and readers, who do not wish for finer bread than is made of wheat, carry away with them is, to quote Bradley once again,

the impression that the heroic being, though in one sense and outwardly he has failed, is yet in another sense superior to the world in which he appears.[1]

As for the talk of 'cheering himself up', 'approving self-dramatisation', and utter forgetfulness of Desdemona, it seems to spring from a complete misunderstanding of all he says and does after his realization of her innocence. Why, for example, does he kill himself? For the same reason that he kills Desdemona: as an act of justice for infidelity to love. It is the same 'cause' and he the same minister. This is the meaning of his reference to the 'malignant Turk'. For if that infidel deserved death merely for beating an ordinary Venetian and speaking disrespectfully of Venice, how much more does his infidel self deserve it for murdering an incomparable Venetian girl and traducing her honour! He does not commit suicide; he executes himself. Yet this, it may be said, is an easy escape from an intolerable situation, a cheap retribution for so terrible a crime; even, it crosses his mind for a moment, a 'happiness'—

> to take arms against a sea of troubles,
> And by opposing, end them!

The words are Hamlet's, for the same thought had been his. But, like Hamlet, Othello knows that Death is not the end. For him indeed, as he tells us a few lines earlier, it is the gate of Hell and the horror that awaits him there is not the physical torture—the scourging, the roasting on sulphur, the drowning 'in steep-down

[1] Bradley, *op. cit.* p. 324.

gulfs of liquid fire'. These he begs for, for they will help him to forget a greater torture: that last piteous look in her eyes, the look which will hurl his soul from heaven and condemn him to the spiritual torment of an eternity of divorce from her love.

Forgetful of Desdemona! The groundlings often show a better understanding of Shakespeare than his super-subtle critics. It is reported from Moscow that in 1936, when the great actor Ostuzhev reached the 'bloody period' of Othello's last speech, a miner in the audience cried out 'It wasn't his fault: his kind of love could burn up a city!'[1] This response would I think have pleased Shakespeare, for what the last speech expresses is not self-approbation, still less a desire on the part of the speaker to cheer himself up, but a just, dignified, yet deeply humble summing up of the whole story of his tragic love before the stroke of Justice brings him to the end. Hamlet's last thought is for his 'wounded name', as befits a soldier and renaissance prince. Othello, a prince too and even more essentially the soldier, could not be altogether careless of his honour, could not be unaware how easily malice might distort the facts. Moreover, as Professor Alexander reminds me, it is Shakespeare's way to give his tragic heroes an apologia before death and sometimes to follow that up with a laudatio or epitaph by another character. Brutus and Antony and Coriolanus all speak confidently of their reputation with their last breath, while Hamlet has Horatio, Brutus Antony, Antony Cleopatra, and Coriolanus Aufidius to praise him at the end. Othello is alone. Yet he dismisses his life-long service for Venice in a line. He claims nothing of men but the truth. And he is so far from apologia

[1] Reported in *The Moscow News* and cited by Kenneth Muir in an article on 'The Jealousy of Iago'. See p. 65, *English Miscellany*, ed. Mario Praz (Rome, 1951).

or self-excuse that his reference to the 'base Indian', is best interpreted as an allusion to the ignorant and degraded 'Indians' of the New World, represented by Caliban in *The Tempest*. In any event, however 'Indian' be explained, 'base', which means 'black' as well as 'debased' or 'vile',[1] is sufficient evidence of a profound self-abasement. The proud Moor, who when we first see him tells us he fetches his 'life and being from men of royal siege', now ranks himself with the lowest type of dark-skinned creature known to the world of that day. Yet the last thought is not of sorrow or degradation. When his

> subdued eyes,
> Albeit unuséd to the melting mood,
> Drop tears as fast as the Arabian trees
> Their medicinable gum,

they are no longer the 'cruel tears' that subdued him after kissing her at the beginning of the scene, not even tears for the now 'tragic loading' of the bed. Nor does he weep for himself, in order to cut a pathetic figure, least of all that! The tears are tears of joy—that the devil has been proved false and she true, that her soul is in bliss, that she had loved him after all.[2] And so we come to his last words:

> I kissed thee ere I killed thee: no way but this,
> Killing myself, to die upon a kiss;

and to Cassio's epitaph, brief but sufficient:

> For he was great of heart.

[1] 'Is black so base a hue?' asks Aaron quibblingly in *Titus Andronicus* (4. 2. 72).
[2] This point also I owe to our records of Ostuzhev's performances. See M. M. Morozov, *Shakespeare on the Soviet Stage*, Soviet News, London, 1947, p. 29.

1955   J. D. W.

THE STAGE-HISTORY OF
OTHELLO

Popularity on the stage has marked the play from the outset. Performances at Court are attested as early as 1 November 1604 at Whitehall; again in 1612–13 during the festivities gracing the marriage of the Princess Elizabeth to the Elector Palatine; in 1636 it was presented at Hampton Court. In April 1610 a foreign visitor saw it at the Globe, and it was staged in Oxford in September; in 1629 and 1635 it was shown at Blackfriars Theatre.[1] In this period Burbage and Swanston were Othello and Taylor was Iago.[2] After the Restoration Pepys saw 'the Moor of Venice' at the Cockpit on 11 October 1660 with Burt as the Moor; on 8 December it was shown at the Theatre, formerly a tennis-court, in Vere Street. Pepys saw the play again on 6 February 1669, at the six-year old Theatre Royal, Drury Lane, Burt once more Othello; Hart was Cassio, Mohun Iago, and Mrs Hughes (probably the first woman ever seen on the stage) Desdemona. Clun, wrote Pepys, had been a much better Iago earlier, and Burt he thought poorer than before. Actually Burt was superseded soon by Hart, while Kynaston took on Cassio.[3] In 1674 and 1675,

---

[1] For the sources of information see Sir E. K. Chambers, *William Shakespeare: Facts and Problems* (1930), ii. 336, 343, 348, 352, 353; and for the Oxford production an article by G. Tillotson in the *Times Literary Supplement*, 20 July 1933, reprinted in his *Essays in Criticism and Research* (1942), pp. 41–8.

[2] See Chambers, *The Elizabethan Stage*, ii. 309; iv. 371.

[3] See Downes, *Roscius Anglicanus* (1708), pp. 6–7; Rev.

after the Duke's and King's companies had combined, in 1683 and 1684, royalty witnessed the play at Drury Lane; and again in Whitehall in 1686.[1]

Only seven years in the eighteenth century have left us no notice of an *Othello* in London.[2] On 21 May 1703 Betterton took the Moor at Lincoln's Inn Fields with Mrs Bracegirdle as Desdemona. He had doubtless played the part previously in 1683 and after; he now continued in it here, at the Queen's Theatre, Haymarket, and at Drury Lane till 1709 with her and Mrs Bradshaw successively. His final Othello was on 15 September 1709 at the Queen's Theatre. Steele in the *Tatler* described his presentation of the Moor as so moving and convincing in its truth to life that he could not imagine a better rendering.[3] In his last performance at Drury Lane, on 24 March, Colley Cibber was Iago, a part which he carried on in the Lane till 1732. We learn from his *Apology* that he thought himself well fitted for it; but Thomas Davies declares that he was only 'endured on account of his merit in comedy'.[4] Betterton's chief successors till about mid-century were Barton Booth, his 1709 Cassio, who played Othello till 1727 ('his masterpiece', said Cibber[5]); and Quin, who was at Lincoln's Inn Fields till 1733, and then at

---

John Genest, *Some Account of the English Stage, 1660–1830* (1832), i. 338–9; and on Burt and Hart, Thomas Davies, *Dramatic Miscellanies* (1783), i. 220–1.

[1] See Allardyce Nicoll, *History of Restoration Drama*, 2nd ed. (1928), pp. 307–8, 311–12, 313; cf. also Downes, *op. cit.* pp. 39–40; Genest, *op. cit.* i. 401.

[2] See the lists in C. B. Hogan, *Shakespeare in the Theatre: London, 1701–50* (1952); and in Genest, *op. cit. passim*.

[3] Cited in R. W. Lowe, *Thomas Betterton* (1891), p. 130.

[4] See Cibber, *Apology for his Life*, ed. R. W. Lowe (1889), i. 222–3; Davies, *op. cit.* iii. 469.

[5] Cibber, *op. cit.* ii, 243.

Drury Lane; his final appearance in the part being in
February 1751, at Covent Garden. Ryan was the most
frequent Iago of this period, first at Lincoln's Inn Fields
in a dozen different years while Cibber was in the Lane,
and then at Covent Garden for another eighteen years
after his time. Other Othellos of the 1730's and 1740's
were Delane and Theophilus Cibber at Goodman's
Fields, Covent Garden, Drury Lane and the Haymarket. Miss Santlow, later Mrs Booth, and Mrs
Thurmond had played Desdemona with Booth, and
after his time Mrs Giffard was in the part with Quin,
Delane, and lesser Othellos. Overlapping her came
Mrs Theophilus Cibber as Quin's partner, and later
Garrick's and Barry's. In 1736 and 1737 at Drury
Lane her husband acted with her as Cassio. She herself
went on till as late as 1761, when Sheridan was
Othello—a poor one, according to Gentleman,[1] and he
only figured later in the part twice. Garrick himself
failed in it; his stature was against him. On his first
attempt, at Drury Lane on 7 March 1745, his small
figure, blackened face and huge turban irresistibly put
the audience in mind of the negro boy with a tea-kettle
in one of Hogarth's series of pictures of *The Harlot's
Progress*, and Quin's exclamation, 'But where's the
kettle?' dissolved the house in laughter. After one
more attempt on the 9th, and another on 20 June 1746
(at Covent Garden) he never again tried the part in
London. In his 1745 performances, Macklin was Iago,[2]
and Mrs Cibber Desdemona. From the outset Quin
won much more favour than Garrick, but Spranger
Barry eclipsed both. In the winter of 1745 in Dublin
Garrick and Sheridan had alternated as Othello and
Iago. Next year, after Barry's first appearance as the

[1] F. Gentleman, *The Dramatic Censor* (1770), i. 152.
[2] Iago once before at the Haymarket in 1744, and
subsequently both at Covent Garden and at Drury Lane.

Moor at Drury Lane on 4 October, he entirely displaced
Garrick; the play ran for ten nights till 26 November.
Garrick was seen only seven more times in *Othello* (in
the Lane, 1749–50 and 1753), and now as Iago; in his
last, on 2 April, Mossop[1] was Othello and Miss
Bellamy Desdemona; they had played thus together
the previous year in the Lane. Barry, 'born for the
Moor',[2] continued triumphantly till 1774 in over
twenty separate revivals. In December 1750, at
Covent Garden, where in October Quin, Ryan and
Mrs Cibber had acted Othello, Iago and Desdemona,
Barry and Macklin played Othello and Iago, while
Mrs Macklin was Emilia; the next year Barry had
Quin as Iago. In 1756–8 Barry had first Miss Nossiter,
and then Mrs Bellamy as Desdemona; the last had
played this part with Murphy (Othello) and Ryan
(Iago) in 1754, and she acted it nine more times later.
After absence in Dublin, Barry resumed his Othellos
in London in 1766 (first at the Haymarket Opera
House) with Mrs Dancer as Desdemona; she had
previously been Emilia. From 1767 each year but one
saw him at Drury Lane, but he gave his last rendering
at Covent Garden on 9 February 1775. Mrs Dancer,
whom he married in 1768, mostly paired with him
till he ceased, and she was last seen as Desdemona in
1780.

J. P. Kemble's first Othello was on 8 March 1785 at
Drury Lane; but Mrs Siddons, who acted Desdemona,
had been seen in the part four times before, from 1777
onwards, in provincial theatres.[3] Her brother was with

[1] Gentleman, *op. cit.* i. 155, ranked him 'second to, but
far beneath', Barry.

[2] Gentleman, *op. cit.* i. 150.

[3] From a list of Mrs Siddons's Shakespearian parts
compiled by Mr Hogan and supplied for use in this edition
of the plays to the late Mr Harold Child.

her again in the Drury Lane *Othellos* of 1787 and 1791.
She was at the Haymarket in 1792 and 1793 when he
was the Moor and Bensley was Iago.[1] The next year
all three were together at the rebuilt Drury Lane, and
the brother and sister again in March 1797. In
September Elliston[2] was Othello at the Haymarket
with Miss De Camp as Desdemona and her future
husband, Charles Kemble, as Cassio. In 1804 the two
Kembles and Mrs Siddons were at Covent Garden in
the same roles. This was the sister's last Desdemona.
Kemble's last Othello, also at Covent Garden, was on
22 May 1805, Charles once more Cassio, but Mrs
Henry Siddons in the great tragic actress's place.
Charles Kemble was Cassio till 1822, and acted in
turn with C. M. Young, Macready, and Kean, while
the elder brother was twice Iago, December–January,
1807–8.

Edmund Kean surmounted the obstacle of short
height[3] which helped to defeat Garrick, and the Moor
was one of his best characters—his 'masterpiece',
thought Hazlitt, 'beyond all praise', though he saw
some defects in his later as contrasted with his earliest
manner.[4] First appearing in the part at Drury Lane

[1] On his Iago see Introduction, p. xxv.

[2] In *The Essays of Elia* ('*Ellistoniana*'), Lamb extols him
chiefly as a comedian, but Leigh Hunt thought only
Garrick excelled him in tragedy.

[3] See A. C. Sprague, *Shakespearian Players and Performances* (British ed., 1954), pp. 71–2.

[4] See Hazlitt, *A View of the English Stage* (1818), in
Complete Works, ed. Waller and Glover, VIII (1903), p. 177
(from the *Morning Chronicle*, 9 May 1814), p. 357 (from
the *Examiner*, 23 Feb. 1817) for the earlier manner; and
ibid. pp. 271–2 (from the *Examiner*, 7 Jan. 1816), *ibid.*
pp. 472–3 (from the *London Magazine*, Sept. 1820) for
the later.

on 5 May 1814, he took Iago from the second night until 9 July—eight times in all—twice with Elliston as Othello. His Iago was at first preferred, but opinion quickly veered round and his many subsequent Othellos were a series of triumphs. Iago he took again only in October 1814, and twice in the 'twenties; while each year till 1823 at Drury Lane and some ten later revivals in London saw him in the title part. Soon after his first acting of it C. M. Young was giving the two parts alternately at Covent Garden (May–June 1814); and here on 10 October 1816, Macready was seen for the first time as the Moor in London to Young's Iago. *The Times* was enthusiastic, but Hazlitt thought him 'effeminate'.[1] On the 15th and the 24th they exchanged and alternated the parts, both of them new for Macready. The year 1817 was marked by young J. B. Booth's attempt at Iago to Kean's Othello at Drury Lane on 20 February, when Kean deliberately gave him no chance, so that he cut the next performance two days later.[2] Returning to Covent Garden, he played Iago there in July to Young's Othello and Miss O'Neill's Desdemona. The Lane theatre saw Kean's second Iago in January 1822, and another of his Othellos in November; in May, Macready and Young paired in the Garden. January 1825 was long remembered at Drury Lane for the tumult when Kean defied the outcry against him by playing Othello there on the 28th, eleven days after Alderman Cox had obtained damages from him for adultery; but at the end of an inaudible performance he won over the audience by

---

[1] *View of the Stage*, *op. cit.* viii. 339 (from the *Examiner*, 13 October 1816).

[2] See H. N. Hillebrand, *Edmund Kean* (1933), pp. 167–9; Giles Playfair, *Kean* (1950), pp. 170–2. The two had acted the two parts together before, on Christmas Eve, 1816, in Brighton (see Sprague, *op. cit.* p. 76).

the courage and dignity of his speech from the stage.[1]
Kean and Young gave *Othello* together in December
1827 at Covent Garden and at Drury Lane in December–
January 1829–30. On the first occasion Charles Kemble
was Cassio; he had acted his first Othello with Young
at the same theatre in October. But Kean was nearing
his end. A prolonged contest with Macready (Iago) in
the Lane at the end of 1832 was the last great display
of his powers as the Moor. On 25 March 1833, with
Charles Kean as Iago and Ellen Tree as Desdemona,
though utterly unfit to act at all, he struggled through
to the end of the great 'Farewell' speech in 3. 3, then
suddenly collapsed and was carried off the stage.[2]

Kean's career was at an end, but a regular spate of
London *Othellos* went on till the 1850's. At the end
of 1835 Charles Kemble was playing the Moor at
Covent Garden; the following October he took Cassio
there with Macready, Vandenhoff and Helen Faucit
in the leading parts; in November, the great American
actor, Edwin Forrest, was in the Lane with Booth. In
1837 Samuel Phelps came to London; on 14 September
he played his first Othello there to Elton's Iago at the
Haymarket, and from 31 October his second, with
Macready and Helen Faucit, at Covent Garden. The
three reappeared at the Haymarket on 19 August 1839
(Mrs Warner Emilia); the two men now exchanged

---

[1] See, for details, Hillebrand, pp. 248–53; W. MacQueen
Pope, *Theatre Royal, Drury Lane* (1945), pp. 257–8; and
cf. the Stage-History in *Richard III* (New Shakespeare ed.),
p. lvi.

[2] For these last Othellos by Kean see Hillebrand,
pp. 326–7; MacQueen Pope, *op. cit.* pp. 264–5; Playfair,
op. cit. pp. 313–15; and for his acting, A. C. Sprague,
op. cit. pp. 71–86—invaluable for its record of detailed
impressions made on a variety of contemporaries, some of
them famous.

parts, but on 2 September Phelps reverted to the Moor.
Three years later, on 20 October, the same foursome
acted at Drury Lane, and in March 1843 Phelps gave
Iago there to J. R. Anderson's Othello. With 1844
began Phelps's great series of revivals at Sadler's Wells
and in all but three of his seventeen years as manager he
staged the play there. Between May 1844 and April
1845, he produced it ten times, Miss Cooper and Mrs
Warner being Desdemona and Emilia, and he and
Marston the Moor and his Ancient. In March 1847
Laura Addison acted Desdemona, and in October 1849
took Emilia; in December 1850 Phelps gave Othello
to Hoskins and played Iago. Meanwhile Edwin
Forrest had returned in 1845 and was at the Princess's
Theatre with Charlotte Cushman; in 1847 she
partnered Macready there, and the next year the same
theatre saw him and Fanny Kemble as the principals.
Charles Kean (previously Othello at Drury Lane in
1838) paired with Wallack, first as the Moor's Ancient
and then as the Moor at the Haymarket in 1849, while
Miss Addison and Ellen Tree (now Mrs Kean)
similarly exchanged Desdemona and Emilia. Miss
Addison was with J. R. Anderson and Vandenhoff at
Drury Lane in 1850 and back at the Haymarket with
Wallack in 1851. Macready's last Othellos were at the
latter theatre in the 1850–1 season. Though very
frequent, it was one of his less successful parts; his Iago,
though much less often played, was much superior—
according to Archer, 'universally admired'.[1] On the
other hand the Moor was one of Phelps's finest
characters; his success as Iago also showed his versatility. At Sadler's Wells his final appearance as Othello,
with a very feeble supporting cast, was on 2 November
1861, but he went on acting both characters for over

[1] W. Archer, *William Charles Macready* (1890), pp.
202–3; cf. J. C. Trewin, *Mr Macready* (1955), p. 246.

ten more years. He was at Drury Lane with Creswick
and Mrs Vezin in 1864, and with Charles Dillon,
alternating the two parts, in 1868–9;[1] in Manchester
with Charles Calvert at the Prince's Theatre in
November 1869; and back in London at the Princess's
Theatre in September 1872.[2]

Some very diverse Othellos and Iagos were seen in
London in the 1860's and 1870's. Fechter played the
two parts successively at the Princess's Theatre in
1861–2; the much greater Salvini was the Moor to
Edwin Booth's Iago at Drury Lane in 1875;[3] between
the two revivals the African, Ira Aldridge, was with
Madge Kendal at the Haymarket in 1865. Prior to
these Hermann Vezin had played Othello at the
Surrey Theatre in 1859. Henry Irving, a Cassio in
his pre-London days, first undertook Othello for Mrs
Bateman at the Lyceum on 14 February 1876 to
Isabel Bateman's Desdemona and Kate Bateman's
Emilia. The play had a run of forty-nine performances,
but Irving as the Moor was a failure. As manager he
revived the play, however, in 1881, and it was shown
twenty-one times in May and June, when Edwin
Booth, who in January and February had been taking
Othello and Iago in succession with Maud Milton at

---

[1] See John Coleman, *Memoirs of Samuel Phelps* (1886),
p. 320.

[2] *Op. cit.* pp. 252, 321. He may have also included
Othello in his farewell repertory at Manchester in 1877
(see W. May Phelps and J. Forbes-Robertson, *The Life and
Life-work of Samuel Phelps*, 1886, p. 307). For criticism
of his acting through the years, see *ibid.* pp. 180–1, 198–202,
322–4.

[3] The acting of these three is studied in detail in A. C.
Sprague's *Shakespeare and the Actors* (1944), pp. 185–223;
see also M. Rosenberg's article in the *Philological Quarterly*
(January 1954), pp. 72–5.

the Princess's Theatre, joined him. Irving and he
alternated the two leading parts, changing round every
second week; William Terriss was Cassio and Ellen
Terry Desdemona. (In this same May, John McCullough and Vezin were showing *Othello* at Drury Lane.)
Irving's Iago, an original conception where Booth's
followed more traditional lines deriving from Kean,
was one of his great achievements; but his Othello
remained one of his poorest, and Irving never staged
the play again, though thereby he sacrificed, not only
his Iago, but Ellen Terry's very moving rendering of
Desdemona.[1] She had acted the part once before, with
Walter Montgomery, in 1863.

The year before Irving's second *Othello* saw the first
of twenty-one revivals up to the present, in the Stratford
Memorial Theatre, then one year old, Barry Sullivan
the Moor. Six years later Benson played the part there
in his first year as Director. On 17 April 1890 he
appeared in it at the Globe in London (Mrs Benson
Desdemona) while Osmond Tearle was producing the
play and acting Othello in Stratford. In 1902, from
15 December, Forbes-Robertson was at the Lyric
Theatre with his wife, Gertrude Elliot, Lena Ashwell
taking Emilia. Though Othello was one of his finest
Shakespearian characters, he played it only once again,
in one of his three farewell Shakespeare performances
at Drury Lane, on 19 May 1913. Meanwhile Benson
had staged the play six more times in Stratford. For
the 1907 production Lewis Waller and Evelyn Millard

---

[1] For the 1881 revival see Laurence Irving's *Henry
Irving* (1951), pp. 270–1; and for Irving's and Booth's
parts Dutton Cook, *Nights at the Play* (1883), ii. 105–9;
297–305, 317–20, 324–7. For Booth as Iago, see also
A. C. Sprague, *Shakespearian Plays and Performances*,
pp. 125–35; he brings out the expressiveness of his detailed
touches and the versatility of his rendering as a whole.

came down from London (with Lyall Swete as Iago),
where the previous year H. B. Irving had been Iago
with them at the Lyric Theatre. In the year of Waller's
visit to Stratford Oscar Asche and Lily Brayton were
the leading figures in their production of *Othello* at His
Majesty's; in 1911 they came to Stratford, Asche
producing for Benson as well as taking the Moor in
the spring Festival. The next year Beerbohm Tree
acted his only Othello at His Majesty's in a sumptuously
mounted production; Laurence Irving took Iago and
Phyllis Neilson-Terry Desdemona. During the first
world war Ben Greet produced the play each year at
the 'Old Vic', 1915–17, and in 1916 in Stratford also
in place of Benson, away in France, when Robert
Atkins played Iago. Atkins produced the Old Vic
Othello in 1921–2 and 1924; in the Vic's 1920 revival
Matheson Lang and his wife (Hutin Britton) had been
the principals and Russell Thorndike the producer.
In 1921 Godfrey Tearle had the title part at the Court
Theatre (Basil Rathbone Iago), and in 1925 at the
Prince's Theatre for the Fellowship of Players, with
Cedric Hardwicke as Iago. In 1922 Baliol Holloway
was Othello in Stratford with Dorothy Green as
Emilia; years afterwards she wrote[1] that Ethel Car-
rington, the Desdemona, was 'outstanding'. In 1930
the African, Paul Robeson, partnered Peggy Ash-
croft at the Savoy Theatre, when Ralph Richardson
played Roderigo.[2] This same year *Othello* was the
Birthday play at Stratford—Wilfrid Walter the Moor;
George Hayes, Iago; and Joyce Bland, Desdemona;
while Eric Maxon acted Cassio. In 1932 Walter was
the Old Vic Othello, with Richardson as Iago, and
Edith Evans as Emilia; concurrently Ernest Milton

---

[1] In her Foreword to Ruth Ellis's *The Stratford Memorial
Theatre* (1948), p. xiii.

[2] See Introduction above, pp. ix–xii.

was Othello at St James's. The next Othello at the
Old Vic was Abraham Sofaer in 1935 with Maurice
Evans as Iago; in 1938 it was Ralph Richardson with
Laurence Olivier as Iago. Since 1940 other notable
Othellos have been Donald Wolfit (first in 1940 at the
Kingsway Theatre and in several revivals since at other
theatres); Baliol Holloway again (Stratford, 1943,
alternating as Othello and Iago with Abraham Sofaer);
George Skillan (Stratford, 1945); Godfrey Tearle
(Stratford, 1948 and 1949); and Anthony Quayle
(Stratford, November, 1952 prior to an Australian
tour,[1] and in 1954). Quayle had played Iago to Godfrey
Tearle's 1948 Othello, and to Jack Hawkins's Moor
at Piccadilly Theatre, 1947. In Stratford he had
Leo McKern as Iago in 1952, and an excellent
Desdemona in Barbara Jefford in 1950 and 1952.[2]
Mention may also be made of the partnership of
Frederick Valk and Bernard Miles in the 1942 Old
Vic revival, with Hermione Hannen as Desdemona.[3]

In New York the first known staging was at the end
of 1751. The finest players of Othello and Iago—each
seen in both roles—were Edwin Forrest (in almost
every year from 1826 to 1871) and Edwin Booth (from
1860 to 1891). The latter's partnership with Lawrence
Barrett from 1888, now as the Moor, now as Iago,
ended tragically on 18 March 1891, when Barrett as
Othello broke down in the course of his performance,
dying two days later. Booth bravely continued their
planned programmes of plays, though himself under
sentence of death; he gave his last Othello on 1 April,
three days before finally retiring. John McCullough,

[1] See T. C. Kemp in Kemp and Trewin's *The Stratford
Festival* (1953), p. 255.   [2] *Ibid.*
[3] See Harcourt Williams, *The Old Vic Saga* (1949),
pp. 171–2; Gordon Crosse, *Shakespearean Playgoing, 1890–
1952* (1953), pp. 125–6.

regarded by many as Forrest's best successor, played
Othello for ten years from 1864; Salvini gave his very
original rendering of the Moor in New York during
three separate seasons in the 1870's and 1880's.[1] In
the present century *Othello* was a regular feature in
R. B. Mansell's repertory. The most notable was the
production of the Theatre Guild at the Shubert Theatre,
New York from 19 October 1943. Paul Robeson was
Othello, Jose Ferrer Iago, and Uta Hagen (Mrs Ferrer)
Desdemona. It had the record (or near-record) run of
250 performances.[2]

C. B. YOUNG

March 1955

[1] The facts above are from G. C. D. Odell's *Annals of the
New York Stage* (15 vols.; still in progress), i. 44 *et passim.*
[2] Information received through Mr Hogan from Dr Van
Lennep of Harvard.

TO THE READER

A bracket at the beginning of a speech signifies an
'aside'.

TO THE READER

OTHELLO

The scene: Venice; Cyprus

CHARACTERS IN THE PLAY

DUKE OF VENICE
BRABANTIO, *a senator, father to Desdemona*
Other Senators
GRATIANO, *brother to Brabantio*
LODOVICO, *kinsman to Brabantio*
OTHELLO, *a noble Moor in the service of the Venetian state*
CASSIO, *his lieutenant*
IAGO, *his ancient*
RODERIGO, *a Venetian gentleman*
MONTANO, *Othello's predecessor as governor of Cyprus*
Clown, servant to Othello

DESDEMONA, *daughter to Brabantio and wife to Othello*
EMILIA, *wife to Iago*
BIANCA, *mistress to Cassio*

Sailor, Messenger, Herald, Officers, Gentlemen, Musicians, and Attendants

OTHELLO

Venice. A street

Enter RODERIGO and IAGO

Roderigo. Tush, never tell me; I take it much unkindly
That thou, Iago, who hast had my purse
As if the strings were thine, shouldst know of this.

Iago. 'Sblood, but you'll not hear me.
If ever I did dream of such a matter,
Abhor me.

Roderigo. Thou told'st me thou didst hold him in
    thy hate.

Iago. Despise me if I do not. Three great ones of
    the city,
In personal suit to make me his lieutenant,
Off-capped to him; and, by the faith of man,   10
I know my price: I am worth no worse a place.
But he, as loving his own pride and purposes,
Evades them with a bombast circumstance
Horribly stuffed with epithets of war;
And, in conclusion,
Nonsuits my mediators: for, 'Certes,' says he,
'I have already chose my officer.'
And what was he?
Forsooth, a great arithmetician,
One Michael Cassio, a Florentine,   20
A fellow almost damned in a fair wife,
That never set a squadron in the field,
Nor the division of a battle knows
More than a spinster—unless the bookish theoric,
Wherein the togéd consuls can propose

1-2

As masterly as he; mere prattle without practice
Is all his soldiership. But he, sir, had th'election;
And I, of whom his eyes had seen the proof
At Rhodes, at Cyprus, and on other grounds
30 Christian and heathen, must be be-lee'd and calmed
By debitor-and-creditor: this counter-caster,
He, in good time, must his lieutenant be,
And I—God bless the mark!—his Moorship's ancient.
  Roderigo. By heaven, I rather would have been
      his hangman.
  Iago. Why, there's no remedy: 'tis the curse
      of service;
Preferment goes by letter and affection,
And not by old gradation, where each second
Stood heir to th'first. Now, sir, be judge yourself
Whether I in any just term am affined
40 To love the Moor.
  Roderigo.   I would not follow him then.
  Iago. O, sir, content you.
I follow him to serve my turn upon him.
We cannot all be masters, nor all masters
Cannot be truly followed. You shall mark
Many a duteous and knee-crooking knave
That, doting on his own obsequious bondage,
Wears out his time, much like his master's ass,
For nought but provender, and, when he's old, cashiered.
Whip me such honest knaves. Others there are
50 Who, trimmed in forms and visages of duty,
Keep yet their hearts attending on themselves;
And, throwing but shows of service on their lords,
Do well thrive by them; and, when they've lined
      their coats,
Do themselves homage. These fellows have some soul,
And such a one do I profess myself:

For, sir,
It is as sure as you are Roderigo,
Were I the Moor, I would not be Iago;
In following him, I follow but myself;
Heaven is my judge, not I for love and duty,   60
But seeming so, for my peculiar end;
For when my outward action doth demonstrate
The native act and figure of my heart
In compliment extern, 'tis not long after
But I will wear my heart upon my sleeve
For daws to peck at—I am not what I am.

Roderigo. What a full fortune does the thick-lips owe,
If he can carry't thus!

Iago.   Call up her father,
Rouse him, make after him, poison his delight,
Proclaim him in the streets, incense her kinsmen,   70
And, though he in a fertile climate dwell,
Plague him with flies; though that his joy be joy,
Yet throw such changes of vexation on't
As it may lose some colour.

Roderigo. Here is her father's house; I'll call aloud.

Iago. Do; with like timorous accent and dire yell
As when, by night and negligence, the fire
Is spied in populous cities.

Roderigo. What, ho, Brabantio! Signior Brabantio, ho!

Iago. Awake! what, ho, Brabantio! thieves!
     thieves! thieves!   80
Look to your house, your daughter, and your bags!
Thieves! thieves!

BRABANTIO appears above, at a window

Brabantio. What is the reason of this terrible summons?
What is the matter there?

Roderigo. Signior, is all your family within?

Iago. Are your doors locked?

Brabantio.   Why, wherefore ask you this?

Iago. 'Zounds, sir, you're robbed; for shame, put
    on your gown;
Your heart is burst; you have lost half your soul;
Even now, now, very now, an old black ram
90 Is tupping your white ewe. Arise, arise;
Awake the snorting citizens with the bell,
Or else the devil will make a grandsire of you.
Arise, I say.

Brabantio.   What, have you lost your wits?

Roderigo. Most reverend signior, do you know
    my voice?

Brabantio. Not I; what are you?

Roderigo. My name is Roderigo.

Brabantio.   The worser welcome:
I have charged thee not to haunt about my doors;
In honest plainness thou hast heard me say
My daughter is not for thee; and now, in madness,
100 Being full of supper and distempering draughts,
Upon malicious knavery dost thou come
To start my quiet.

Roderigo. Sir, sir, sir—

Brabantio.   But thou must needs be sure
My spirit and my place have in them power
To make this bitter to thee.

Roderigo.   Patience, good sir.

Brabantio. What tell'st thou me of robbing? This
    is Venice:
My house is not a grange.

Roderigo.   Most grave Brabantio,
In simple and pure soul I come to you.

Iago. 'Zounds, sir, you are one of those that will not
110 serve God, if the devil bid you. Because we come to do

you service and you think we are ruffians, you'll have
your daughter covered with a Barbary horse; you'll
have your nephews neigh to you; you'll have coursers
for cousins, and jennets for germans.

Brabantio. What profane wretch art thou?

Iago. I am one, sir, that comes to tell you your
daughter and the Moor are now making the beast with
two backs.

Brabantio. Thou art a villain.

Iago.   You are a senator.

Brabantio. This thou shalt answer; I know
thee, Roderigo.   120

Roderigo. Sir, I will answer anything. But
I beseech you,
If't be your pleasure and most wise consent,
As partly I find it is, that your fair daughter,
At this odd-even and dull watch o' th'night,
Transported with no worse nor better guard
But with a knave of common hire, a gondolier,
To the gross clasps of a lascivious Moor—
If this be known to you, and your allowance,
We then have done you bold and saucy wrong;
But if you know not this, my manners tell me   130
We have your wrong rebuke. Do not believe
That, from the sense of all civility,
I thus would play and trifle with your reverence.
Your daughter, if you have not given her leave,
I say again, hath made a gross revolt,
Tying her duty, beauty, wit, and fortunes
In an extravagant and wheeling stranger
Of here and everywhere. Straight satisfy yourself.
If she be in her chamber or your house,
Let loose on me the justice of the state   140
For thus deluding you.

Brabantio.   Strike on the tinder, ho!
Give me a taper! call up all my people!
This accident is not unlike my dream;
Belief of it oppresses me already.
Light, I say! light!   *[he goes in*
 Iago.   Farewell, for I must leave you:
It seems not meet nor wholesome to my place
To be produced—as, if I stay, I shall—
Against the Moor; for I do know the state,
However this may gall him with some check,
150 Cannot with safety cast him; for he's embarked
With such loud reason to the Cyprus wars,
Which even now stand in act, that, for their souls,
Another of his fathom they have none
To lead their business: in which regard,
Though I do hate him as I do hell-pains,
Yet, for necessity of present life,
I must show out a flag and sign of love,
Which is indeed but sign. That you shall surely
  find him,
Lead to the Sagittary the raiséd search,
160 And there will I be with him. So farewell. *[he goes*

  Enter, below, BRABANTIO, *and Servants*
     with torches

 Brabantio. It is too true an evil: gone she is;
And what's to come of my despiséd time
Is nought but bitterness. Now, Roderigo,
Where didst thou see her? O unhappy girl!
With the Moor, say'st thou? Who would be a father!
How didst thou know 'twas she? O, she deceives me
Past thought! What said she to you? Get more tapers.
Raise all my kindred. Are they married, think you?
 Roderigo. Truly, I think they are.

Brabantio. O heaven! How got she out? O treason
 of the blood!   170
Fathers, from hence trust not your daughters' minds
By what you see them act! Is there not charms
By which the property of youth and maidhood
May be abused? Have you not read, Roderigo,
Of some such thing?
 Roderigo.   Yes, sir, I have indeed.
 Brabantio. Call up my brother. O, that you had
 had her!
Some one way, some another. Do you know
Where we may apprehend her and the Moor?
 Roderigo. I think I can discover him, if you please
To get good guard and go along with me.   180
 Brabantio. Pray you, lead on. At every house I'll call;
I may command at most. Get weapons, ho!
And raise some special officers of night.
On, good Roderigo; I'll deserve your pains. [*they go*

[1. 2.]   *Another street*

Enter OTHELLO, IAGO, *and Attendants with torches*

 Iago. Though in the trade of war I have slain men,
Yet do I hold it very stuff o'th'conscience
To do no contrived murder. I lack iniquity
Sometimes to do me service. Nine or ten times
I had thought t'have jerked him here under the ribs.
 Othello. 'Tis better as it is.
 Iago.   Nay, but he prated,
And spoke such scurvy and provoking terms
Against your honour
That, with the little godliness I have,

10 I did full hard forbear him. But I pray, sir,
Are you fast married? For be sure of this,
That the magnifico is much beloved,
And hath in his effect a voice potential
As double as the duke's. He will divorce you,
Or put upon you what restraint and grievance
The law, with all his might to enforce it on,
Will give him cable.
   Othello.   Let him do his spite;
My services which I have done the signiory
Shall out-tongue his complaints. 'Tis yet to know—
20 Which, when I know that boasting is an honour,
I shall promulgate—I fetch my life and being
From men of royal siege; and my demerits
May speak unbonneted to as proud a fortune
As this that I have reached. For know, Iago,
But that I love the gentle Desdemona,
I would not my unhoused free condition
Put into circumscription and confine
For the sea's worth. But look what lights come yond!
   Iago. Those are the raised father and his friends.
30 You were best go in.
   Othello.   Not I; I must be found.
My parts, my title, and my perfect soul,
Shall manifest me rightly. Is it they?
   Iago. By Janus, I think no.

     Enter CASSIO, and certain Officers with torches

   Othello. The servants of the duke, and my lieutenant!
The goodness of the night upon you, friends!
What is the news?
   Cassio.   The duke does greet you, general,
And he requires your haste-post-haste appearance
Even on the instant.

Othello.   What is the matter, think you?
  Cassio. Something from Cyprus, as I may divine.
It is a business of some heat: the galleys   40
Have sent a dozen sequent messengers
This very night at one another's heels;
And many of the consuls, raised and met,
Are at the duke's already. You have been hotly
          called for;
When, being not at your lodging to be found,
The senate hath sent about three several quests
To search you out.
  Othello.   'Tis well I am found by you.
I will but spend a word here in the house,
And go with you.   [*he goes in*
  Cassio.   Ancient, what makes he here?
  Iago. Faith, he tonight hath boarded a land carack; 50
If it prove lawful prize, he's made for ever.
  Cassio. I do not understand.
  Iago.   He's married.
  Cassio.   To who?

          Re-enter OTHELLO

  Iago. Marry, to—Come, captain, will you go?
  Othello.   Have with you.
  Cassio. Here comes another troop to seek for you.
  Iago. It is Brabantio. General, be advised;
He comes to bad intent.

      Enter BRABANTIO, RODERIGO, *and Officers with*
                torches and weapons

  Othello.   Holla! stand there!
  Roderigo. Signior, it is the Moor.
  Brabantio.   Down with him, thief!
                              [*they draw on both sides*

Iago. You, Roderigo! come sir, I am for you.

Othello. Keep up your bright swords, for the dew
    will rust them.

60 Good signior, you shall more command with years
Than with your weapons.

Brabantio. O thou foul thief, where hast thou stowed
    my daughter?
Damned as thou art, thou hast enchanted her:
For I'll refer me to all things of sense,
If she in chains of magic were not bound,
Whether a maid so tender, fair, and happy,
So opposite to marriage that she shunned
The wealthy curléd darlings of our nation,
Would ever have, t'incur a general mock,
70 Run from her guardage to the sooty bosom
Of such a thing as thou—to fear, not to delight.
Judge me the world, if 'tis not gross in sense
That thou hast practised on her with foul charms,
Abused her delicate youth with drugs or minerals
That weaken motion: I'll have't disputed on;
'Tis probable and palpable to thinking.
I therefore apprehend and do attach thee
For an abuser of the world, a practiser
Of arts inhibited and out of warrant.
80 Lay hold upon him. If he do resist,
Subdue him at his peril.

  Othello.   Hold your hands,
Both you of my inclining and the rest:
Were it my cue to fight, I should have known it
Without a prompter. Where will you that I go
To answer this your charge?

  Brabantio.   To prison, till fit time
Of law and course of direct session
Call thee to answer.

Othello.   What if I do obey?
How may the duke be therewith satisfied,
Whose messengers are here about my side,
Upon some present business of the state   90
To bring me to him?
  1 *Officer.*   'Tis true, most worthy signior;
The duke's in council, and your noble self,
I am sure, is sent for.
  Brabantio.   How! the duke in council!
In this time of the night! Bring him away.
Mine's not an idle cause: the duke himself,
Or any of my brothers of the state,
Cannot but feel this wrong as 'twere their own;
For if such actions may have passage free,
Bond-slaves and pagans shall our statesmen be. [*they go*

[1. 3.]   *A council-chamber*

The Duke and Senators sitting at a table;
Officers attending

  Duke. There is no composition in these news
That gives them credit.
  1 *Senator.*   Indeed they are disproportioned:
My letters say a hundred and seven galleys.
  Duke. And mine, a hundred and forty.
  2 *Senator.*   And mine, two hundred;
But though they jump not on a just account—
As in these cases where the aim reports
'Tis oft with difference—yet do they all confirm
A Turkish fleet, and bearing up to Cyprus.
  Duke. Nay, it is possible enough to judgement;
I do not so secure me in the error,   10

But the main article I do approve
In fearful sense.

Sailor [*without*]. What, ho! what, ho! what, ho!

1 *Officer*. A messenger from the galleys.

Enter Sailor

Duke.   Now, what's the business?

Sailor. The Turkish preparation makes for Rhodes;
So was I bid report here to the state
By Signior Angelo.

Duke. How say you by this change?

1 *Senator*.   This cannot be,
By no assay of reason; 'tis a pageant
To keep us in false gaze. When we consider
20 Th'importancy of Cyprus to the Turk,
And let ourselves again but understand
That, as it more concerns the Turk than Rhodes,
So may he with more facile question bear it,
For that it stands not in such warlike brace,
But altogether lacks th'abilities
That Rhodes is dressed in—if we make thought of this,
We must not think the Turk is so unskilful
To leave that latest which concerns him first,
Neglecting an attempt of ease and gain
30 To wake and wage a danger profitless.

Duke. Nay, in all confidence, he's not for Rhodes.

1 *Officer*. Here is more news.

Enter a Messenger

Messenger. The Ottomites, reverend and gracious,
Steering with due course toward the isle of Rhodes,
Have there injointed with an after fleet.

1 *Senator*. Ay, so I thought. How many, as
    you guess?

Messenger. Of thirty sail; and now they do re-stem
Their backward course, bearing with frank appearance
Their purposes toward Cyprus. Signior Montano,
Your trusty and most valiant servitor,   40
With his free duty recommends you thus,
And prays you to relieve him.
    Duke. 'Tis certain then for Cyprus.
Marcus Luccicos, is not he in town?
    1 *Senator*. He's now in Florence.
    Duke. Write from us to him; post-post-
      haste dispatch.
    1 *Senator*. Here comes Brabantio and the
      valiant Moor.

    Enter BRABANTIO, OTHELLO, IAGO, RODERIGO,
             and Officers

    Duke. Valiant Othello, we must straight employ you
Against the general enemy Ottoman.
[*to Brabantio*] I did not see you; welcome,
      gentle signior;   50
We lacked your counsel and your help tonight.
    Brabantio. So did I yours. Good your grace,
      pardon me:
Neither my place nor aught I heard of business
Hath raised me from my bed, nor doth the general care
Take hold on me; for my particular grief
Is of so flood-gate and o'erbearing nature
That it engluts and swallows other sorrows,
And yet is still itself.
    Duke.   Why, what's the matter?
    Brabantio. My daughter! O, my daughter!
    All.   Dead?
    Brabantio.   Ay, to me:
She is abused, stolen from me and corrupted   60

By spells and medicines bought of mountebanks;
For nature so preposterously to err,
Being not deficient, blind, or lame of sense,
Sans witchcraft could not.

   Duke. Whoe'er he be that in this foul proceeding
Hath thus beguiled your daughter of herself,
And you of her, the bloody book of law
You shall yourself read in the bitter letter
After your own sense, yea, though our proper son
70 Stood in your action.

   Brabantio.   Humbly I thank your grace.
Here is the man: this Moor, whom now, it seems,
Your special mandate for the state affairs
Hath hither brought.

   All.   We are very sorry for't.

   Duke [*to Othello*]. What in your own part can you
     say to this?

   Brabantio. Nothing, but this is so.

   Othello. Most potent, grave, and reverend signiors,
My very noble and approved good masters,·
That I have ta'en away this old man's daughter,
It is most true; true, I have married her:
80 The very head and front of my offending
Hath this extent, no more. Rude am I in
     my speech,
And little blest with the soft phrase of peace:
For since these arms of mine had seven years' pith
Till now some nine moons wasted, they have used
Their dearest action in the tented field;
And little of this great world can I speak
More than pertains to feats of broil and battle;
And therefore little shall I grace my cause
In speaking for myself. Yet, by your patience,
90 I will a round unvarnished tale deliver

Of my whole course of love: what drugs,
    what charms,
What conjuration, and what mighty magic—
For such proceedings I am charged withal—
I won his daughter.
  Brabantio.   A maiden never bold;
Of spirit so still and quiet that her motion
Blushed at herself; and she—in spite of nature,
Of years, of country, credit, everything—
To fall in love with what she feared to look on!
It is a judgement maimed and most imperfect
That will confess perfection so could err   100
Against all rules of nature, and must be driven
To find out practices of cunning hell
Why this should be. I therefore vouch again
That with some mixtures powerful o'er the blood,
Or with some dram conjured to this effect,
He wrought upon her.
  Duke.   To vouch this is no proof,
Without more wider and more overt test
Than these thin habits and poor likelihoods
Of modern seeming do prefer against him.
  1 *Senator.* But, Othello, speak: 110
Did you by indirect and forcéd courses
Subdue and poison this young maid's affections?
Or came it by request and such fair question
As soul to soul affordeth?
  Othello.   I beseech you,
Send for the lady to the Sagittary,
And let her speak of me before her father;
If you do find me foul in her report,
The trust, the office I do hold of you,
Not only take away, but let your sentence
Even fall upon her life.

2

120 *Duke.*   Fetch Desdemona hither.
    Othello. Ancient, conduct them; you best know
        the place.   [*Iago departs with attendants*
    And till she come, as truly as to heaven
    I do confess the vices of my blood,
    So justly to your grave ears I'll present
    How I did thrive in this fair lady's love,
    And she in mine.
    Duke. Say it, Othello.
    Othello. Her father loved me, oft invited me,
    Still questioned me the story of my life
130 From year to year—the battles, sieges, fortunes,
    That I have passed.
    I ran it through, even from my boyish days
    To th'very moment that he bade me tell it:
    Wherein I spake of most disastrous chances,
    Of moving accidents by flood and field,
    Of hair-breadth scapes i'th'imminent deadly breach,
    Of being taken by the insolent foe,
    And sold to slavery; of my redemption thence,
    And portance in my travels' history:
140 Wherein of antres vast and deserts idle,
    Rough quarries, rocks, and hills whose heads
        touch heaven,
    It was my hint to speak—such was the process;
    And of the Cannibals that each other eat,
    The Anthropophagi, and men whose heads
    Do grow beneath their shoulders. This to hear
    Would Desdemona seriously incline;
    But still the house affairs would draw her thence,
    Which ever as she could with haste dispatch
    She'ld come again, and with a greedy ear
150 Devour up my discourse; which I observing,
    Took once a pliant hour, and found good means

To draw from her a prayer of earnest heart
That I would all my pilgrimage dilate,
Whereof by parcels she had something heard,
But not intentively. I did consent,
And often did beguile her of her tears
When I did speak of some distressful stroke
That my youth suffered. My story being done,
She gave me for my pains a world of sighs:
She swore, in faith 'twas strange, 'twas
       passing strange;   160
'Twas pitiful, 'twas wondrous pitiful;
She wished she had not heard it, yet she wished
That heaven had made her such a man; she
       thanked me,
And bade me, if I had a friend that loved her,
I should but teach him how to tell my story,
And that would woo her. Upon this hint I spake;
She loved me for the dangers I had passed,
And I loved her that she did pity them.
This only is the witchcraft I have used.
Here comes the lady; let her witness it.   170

Enter DESDEMONA, IAGO, *and Attendants*

Duke. I think this tale would win my daughter too.
Good Brabantio,
Take up this mangled matter at the best:
Men do their broken weapons rather use
Than their bare hands.

     Brabantio.   I pray you, hear her speak.
If she confess that she was half the wooer,
Destruction on my head, if my bad blame
Light on the man! Come hither, gentle mistress:
Do you perceive in all this company
Where most you owe obedience?

180 *Desdemona.*   My noble father,
     I do perceive here a divided duty.
     To you I am bound for life and education;
     My life and education both do learn me
     How to respect you. You are the lord of duty;
     I am hitherto your daughter. But here's my husband;
     And so much duty as my mother showed
     To you, preferring you before her father,
     So much I challenge that I may profess
     Due to the Moor my lord.
         Brabantio.   God bu'y! I've done.
190 Please it your grace, on to the state affairs.
     I had rather to adopt a child than get it.
     Come hither, Moor:
     I here do give thee that with all my heart,
     Which, but thou hast already, with all my heart
     I would keep from thee. For your sake, jewel,
     I am glad at soul I have no other child;
     For thy escape would teach me tyranny,
     To hang clogs on them. I have done, my Lord.
         Duke. Let me speak like yourself, and lay a sentence
200 Which, as a grise or step, may help these lovers
     Into your favour.
     When remedies are past, the griefs are ended
     By seeing the worst, which late on hopes depended.
     To mourn a mischief that is past and gone
     Is the next way to draw new mischief on.
     What cannot be preserved when Fortune takes,
     Patience her injury a mockery makes.
     The robbed that smiles steals something from the thief;
     He robs himself that spends a bootless grief.
210 *Brabantio.* So let the Turk of Cyprus us beguile,
     We lose it not so long as we can smile.
     He bears the sentence well that nothing bears

But the free comfort which from thence he hears;
But he bears both the sentence and the sorrow
That to pay grief must of poor patience borrow.
These sentences, to sugar or to gall,
Being strong on both sides, are equivocal.
But words are words: I never yet did hear
That the bruised heart was piecéd through the ear.
I humbly beseech you, proceed to th'affairs of state.   220

Duke. The Turk with a most mighty preparation makes
for Cyprus. Othello, the fortitude of the place is best
known to you; and though we have there a substitute of
most allowed sufficiency, yet opinion, a sovereign
mistress of effects, throws a more safer voice on you:
you must therefore be content to slubber the gloss of
your new fortunes with this more stubborn and
boisterous expedition.

Othello. The tyrant Custom, most grave senators,
Hath made the flinty and steel couch of war   230
My thrice-driven bed of down. I do agnize
A natural and prompt alacrity
I find in hardness; and do undertake
These present wars against the Ottomites.
Most humbly therefore bending to your state,
I crave fit disposition for my wife,
Due reference of place and exhibition,
With such accommodation and besort
As levels with her breeding.

Duke.   Why, if you please,
Be't at her father's.

Brabantio.   I'll not have it so.   240

Othello. Nor I.

Desdemona.   Nor I; I would not there reside,
To put my father in impatient thoughts
By being in his eye. Most gracious duke,

To my unfolding lend your prosperous ear,
And let me find a charter in your voice
T'assist my simpleness.
 Duke. What would you, Desdemona?
 Desdemona. That I did love the Moor to live with him,
My downright violence and scorn of fortunes
250 May trumpet to the world. My heart's subdued
Even to the very quality of my lord.
I saw Othello's visage in his mind,
And to his honours and his valiant parts
Did I my soul and fortunes consecrate.
So that, dear lords, if I be left behind,
A moth of peace, and he go to the war,
The rights for why I love him are bereft me,
And I a heavy interim shall support
By his dear absence. Let me go with him.
260 *Othello.* Let her have your voice.
Vouch with me, heaven, I therefore beg it not
To please the palate of my appetite;
Nor to comply with heat and young affects
In my distinct and proper satisfaction;
But to be free and bounteous to her mind.
And heaven defend your good souls that you think
I will your serious and great business scant
For she is with me. No, when light-winged toys
Of feathered Cupid seel with wanton dullness
270 My speculative and officed instruments,
That my disports corrupt and taint my business,
Let housewives make a skillet of my helm,
And all indign and base adversities
Make head against my estimation!
 Duke. Be it as you shall privately determine,
Either for her stay or going; th'affair cries haste,
And speed must answer it.

1 *Senator.* You must away tonight.

Othello.   With all my heart.

Duke. At nine i'th'morning here we'll meet again.

Othello, leave some officer behind,   280

And he shall our commission bring to you;

With such things else of quality and respect

As doth import you.

Othello.   So please your grace, my ancient:

A man he is of honesty and trust;

To his conveyance I assign my wife,

With what else needful your good grace shall think

To be sent after me.

Duke.   Let it be so.

Good night to everyone. [*to Brabantio*] And,
     noble signior,

If virtue no delighted beauty lack,

Your son-in-law is far more fair than black.   290

1 *Senator.* Adieu, brave Moor; use Desdemona well.

Brabantio. Look to her, Moor, if thou hast eyes
     to see:

She has deceived her father, and may thee.

Othello. My life upon her faith!

                    [*Duke, Senators, Officers, &c. depart*

                         Honest Iago,

My Desdemona must I leave to thee;

I prithee, let thy wife attend on her,

And bring them after in the best advantage.

Come, Desdemona, I have but an hour

Of love, of worldly matter and direction,

To spend with thee: we must obey the time.   300

                    [*Othello and Desdemona go out*

Roderigo. Iago!

Iago. What say'st thou, noble heart?

Roderigo. What will I do, think'st thou?

Iago. Why, go to bed and sleep.

Roderigo. I will incontinently drown myself.

Iago. If thou dost, I shall never love thee after. Why, thou silly gentleman!

Roderigo. It is silliness to live when to live is torment; and then have we a prescription to die when death is 310 our physician.

Iago. O villanous! I have looked upon the world for four times seven years; and since I could distinguish betwixt a benefit and an injury, I never found a man that knew how to love himself. Ere I would say I would drown myself for the love of a guinea-hen, I would change my humanity with a baboon.

Roderigo. What should I do? I confess it is my shame to be so fond, but it is not in my virtue to amend it.

Iago. Virtue! a fig! 'tis in ourselves that we are thus or 320 thus. Our bodies are gardens, to the which our wills are gardeners; so that if we will plant nettles or sow lettuce, set hyssop and weed up tine, supply it with one gender of herbs or distract it with many, either to have it sterile with idleness or manured with industry— why, the power and corrigible authority of this lies in our wills. If the beam of our lives had not one scale of reason to poise another of sensuality, the blood and baseness of our natures would conduct us to most preposterous conclusions. But we have reason to cool our 330 raging motions, our carnal stings, our unbitted lusts; whereof I take this, that you call love, to be a set or scion.

Roderigo. It cannot be.

Iago. It is merely a lust of the blood and a permission of the will. Come, be a man. Drown thyself! Drown cats and blind puppies. I have professed me thy friend, and I confess me knit to thy deserving with cables of

perdurable toughness. I could never better stead thee
than now. Put money in thy purse; follow thou these
wars; defeat thy favour with an usurped beard. I say, 340
put money in thy purse. It cannot be that Desdemona
should long continue her love to the Moor—put money
in thy purse—nor he his to her: it was a violent commencement, and thou shalt see an answerable sequestration—put but money in thy purse. These Moors are
changeable in their wills—fill thy purse with money.
The food that to him now is as luscious as locusts, shall
be to him shortly as bitter as coloquintida. She must
change for youth: when she is sated with his body, she
will find the error of her choice. Therefore put money 350
in thy purse. If thou wilt needs damn thyself, do it
a more delicate way than drowning. Make all the
money thou canst. If sanctimony and a frail vow betwixt
an erring barbarian and a supersubtle Venetian be not
too hard for my wits and all the tribe of hell, thou shalt
enjoy her; therefore make money. A pox of drowning
thyself! 'Tis clean out of the way. Seek thou rather to
be hanged in compassing thy joy than to be drowned
and go without her.

Roderigo. Wilt thou be fast to my hopes, if I depend 360
on the issue?

Iago. Thou art sure of me. Go, make money. I have
told thee often, and I re-tell thee again and again, I hate
the Moor. My cause is hearted; thine hath no less
reason. Let us be conjunctive in our revenge against
him. If thou canst cuckold him, thou dost thyself a
pleasure, me a sport. There are many events in the
womb of time, which will be delivered. Traverse! go;
provide thy money. We will have more of this tomorrow. Adieu.   370

Roderigo. Where shall we meet i'th'morning?

Iago. At my lodging.

Roderigo. I'll be with thee betimes.

Iago. Go to; farewell. Do you hear, Roderigo?

Roderigo. What say you?

Iago. No more of drowning, do you hear?

Roderigo. I am changed.

Iago. Go to; farewell. Put money enough in your purse.

380 *Roderigo.* I'll sell all my land.   [*goes*

Iago. Thus do I ever make my fool my purse;
For I mine own gained knowledge should profane
If I would time expend with such a snipe
But for my sport and profit. I hate the Moor;
And it is thought abroad that 'twixt my sheets
He's done my office. I know not if't be true;
Yet I, for mere suspicion in that kind,
Will do as if for surety. He holds me well;
The better shall my purpose work on him.

390 Cassio's a proper man: let me see now;
To get his place, and to plume up my will
In double knavery. How? How? Let's see:
After some time to abuse Othello's ear
That he is too familiar with his wife;
He hath a person and a smooth dispose
To be suspected—framed to make women false.
The Moor is of a free and open nature
That thinks men honest that but seem to be so,
And will as tenderly be led by th'nose

400 As asses are.
I have't. It is engendered. Hell and night
Must bring this monstrous birth to the world's light.

          [*goes*

[2. 1.]   *A sea-port in Cyprus. An open place*
near the quay

Enter MONTANO and two Gentlemen

Montano. What from the cape can you discern at sea?
1 *Gentleman.* Nothing at all: it is a high-wrought flood;
I cannot 'twixt the heaven and the main
Descry a sail.
    Montano. Methinks the wind hath spoke aloud
         at land;
A fuller blast ne'er shook our battlements.
If it hath ruffianed so upon the sea,
What ribs of oak, when mountains melt on them,
Can hold the mortise? What shall we hear of this?
    2 *Gentleman.* A segregation of the Turkish fleet: 10
For do but stand upon the foaming shore,
The chidden billow seems to pelt the clouds;
The wind-shaked surge, with high and
         monstrous mane,
Seems to cast water on the burning Bear,
And quench the guards of th'ever-fixéd pole.
I never did like molestation view
On the enchaféd flood.
    Montano.   If that the Turkish fleet
Be not ensheltered and embayed, they are drowned;
It is impossible they bear it out.

Enter a third Gentleman

3 *Gentleman.* News, lads! our wars are done: 20
The desperate tempest hath so banged the Turks
That their designment halts. A noble ship of Venice
Hath seen a grievous wreck and sufferance
On most part of their fleet.

Montano. How! is this true?

   3 *Gentleman.*   The ship is here put in,
A Veronesa; Michael Cassio,
Lieutenant to the warlike Moor Othello,
Is come on shore; the Moor himself at sea,
And is in full commission here for Cyprus.

30 *Montano.* I am glad on't; 'tis a worthy governor.

   3 *Gentleman.* But this same Cassio, though he speak
     of comfort
Touching the Turkish loss, yet he looks sadly,
And prays the Moor be safe; for they were parted
With foul and violent tempest.

   Montano.   Pray heaven he be;
For I have served him, and the man commands
Like a full soldier. Let's to the sea-side, ho!
As well to see the vessel that's come in
As to throw out our eyes for brave Othello,
Even till we make the main and th'aerial blue

40 An indistinct regard.

   3 *Gentleman.*   Come, let's do so;
For every minute is expectancy
Of more arrivance.

Enter CASSIO

   Cassio. Thanks you, the valiant of this warlike isle,
That so approve the Moor! O, let the heavens
Give him defence against the elements,
For I have lost him on a dangerous sea.

   Montano. Is he well shipped?

   Cassio. His bark is stoutly timbered, and his pilot
Of very expert and approved allowance;

50 Therefore my hopes, not forfeited to death,
Stand in bold cure.

                 [*a cry heard*: 'A sail, a sail, a sail!'

Enter a fourth Gentleman

Cassio. What noise?
4 *Gentleman.* The town is empty; on the brow
    o'th'sea
Stand ranks of people, and they cry 'A sail!'
  Cassio. My hopes do shape him for the Governor.
                            [guns heard
2 *Gentleman.* They do discharge their shot of courtesy:
Our friends at least.
  Cassio.   I pray you, sir, go forth,
And give us truth who 'tis that is arrived.
  2 *Gentleman.* I shall.   *[goes*
  Montano. But, good lieutenant, is your general wived? 60
  Cassio. Most fortunately: he hath achieved a maid
That paragons description and wild fame;
One that excels the quirks of blazoning pens,
And in th'essential vesture of creation
Does tire the ingener.

Re-enter second Gentleman

               How now! who has put in?
  2 *Gentleman.* 'Tis one Iago, ancient to the general.
  Cassio. He's had most favourable and happy speed:
Tempests themselves, high seas, and howling winds,
The guttered rocks, and congregated sands,
Traitors insteeped to clog the guiltless keel,   70
As having sense of beauty, do omit
Their mortal natures, letting go safely by
The divine Desdemona.
  Montano.   What is she?
  Cassio. She that I spake of, our great
    captain's captain,
Left in the conduct of the bold Iago;

Whose footing here anticipates our thoughts
A se'nnight's speed. Great Jove, Othello guard,
And swell his sail with thine own powerful breath,
That he may bless this bay with his tall ship,
80 Make love's quick pants in Desdemona's arms,
Give renewed fire to our extincted spirits,
And bring all Cyprus comfort.

*Enter DESDEMONA, EMILIA, IAGO, RODERIGO,
and Attendants*

                              O, behold,
The riches of the ship is come on shore!
You men of Cyprus, let her have your knees.
Hail to thee, lady! and the grace of heaven,
Before, behind thee, and on every hand,
Enwheel thee round!
    Desdemona.   I thank you, valiant Cassio.
What tidings can you tell me of my lord?
    Cassio. He is not yet arrived; nor know I aught
90 But that he's well and will be shortly here.
    Desdemona. O, but I fear—How lost you company?
    Cassio. The great contention of the sea and skies
Parted our fellowship. But, hark! a sail!

             [*a cry heard, 'A sail, a sail!', and then guns*
    2 Gentleman. They give their greeting to the citadel:
This likewise is a friend.
    Cassio.   See for the news.

                              [*Gentleman goes*
Good ancient, you are welcome. [*to Emilia*]
        Welcome, mistress.
Let it not gall your patience, good Iago,
That I extend my manners; 'tis my breeding
That gives me this bold show of courtesy. [*kisses her*
100 *Iago.* Sir, would she give you so much of her lips

As of her tongue she oft bestows on me,
You'ld have enough.

Desdemona. Alas, she has no speech.

Iago.   In faith, too much;
I find it still when I have list to sleep.
Marry, before your ladyship, I grant,
She puts her tongue a little in her heart
And chides with thinking.

Emilia. You have little cause to say so.

Iago. Come on, come on; you are pictures out of
doors, bells in your parlours, wild-cats in your kitchens; 110
saints in your injuries, devils being offended; players in
your housewifery, and hussies in your beds.

Desdemona. O, fie upon thee, slanderer!

Iago. Nay, it is true, or else I am a Turk:
You rise to play, and go to bed to work.

Emilia. You shall not write my praise.

Iago.   No, let me not.

Desdemona. What wouldst thou write of me, if thou
    shouldst praise me?

Iago. O gentle lady, do not put me to't;
For I am nothing if not critical.

Desdemona. Come on, assay—There's one gone to
    the harbour?   120

Iago. Ay, madam.

(*Desdemona.* I am not merry; but I do beguile
The thing I am by seeming otherwise.
[*aloud*] Come, how wouldst thou praise me?

Iago. I am about it; but indeed my invention comes
from my pate as birdlime does from frieze—it plucks
out brains and all. But my muse labours, and thus she
is delivered.

    If she be fair and wise, fairness and wit,
        The one's for use, the other useth it.   130

Desdemona. Well praised! How if she be black
    and witty?

Iago. If she be black, and thereto have a wit,
    She'll find a white that shall her blackness hit.

Desdemona. Worse and worse.

Emilia. How if fair and foolish?

Iago. She never yet was foolish that was fair;
    For even her folly helped her to an heir.

Desdemona. These are old fond paradoxes to make
fools laugh i'th'alehouse. What miserable praise hast
140 thou for her that's foul and foolish?

Iago. There's none so foul, and foolish thereunto,
    But does foul pranks which fair and wise
        ones do.

Desdemona. O heavy ignorance! thou praisest the
worst best. But what praise couldst thou bestow on
a deserving woman indeed—one that in the authority
of her merit did justly put on the vouch of very malice
itself?

Iago. She that was ever fair, and never proud,
    Had tongue at will, and yet was never loud,
150   Never lacked gold, and yet went never gay,
    Fled from her wish, and yet said 'Now
        I may';
    She that, being angered, her revenge
        being nigh,
    Bade her wrong stay, and her displeasure fly;
    She that in wisdom never was so frail
    To change the cod's head for the
        salmon's tail;
    She that could think, and ne'er disclose
        her mind,
    See suitors following, and not look behind;
    She was a wight, if ever such wight were—

Desdemona. To do what?

Iago. To suckle fools and chronicle small beer.   160

Desdemona. O most lame and impotent conclusion!
Do not learn of him, Emilia, though he be thy husband.
How say you, Cassio? Is he not a most profane and
liberal counsellor?

Cassio. He speaks home, madam. You may relish him
more in the soldier than in the scholar.

(*Iago.* He takes her by the palm. Ay, well said,
whisper. With as little a web as this will I ensnare as
great a fly as Cassio. Ay, smile upon her, do; I will
gyve thee in thine own courtship. You say true: 'tis so,   170
indeed. If such tricks as these strip you out of your
lieutenantry, it had been better you had not kissed your
three fingers so oft, which now again you are most apt
to play the sir in. Very good; well kissed! an excellent
courtesy! 'tis so, indeed. Yet again your fingers to your
lips? Would they were clyster-pipes for your sake!

                          [*trumpets within*

[*aloud*] The Moor! I know his trumpet.

Cassio.   'Tis truly so.

Desdemona. Let's meet him and receive him.

Cassio.   Lo where he comes!

Enter OTHELLO and Attendants

Othello. O my fair warrior!

Desdemona.   My dear Othello!

Othello. It gives me wonder great as my content   180
To see you here before me. O my soul's joy!
If after every tempest come such calms,
May the winds blow till they have wakened death!
And let the labouring bark climb hills of seas
Olympus-high and duck again as low
As hell's from heaven! If it were now to die,

'Twere now to be most happy; for I fear,
My soul hath her content so absolute
That not another comfort like to this
190 Succeeds in unknown fate.
    Desdemona.   The heavens forbid
But that our loves and comforts should increase,
Even as our days do grow!
    Othello.   Amen to that, sweet powers!
I cannot speak enough of this content:
It stops me here; it is too much of joy.
And this, and this, the greatest discords be   *[they kiss*
That e'er our hearts shall make!
    (*Iago*. O, you are well tuned now! But I'll set down
the pegs that make this music, as honest as I am.
    Othello. Come, let's to the castle.
200 News, friends: our wars are done; the Turks
       are drowned.
How does my old acquaintance of this isle?
Honey, you shall be well desired in Cyprus;
I have found great love amongst them. O my sweet,
I prattle out of fashion, and I dote
In mine own comfort. I prithee, good Iago,
Go to the bay, and disembark my coffers;
Bring thou the master to the citadel;
He is a good one, and his worthiness
Does challenge much respect. Come, Desdemona,
210 Once more well met at Cyprus.
                        [all but Iago and Roderigo depart
    Iago. Do thou meet me presently at the harbour.
Come hither. If thou be'st valiant—as they say base
men being in love have then a nobility in their natures
more than is native to them—list me. The lieutenant
tonight watches on the court of guard. First, I must
tell thee this: Desdemona is directly in love with him.

Roderigo. With him! why, 'tis not possible.

Iago. Lay thy finger thus, and let thy soul be instructed. Mark me with what violence she first loved the Moor but for bragging and telling her fantastical 220 lies. And will she love him still for prating?—let not thy discreet heart think it. Her eye must be fed; and what delight shall she have to look on the devil? When the blood is made dull with the act of sport, there should be—again to inflame it and to give satiety a fresh appetite—loveliness in favour, sympathy in years, manners, and beauties; all which the Moor is defective in. Now, for want of these required conveniencies, her delicate tenderness will find itself abused, begin to heave the gorge, disrelish and abhor the Moor. Very nature 230 will instruct her in it and compel her to some second choice. Now, sir, this granted—as it is a most pregnant and unforced position—who stands so eminent in the degree of this fortune as Cassio does?—a knave very voluble; no further conscionable than in putting on the mere form of civil and humane seeming, for the better compassing of his salt and most hidden loose affection. Why, none; why, none—a slipper and subtle knave; a finder-out of occasions; that has an eye can stamp and counterfeit advantages, though true advantage never 240 present itself; a devilish knave! Besides, the knave is handsome, young, and hath all those requisites in him that folly and green minds look after; a pestilent complete knave; and the woman hath found him already.

Roderigo. I cannot believe that in her; she's full of most blest condition.

Iago. Blest fig's-end! The wine she drinks is made of grapes. If she had been blest, she would never have loved the Moor. Blest pudding! Didst thou not see her paddle with the palm of his hand? Didst not mark that? 250

Roderigo. Yes, that I did; but that was but courtesy.

Iago. Lechery, by this hand; an index and obscure prologue to the history of lust and foul thoughts. They met so near with their lips that their breaths embraced together—villanous thoughts, Roderigo! When these mutualities so marshal the way, hard at hand comes the master and main exercise, th'incorporate conclusion. Pish! But, sir, be you ruled by me. I have brought you from Venice. Watch you tonight; for the command, 260 I'll lay't upon you. Cassio knows you not; I'll not be far from you. Do you find some occasion to anger Cassio, either by speaking too loud or tainting his discipline, or from what other course you please which the time shall more favourably minister.

Roderigo. Well.

Iago. Sir, he's rash and very sudden in choler, and haply may strike at you—provoke him that he may; for even out of that will I cause these of Cyprus to mutiny, whose qualification shall come into no true taste again 270 but by the displanting of Cassio. So shall you have a shorter journey to your desires by the means I shall then have to prefer them, and the impediment most profitably removed, without the which there were no expectation of our prosperity.

Roderigo. I will do this, if you can bring it to any opportunity.

Iago. I warrant thee. Meet me by and by at the citadel. I must fetch his necessaries ashore. Farewell.

Roderigo. Adieu.   [*goes*

280 *Iago.* That Cassio loves her, I do well believe't;
That she loves him, 'tis apt and of great credit.
The Moor, howbeit that I endure him not,
Is of a constant, loving, noble nature;
And I dare think he'll prove to Desdemona

A most dear husband. Now, I do love her too,
Not out of absolute lust—though peradventure
I stand accountant for as great a sin—
But partly led to diet my revenge
For that I do suspect the lusty Moor
Hath leaped into my seat, the thought whereof   290
Doth like a poisonous mineral gnaw my inwards;
And nothing can or shall content my soul
Till I am evened with him, wife for wife;
Or failing so, yet that I put the Moor
At least into a jealousy so strong
That judgement cannot cure. Which thing to do,
If this poor trash of Venice, whom I leash
For his quick hunting, stand the putting on,
I'll have our Michael Cassio on the hip,
Abuse him to the Moor in the rank garb—   300
For I fear Cassio with my night-cap too—
Make the Moor thank me, love me, and reward me,
For making him egregiously an ass,
And practising upon his peace and quiet
Even to madness. 'Tis here, but yet confused;
Knavery's plain face is never seen till used.   [goes

[2. 2.]   *A street*

Enter a Herald with a proclamation; people following

Herald. It is Othello's pleasure, our noble and valiant
general, that, upon certain tidings now arrived im-
porting the mere perdition of the Turkish fleet, every
man put himself into triumph; some to dance, some to
make bonfires, each man to what sport and revels his
addiction leads him: for, besides these beneficial news,

it is the celebration of his nuptial. So much was his pleasure should be proclaimed. All offices are open, and there is full liberty of feasting from this present hour of
10 five till the bell have told eleven. Heaven bless the isle of Cyprus and our noble general Othello! [*he moves on*

[2. 3.]   *A hall in the citadel*

Enter OTHELLO, DESDEMONA, CASSIO, *and Attendants*

Othello. Good Michael, look you to the guard tonight.
Let's teach ourselves that honourable stop,
Not to outsport discretion.
    Cassio. Iago hath direction what to do;
But notwithstanding with my personal eye
Will I look to't.
    Othello.   Iago is most honest.
Michael, good night; tomorrow with your earliest
Let me have speech with you. Come, my dear love,
The purchase made, the fruits are to ensue;
10 That profit's yet to come 'tween me and you.
Good night.
            [*Othello, Desdemona, and Attendants depart*

                    Enter IAGO

    Cassio. Welcome, Iago; we must to the watch.
    Iago. Not this hour, lieutenant; 'tis not yet ten o'clock. Our general cast us thus early for the love of his Desdemona; who let us not therefore blame: he hath not yet made wanton the night with her, and she is sport for Jove.
    Cassio. She's a most exquisite lady.
    Iago. And, I'll warrant her, full of game.

Cassio. Indeed she's a most fresh and delicate creature.   20

Iago. What an eye she has! methinks it sounds a parley
to provocation.

Cassio. An inviting eye; and yet methinks right
modest.

Iago. And when she speaks, is it not an alarum to love?

Cassio. She is indeed perfection.

Iago. Well, happiness to their sheets! Come, lieutenant, I have a stoup of wine; and here without are
a brace of Cyprus gallants that would fain have a
measure to the health of black Othello.   30

Cassio. Not tonight, good Iago; I have very poor and
unhappy brains for drinking. I could well wish
courtesy would invent some other custom of entertainment.

Iago. O, they are our friends—but one cup; I'll drink
for you.

Cassio. I have drunk but one cup tonight, and that was
craftily qualified too, and behold what innovation it
makes here. I am unfortunate in the infirmity and dare
not task my weakness with any more.   40

Iago. What, man! 'Tis a night of revels; the gallants
desire it.

Cassio. Where are they?

Iago. Here at the door; I pray you, call them in.

Cassio. I'll do't; but it dislikes me.   [*goes*

Iago. If I can fasten but one cup upon him,
With that which he hath drunk tonight already,
He'll be as full of quarrel and offence
As my young mistress' dog. Now my sick fool Roderigo,
Whom love hath turned almost the wrong side out,   50
To Desdemona hath tonight caroused
Potations pottle-deep; and he's to watch.
Three else of Cyprus, noble swelling spirits,

That hold their honours in a wary distance,
The very elements of this warlike isle,
Have I tonight flustered with flowing cups;
And they watch too. Now, 'mongst this flock
          of drunkards,
Am I to put our Cassio in some action
That may offend the isle. But here they come;
60 If consequence do but approve my dream,
My boat sails freely, both with wind and stream.

*Re-enter CASSIO; with him MONTANO and Gentle-
men; Servants following with wine*

Cassio. 'Fore God, they have given me a rouse
already.

Montano. Good faith, a little one; not past a pint, as
I am a soldier.

Iago. Some wine, ho!
          [*sings*] And let me the canakin clink, clink;
                    And let me the canakin clink;
                    A soldier's a man;
70   O, man's life's but a span;
                    Why, then, let a soldier drink.
Some wine, boys!

Cassio. 'Fore God, an excellent song.

Iago. I learned it in England, where indeed they are
most potent in potting; your Dane, your German, and
your swag-bellied Hollander—Drink, ho!—are nothing
to your English.

Cassio. Is your Englishman so exquisite in his
drinking?

80 *Iago.* Why, he drinks you with facility your Dane
dead drunk; he sweats not to overthrow your Almain;
he gives your Hollander a vomit ere the next pottle can
be filled.

Cassio. To the health of our general!

Montano. I am for it, lieutenant, and I'll do you justice.

Iago. O sweet England!

[*sings*] King Stephen was and-a worthy peer,
  His breeches cost him but a crown;
 He held them sixpence all too dear,   90
  With that he called the tailor lown.

 He was a wight of high renown,
  And thou art but of low degree;
 'Tis pride that pulls the country down;
  Then take thy auld cloak about thee.

Some wine, ho!

Cassio. Why, this is a more exquisite song than the other.

Iago. Will you hear't again?

Cassio. No; for I hold him to be unworthy of his place 100 that does those things. Well, God's above all; and there be souls must be saved, and there be souls must not be saved.

Iago. It's true, good lieutenant.

Cassio. For mine own part—no offence to the general, nor any man of quality—I hope to be saved.

Iago. And so do I too, lieutenant.

Cassio. Ay, but, by your leave, not before me; the lieutenant is to be saved before the ancient. Let's have no more of this; let's to our affairs. God forgive us our 110 sins! Gentlemen, let's look to our business. Do not think, gentlemen, I am drunk; this is my ancient; this is my right hand, and this is my left hand. I am not drunk now: I can stand well enough, and I speak well enough.

All. Excellent well.

Cassio. Why, very well then; you must not think then
that I am drunk.   *[goes out*

Montano. To th'platform, masters; come, let's set the
120 watch.

Iago. You see this fellow that is gone before:
He is a soldier fit to stand by Caesar
And give direction; and do but see his vice—
'Tis to his virtue a just equinox,
The one as long as th'other. 'Tis pity of him.
I fear the trust Othello puts him in,
On some odd time of his infirmity,
Will shake this island.

    Montano.   But is he often thus?

    Iago. 'Tis evermore the prologue to his sleep:
130 He'll watch the horologe a double set,
If drink rock not his cradle.

    Montano.   It were well
The general were put in mind of it.
Perhaps he sees it not, or his good nature
Prizes the virtue that appears in Cassio,
And looks not on his evil: is not this true?

Enter RODERIGO

(*Iago.* How, now, Roderigo!
I pray you, after the lieutenant; go.   *[Roderigo goes*

    Montano. And 'tis great pity that the noble Moor
Should hazard such a place as his own second
140 With one of an ingraft infirmity:
It were an honest action to say
So to the Moor.

    Iago.   Not I, for this fair island:
I do love Cassio well, and would do much
To cure him of this evil. *[a cry within,* 'Help! Help!'
                       But hark! what noise?

Re-enter CASSIO, pursuing RODERIGO

Cassio. 'Zounds, you rogue, you rascal!

Montano. What's the matter, lieutenant?

Cassio. A knave teach me my duty! I'll beat the knave
Into a twiggen bottle.

Roderigo.   Beat me!

Cassio.   Dost prate, rogue?
                         [*striking Roderigo*

Montano. Nay, good lieutenant; pray sir, hold
    your hand.

Cassio. Let go, sir, or I'll knock you o'er the mazard.   150

Montano. Come, come, you're drunk.

Cassio. Drunk!   [*they fight*

(*Iago.* Away, I say; go out and cry a mutiny.
                            [*Roderigo goes*

[*aloud*] Nay, good lieutenant! God's will, gentlemen!
Help, ho!—lieutenant—sir—Montano—sir—
Help, masters!—Here's a goodly watch indeed!
                         [*a bell rings*

Who's that that rings the bell?—Diablo, ho!
The town will rise. God's will, lieutenant, hold;
You will be shamed for ever.

Re-enter OTHELLO and Attendants

Othello. What is the matter here?

Montano.   'Zounds, I bleed still.   160
I am hurt to th'death. He dies.
                         [*assailing Cassio again*

Othello.   Hold, for your lives!

Iago. Hold, ho! Lieutenant—sir—Montano—
    gentlemen—
Have you forgot all sense of place and duty?
The general speaks to you; hold, hold, for shame!

Othello. Why, how now, ho! from whence ariseth this?
Are we turned Turks, and to ourselves do that
Which heaven hath forbid the Ottomites?
For Christian shame, put by this barbarous brawl.
He that stirs next to carve for his own rage
170 Holds his soul light; he dies upon his motion.
Silence that dreadful bell; it frights the isle
From her propriety. What is the matter, masters?
Honest Iago, that look'st dead with grieving,
Speak who began this; on thy love, I charge thee.

Iago. I do not know. Friends all but now, even now,
In quarter and in terms like bride and groom
Divesting them for bed; and then, but now,
As if some planet had unwitted men,
Swords out, and tilting one at other's breast,
180 In opposition bloody. I cannot speak
Any beginning to this peevish odds;
And would in action glorious I had lost
Those legs that brought me to a part of it!

Othello. How comes it, Michael, you are thus forgot?
Cassio. I pray you, pardon me; I cannot speak.
Othello. Worthy Montano, you were wont be civil;
The gravity and stillness of your youth
The world hath noted, and your name is great
In mouths of wisest censure: what's the matter
190 That you unlace your reputation thus,
And spend your rich opinion for the name
Of a night-brawler? give me answer to it.

Montano. Worthy Othello, I am hurt to danger;
Your officer, Iago, can inform you—
While I spare speech, which something now
     offends me—
Of all that I do know; nor know I aught
By me that's said or done amiss this night—

Unless self-charity be sometimes a vice,
And to defend ourselves it be a sin
When violence assails us.

Othello.   Now, by heaven,   200
My blood begins my safer guides to rule,
And passion, having my best judgement collied,
Assays to lead the way. If I once stir,
Or do but lift this arm, the best of you
Shall sink in my rebuke. Give me to know
How this foul rout began, who set it on,
And he that is approved in this offence,
Though he had twinned with me, both at a birth,
Shall lose me. What! in a town of war,
Yet wild, the people's hearts brimful of fear,   210
To manage private and domestic quarrel,
In night, and on the court and guard of safety!
'Tis monstrous. Iago, who began't?

Montano. If partially affined, or leagued in office,
Thou dost deliver more or less than truth,
Thou art no soldier.

Iago.   Touch me not so near;
I had rather have this tongue cut from my mouth
Than it should do offence to Michael Cassio;
Yet, I persuade myself, to speak the truth
Shall nothing wrong him. This it is, general.   220
Montano and myself being in speech,
There comes a fellow crying out for help,
And Cassio following with determined sword
To execute upon him. Sir, this gentleman
Steps in to Cassio and entreats his pause;
Myself the crying fellow did pursue,
Lest by his clamour—as it so fell out—
The town might fall in fright; he, swift of foot,
Outran my purpose; and I returned the rather

230 For that I heard the clink and fall of swords,
And Cassio high in oath; which till tonight
I ne'er might say before. When I came back—
For this was brief—I found them close together
At blow and thrust; even as again they were
When you yourself did part them.
More of this matter can I not report;
But men are men; the best sometimes forget.
Though Cassio did some little wrong to him,
As men in rage strike those that wish them best,
240 Yet surely Cassio, I believe, received
From him that fled some strange indignity,
Which patience could not pass.
   Othello.   I know, Iago,
Thy honesty and love doth mince this matter,
Making it light to Cassio. Cassio, I love thee;
But never more be officer of mine.

Re-enter DESDEMONA, *attended*

Look if my gentle love be not raised up!
I'll make thee an example.
   Desdemona.   What's the matter?
   Othello. All's well, dear sweeting; come away to bed.
Sir, for your hurts, myself will be your surgeon.
                 [they lead Montano away
250 Iago, look with care about the town,
And silence those whom this vile brawl distracted.
Come, Desdemona: 'tis the soldiers' life
To have their balmy slumbers waked with strife.
              [all but Iago and Cassio depart
   Iago. What, are you hurt, lieutenant?
   Cassio. Ay, past all surgery.
   Iago. Marry, heaven forbid!
   Cassio. Reputation, reputation, reputation! O, I have

lost my reputation! I have lost the immortal part of
myself, and what remains is bestial. My reputation,
Iago, my reputation!　　　　　　　　　　　　　　　260

Iago. As I am an honest man, I thought you had
received some bodily wound; there is more sense in
that than in reputation. Reputation is an idle and most
false imposition; oft got without merit and lost without
deserving. You have lost no reputation at all, unless
you repute yourself such a loser. What, man! there are
ways to recover the general again. You are but now
cast in his mood, a punishment more in policy than in
malice; even so as one would beat his offenceless dog to
affright an imperious lion. Sue to him again, and he's　270
yours.

Cassio. I will rather sue to be despised than to deceive
so good a commander with so light, so drunken, and so
indiscreet an officer. Drunk! and speak parrot! and
squabble! swagger! swear! and discourse fustian with
one's own shadow! O thou invisible spirit of wine, if thou
hast no name to be known by, let us call thee devil!

Iago. What was he that you followed with your
sword? What had he done to you?

Cassio. I know not.　　　　　　　　　　　　　　　280

Iago. Is't possible?

Cassio. I remember a mass of things, but nothing
distinctly; a quarrel, but nothing wherefore. O, that
men should put an enemy in their mouths to steal away
their brains! that we should, with joy, pleasance, revel
and applause, transform ourselves into beasts!

Iago. Why, but you are now well enough. How
came you thus recovered?

Cassio. It hath pleased the devil drunkenness to give
place to the devil wrath: one unperfectness shows me　290
another, to make me frankly despise myself.

Iago. Come, you are too severe a moraller. As the time, the place, and the condition of this country stands, I could heartily wish this had not befallen; but since it is as it is, mend it for your own good.

Cassio. I will ask him for my place again; he shall tell me I am a drunkard! Had I as many mouths as Hydra, such an answer would stop them all. To be now a sensible man, by and by a fool, and presently a beast!
300 O strange! Every inordinate cup is unblest, and the ingredience is a devil.

Iago. Come, come, wine is a good familiar creature, if it be well used; exclaim no more against it. And, good lieutenant, I think you think I love you.

Cassio. I have well approved it, sir. I drunk!

Iago. You or any man living may be drunk at a time. I'll tell you what you shall do. Our general's wife is now the general: I may say so in this respect, for that he hath devoted and given up himself to the contempla-
310 tion, mark and denotement of her parts and graces. Confess yourself freely to her; importune her help to put you in your place again. She is of so free, so kind, so apt, so blessed a disposition, she holds it a vice in her goodness not to do more than she is requested. This broken joint between you and her husband entreat her to splinter; and, my fortunes against any lay worth naming, this crack of your love shall grow stronger than it was before.

Cassio. You advise me well.

320 *Iago.* I protest, in the sincerity of love and honest kindness.

Cassio. I think it freely; and betimes in the morning I will beseech the virtuous Desdemona to undertake for me. I am desperate of my fortunes if they check me here.

Iago. You are in the right. Good night, lieutenant;
I must to the watch.

Cassio. Good night, honest Iago.   [*goes*

Iago. And what's he then that says I play the villain,
When this advice I give is free and honest,   330
Probal to thinking, and indeed the course
To win the Moor again? For 'tis most easy
Th'inclining Desdemona to subdue
In any honest suit. She's framed as fruitful
As the free elements. And then for her
To win the Moor, were't to renounce his baptism,
All seals and symbols of redeeméd sin,
His soul is so enfettered to her love
That she may make, unmake, do what she list,
Even as her appetite shall play the god   340
With his weak function. How am I then a villain
To counsel Cassio to this parallel course,
Directly to his good? Divinity of hell!
When devils will the blackest sins put on,
They do suggest at first with heavenly shows,
As I do now; for while this honest fool
Plies Desdemona to repair his fortunes,
And she for him pleads strongly to the Moor,
I'll pour this pestilence into his ear,
That she repeals him for her body's lust;   350
And by how much she strives to do him good,
She shall undo her credit with the Moor.
So will I turn her virtue into pitch,
And out of her own goodness make the net
That shall enmesh them all.

Enter RODERIGO

                    How now, Roderigo!

Roderigo. I do follow here in the chase, not like a

hound that hunts, but one that fills up the cry. My
money is almost spent; I have been tonight exceedingly
well cudgelled; and I think the issue will be, I shall have
360 so much experience for my pains; and so, with no money
at all and a little more wit, return again to Venice.

    Iago. How poor are they that have not patience!
What wound did ever heal but by degrees?
Thou know'st we work by wit and not by witchcraft,
And wit depends on dilatory time.
Does't not go well? Cassio hath beaten thee,
And thou by that small hurt hast cashiered Cassio.
Though other things grow fair against the sun,
Yet fruits that blossom first will first be ripe.
370 Content thyself awhile. By th'mass, 'tis morning;
Pleasure and action make the hours seem short.
Retire thee; go where thou art billeted.
Away, I say; thou shalt know more hereafter.
Nay, get thee gone.   *[Roderigo goes*
           Two things are to be done:
My wife must move for Cassio to her mistress—
I'll set her on—
Myself the while to draw the Moor apart,
And bring him jump when he may Cassio find
Soliciting his wife. Ay, that's the way;
380 Dull not device by coldness and delay.   *[goes*

    [3. 1.]   *The citadel. Outside Othello's lodging*

        Enter CASSIO *and some Musicians*

    Cassio. Masters, play here; I will content your pains;
Something that's brief; and bid 'Good
       morrow, general'.   *[music*

Enter Clown

Clown. Why, masters, have your instruments been in Naples, that they speak i'th'nose thus?

1 *Musician.* How, sir, how?

Clown. Are these, I pray you, wind instruments?

1 *Musician.* Ay, marry, are they, sir.

Clown. O, thereby hangs a tail.

1 *Musician.* Whereby hangs a tale, sir?

Clown. Marry, sir, by many a wind instrument that 10 I know. But, masters, here's money for you; and the general so likes your music, that he desires you, for love's sake, to make no more noise with it.

1 *Musician.* Well, sir, we will not.

Clown. If you have any music that may not be heard, to't again; but, as they say, to hear music the general does not greatly care.

1 *Musician.* We have none such, sir.

Clown. Then put up your pipes in your bag, for I'll away. Go; vanish into air; away!   [*Musicians go* 20

Cassio. Dost thou hear, my honest friend?

Clown. No, I hear not your honest friend; I hear you.

Cassio. Prithee, keep up thy quillets. There's a poor piece of gold for thee: if the gentlewoman that attends the general's wife be stirring, tell her there's one Cassio entreats her a little favour of speech. Wilt thou do this?

Clown. She is stirring, sir; if she will stir hither, I shall seem to notify unto her.

Cassio. Do, good my friend.   [*Clown goes*

Enter IAGO

                In happy time, Iago.

Iago. You have not been abed then?   30

Cassio. Why, no; the day had broke before we parted.

I have made bold, Iago,
To send in to your wife: my suit to her
Is that she will to virtuous Desdemona
Procure me some access.

 Iago.   I'll send her to you presently;
And I'll devise a mean to draw the Moor
Out of the way, that your converse and business
May be more free.

 Cassio. I humbly thank you for't.   [*Iago goes*]
    I never knew
40 A Florentine more kind and honest.

Enter EMILIA

 Emilia. Good morrow, good lieutenant: I
    am sorry
For your displeasure; but all will sure be well.
The general and his wife are talking of it,
And she speaks for you stoutly. The Moor replies
That he you hurt is of great fame in Cyprus
And great affinity, and that in wholesome wisdom
He might not but refuse you; but he protests he
    loves you,
And needs no other suitor but his liking
To take the safest occasion by the front
50 To bring you in again.

 Cassio.   Yet, I beseech you,
If you think fit, or that it may be done,
Give me advantage of some brief discourse
With Desdemon alone.

 Emilia.   Pray you, come in;
I will bestow you where you shall have time
To speak your bosom freely.

 Cassio.   I am much bound to you.   [*they go*

[3. 2.]   *A room in the citadel*

Enter OTHELLO, IAGO, *and Gentlemen*

Othello. These letters give, Iago, to the pilot,
And by him do my duties to the senate.
That done, I will be walking on the works;
Repair there to me.
    Iago.   Well, my good lord, I'll do't.   [*goes*
    Othello. This fortification, gentlemen, shall we see't?
    Gentlemen. We'll wait upon your lordship.   [*they go*

[3. 3.]   *Before the citadel*

Enter DESDEMONA, CASSIO, *and* EMILIA

Desdemona. Be thou assured, good Cassio, I will do
All my abilities in thy behalf.
    Emilia. Good madam, do; I warrant it grieves
        my husband
As if the case were his.
    Desdemona. O, that's an honest fellow. Do not
        doubt, Cassio,
But I will have my lord and you again
As friendly as you were.
    Cassio.   Bounteous madam,
Whatever shall become of Michael Cassio,
He's never anything but your true servant.
    Desdemona. I know't; I thank you. You do love
        my lord;   10
You have known him long; and be you well assured
He shall in strangeness stand no farther off
Than in a politic distance.
    Cassio.   Ay, but, lady,

That policy may either last so long,
Or feed upon such nice and waterish diet,
Or breed itself so out of circumstance,
That, I being absent, and my place supplied,
My general will forget my love and service.
    Desdemona. Do not doubt that: before Emilia here
20 I give thee warrant of thy place. Assure thee,
If I do vow a friendship, I'll perform it
To the last article. My lord shall never rest:
I'll watch him tame, and talk him out of patience;
His bed shall seem a school, his board a shrift;
I'll intermingle everything he does
With Cassio's suit. Therefore be merry, Cassio;
For thy solicitor shall rather die
Than give thy cause away.

Enter OTHELLO *and* IAGO, *at a distance*

    Emilia. Madam, here comes my lord.
30   *Cassio.* Madam, I'll take my leave.
    Desdemona. Why, stay, and hear me speak.
    Cassio. Madam, not now: I am very ill at ease,
Unfit for mine own purposes.
    Desdemona. Well, do your discretion.   [*Cassio goes*
    Iago. Ha! I like not that.
    Othello. What dost thou say?
    Iago. Nothing, my lord; or if—I know not what.
    Othello. Was not that Cassio parted from my wife?
    Iago. Cassio, my lord! No, sure, I cannot think it,
40 That he would steal away so guilty-like,
Seeing you coming.
    Othello.   I do believe 'twas he.
    Desdemona. How now, my lord!
I have been talking with a suitor here,
A man that languishes in your displeasure.

Othello. Who is't you mean?

Desdemona. Why, your lieutenant, Cassio. Good
　　my lord,
If I have any grace or power to move you,
His present reconciliation take;
For if he be not one that truly loves you,
That errs in ignorance and not in cunning,　　50
I have no judgement in an honest face.
I prithee, call him back.

Othello.　　　　　　　　Went he hence now?

Desdemona. Ay, sooth; so humbled,
That he hath left part of his grief with me
To suffer with him. Good love, call him back.

Othello. Not now, sweet Desdemon; some
　　other time.

Desdemona. But shall't be shortly?

Othello.　　　　　　　The sooner, sweet, for you.

Desdemona. Shall't be tonight at supper?

Othello.　　　　　　　　　No, not tonight.

Desdemona. Tomorrow dinner then?

Othello.　　　　　　　I shall not dine at home:
I meet the captains at the citadel.　　60

Desdemona. Why then, tomorrow night; or
　　Tuesday morn;
On Tuesday noon, or night; on Wednesday morn.
I prithee, name the time; but let it not
Exceed three days. In faith, he's penitent;
And yet his trespass, in our common reason—
Save that, they say, the wars must make example
Out of their best—is not almost a fault
T'incur a private check. When shall he come?
Tell me, Othello. I wonder in my soul
What you would ask me that I should deny,　　70
Or stand so mammering on. What! Michael Cassio,

That came a-wooing with you, and so many a time,
When I have spoke of you dispraisingly,
Hath ta'en your part—to have so much to do
To bring him in! Trust me, I could do much—
  Othello. Prithee, no more. Let him come when
    he will;
I will deny thee nothing.
  Desdemona.   Why, this is not a boon;
'Tis as I should entreat you wear your gloves,
Or feed on nourishing dishes, or keep you warm,
80 Or sue to you to do peculiar profit
To your own person. Nay, when I have a suit
Wherein I mean to touch your love indeed,
It shall be full of poise and difficult weight,
And fearful to be granted.
  Othello.   I will deny thee nothing.
Whereon, I do beseech thee, grant me this,
To leave me but a little to myself.
  Desdemona. Shall I deny you? no; farewell,
    my lord.
  Othello. Farewell, my Desdemona, I'll come straight.
  Desdemona. Emilia, come. Be as your fancies
    teach you;
90 Whate'er you be, I am obedient.
                   [Desdemona and Emilia go
  Othello. Excellent wretch! Perdition catch my soul
But I do love thee; and when I love thee not
Chaos is come again.
  Iago.   My noble lord—
  Othello. What dost thou say, Iago?
  Iago.   Did Michael Cassio,
When you wooed my lady, know of your love?
  Othello. He did, from first to last. Why dost
    thou ask?

Iago. But for a satisfaction of my thought;
No further harm.

  Othello.   Why of thy thought, Iago?

  Iago. I did not think he had been acquainted
    with her.

  Othello. O, yes, and went between us very oft.   100

  Iago. Indeed!

  Othello. Indeed? ay, indeed. Discern'st thou aught
    in that?
Is he not honest?

  Iago. Honest, my lord?

  Othello. Honest? ay, honest.

  Iago. My lord, for aught I know.

  Othello. What dost thou think?

  Iago. Think, my lord?

  Othello. Think, my lord! Alas, thou echo'st me,
As if there were some monster in thy thought   110
Too hideous to be shown. Thou dost
    mean something:
I heard thee say even now, thou likedst not that,
When Cassio left my wife. What didst not like?
And when I told thee he was of my counsel
In my whole course of wooing, thou criedst 'Indeed!'
And didst contract and purse thy brow together,
As if thou then hadst shut up in thy brain
Some horrible conceit. If thou dost love me,
Show me thy thought.

  Iago. My lord, you know I love you.

  Othello.   I think thou dost; 120
And for I know thou'rt full of love, and honest,
And weigh'st thy words before thou giv'st
    them breath,
Therefore these stops of thine fright me the more:
For such things in a false disloyal knave

Are tricks of custom; but in a man that's just
They're close dilations, working from the heart
That passion cannot rule.

    Iago.   For Michael Cassio,
I dare be sworn I think that he is honest.

    Othello. I think so too.

    Iago.   Men should be what they seem;
130 Or those that be not, would they might seem none!

    Othello. Certain, men should be what they seem.

    Iago. Why then, I think Cassio's an honest man.

    Othello. Nay, yet there's more in this.
I prithee, speak to me as to thy thinkings,
As thou dost ruminate, and give thy worst of thoughts
The worst of words.

    Iago.   Good my lord, pardon me:
Though I am bound to every act of duty,
I am not bound to that all slaves are free to.
Utter my thoughts! Why, say they are vile and false—
140 As where's that palace whereinto foul things
Sometimes intrude not? who has a breast so pure,
But some uncleanly apprehensions
Keep leets and law-days, and in session sit
With meditations lawful?

    Othello. Thou dost conspire against thy friend, Iago,
If thou but think'st him wronged and mak'st his ear
A stranger to thy thoughts.

    Iago.   I do beseech you—
Though I perchance am vicious in my guess,
As, I confess, it is my nature's plague
150 To spy into abuses, and oft my jealousy
Shapes faults that are not—that your wisdom then,
From one that so imperfectly conceits,
Would take no notice, nor build yourself a trouble
Out of his scattering and unsure observance.

It were not for your quiet nor your good,
Nor for my manhood, honesty, or wisdom,
To let you know my thoughts.
  Othello.   What dost thou mean?
  Iago. Good name in man and woman, dear
      my lord,
Is the immediate jewel of their souls:
Who steals my purse steals trash—'tis
    something, nothing;   160
'Twas mine, 'tis his, and has been slave to thousands;
But he that filches from me my good name
Robs me of that which not enriches him
And makes me poor indeed.
  Othello.   I'll know thy thoughts!
  Iago. You cannot, if my heart were in your hand;
Nor shall not, while 'tis in my custody.
  Othello. Ha!
  Iago.   O, beware, my lord, of jealousy;
It is the green-eyed monster, which doth mock
The meat it feeds on: that cuckold lives in bliss
Who, certain of his fate, loves not his wronger;   170
But, O, what damnéd minutes tells he o'er
Who dotes, yet doubts, suspects, yet fondly loves!
  Othello. O misery!
  Iago. Poor and content is rich, and rich enough;
But riches fineless is as poor as winter
To him that ever fears he shall be poor.
Good heaven the souls of all my tribe defend
From jealousy!
  Othello.   Why, why is this?
Think'st thou I'ld make a life of jealousy,
To follow still the changes of the moon   180
With fresh suspicions? No; to be once in doubt
Is once resolved. Exchange me for a goat,

When I shall turn the business of my soul
To such exsufflicate and blown surmise
Matching thy inference. 'Tis not to make
    me jealous
To say my wife is fair, loves company,
Is free of speech, sings, plays and dances well;
Where virtue is, these are more virtuous;
Nor from mine own weak merits will I draw
190 The smallest fear or doubt of her revolt;
For she had eyes and chose me. No, Iago:
I'll see before I doubt; when I doubt, prove;
And on the proof, there is no more but this,
Away at once with love or jealousy!

   Iago. I am glad of it; for now I shall have reason
To show the love and duty that I bear you
With franker spirit. Therefore, as I am bound,
Receive it from me. I speak not yet of proof.
Look to your wife; observe her well with Cassio;
200 Wear your eye thus not jealous nor secure:
I would not have your free and noble nature
Out of self-bounty be abused. Look to't:
I know our country disposition well;
In Venice they do let heaven see the pranks
They dare not show their husbands; their
    best conscience
Is not to leave't undone, but keep't unknown.

   Othello. Dost thou say so?

   Iago. She did deceive her father, marrying you;
And when she seemed to shake and fear your looks,
210 She loved them most.

   Othello.   And so she did.

   Iago.   Why then,
She that so young could give out such a seeming,
To seel her father's eyes up close as oak,

He thought 'twas witchcraft—but I am much
　　to blame;
I humbly do beseech you of your pardon
For too much loving you.
　Othello.　　　　　　　I am bound to thee for ever.
　Iago.　I see this hath a little dashed your spirits.
　Othello.　Not a jot, not a jot.
　Iago.　　　　　　　In faith, I fear it has.
I hope you will consider what is spoke
Comes from my love.　But I do see you're moved.
I am to pray you not to strain my speech　　　　　220
To grosser issues nor to larger reach
Than to suspicion.
　Othello.　I will not.
　Iago.　　　　　　Should you do so, my lord,
My speech should fall into such vile success
As my thoughts aimed not at.　Cassio's my
　　worthy friend—
My lord, I see you're moved.
　Othello.　　　　　　　No, not much moved:
I do not think but Desdemona's honest.
　Iago.　Long live she so! and long live you to
　　think so!
　Othello.　And yet, how nature erring from itself—
　Iago.　Ay, there's the point: as—to be bold
　　with you—　　　　　230
Not to affect many proposéd matches
Of her own clime, complexion, and degree,
Whereto we see in all things nature tends—
Foh! one may smell, in such, a will most rank,
Foul disproportion, thoughts unnatural.
But pardon me: I do not in position
Distinctly speak of her; though I may fear
Her will, recoiling to her better judgement,

May fall to match you with her country forms,
240 And happily repent.

    Othello.   Farewell, farewell.
If more thou dost perceive, let me know more;
Set on thy wife to observe. Leave me, Iago.

    Iago [*going*]. My lord, I take my leave.

    Othello. Why did I marry? This honest
      creature doubtless
Sees and knows more, much more, than he unfolds.

    Iago [*returning*]. My lord, I would I might entreat
      your honour
To scan this thing no further. Leave it to time:
Although 'tis fit that Cassio have his place—
For sure he fills it up with great ability—
250 Yet if you please to hold him off awhile,
You shall by that perceive him and his means;
Note if your lady strain his entertainment
With any strong or vehement importunity—
Much will be seen in that. In the mean time,
Let me be thought too busy in my fears—
As worthy cause I have to fear I am—
And hold her free, I do beseech your honour.

    Othello. Fear not my government.

    Iago. I once more take my leave.   [*goes*
260   *Othello.* This fellow's of exceeding honesty,
And knows all qualities, with a learnéd spirit,
Of human dealings. If I do prove her haggard,
Though that her jesses were my dear heart-strings,
I'ld whistle her off and let her down the wind
To prey at fortune. Haply, for I am black
And have not those soft parts of conversation
That chamberers have, or for I am declined
Into the vale of years—yet that's not much—
She's gone; I am abused, and my relief

Must be to loathe her. O curse of marriage,   270
That we can call these delicate creatures ours,
And not their appetites! I had rather be a toad,
And live upon the vapour of a dungeon,
Than keep a corner in the thing I love
For others' uses. Yet, 'tis the plague of great ones;
Prerogatived are they less than the base;
'Tis destiny unshunnable, like death:
Even then this forkéd plague is fated to us
When we do quicken. Look where she comes:

Re-enter DESDEMONA *and* EMILIA

If she be false, O, then heaven mocks itself!   280
I'll not believe't.
  Desdemona.   How now, my dear Othello!
Your dinner, and the generous islanders
By you invited, do attend your presence.
  Othello. I am to blame.
  Desdemona.   Why do you speak so faintly?
Are you not well?
  Othello. I have a pain upon my forehead here.
  Desdemona. Faith, that's with watching; 'twill
    away again:
Let me but bind it hard, within this hour
It will be well.
  Othello.   Your napkin is too little;
    [*he puts the handkerchief from him; and she drops it*
Let it alone. Come, I'll go in with you.   290
  Desdemona. I am very sorry that you are not well.
               [*Othello and Desdemona go*
  Emilia. I am glad I've found this napkin:
This was her first remembrance from the Moor;
My wayward husband hath a hundred times
Wooed me to steal it; but she so loves the token,

For he conjured her she should ever keep it,
That she reserves it evermore about her
To kiss and talk to. I'll have the work ta'en out,
And give't Iago. What he will do with it
300 Heaven knows, not I:
I nothing but to please his fantasy.

Re-enter IAGO

Iago. How now! What do you here alone?
Emilia. Do not you chide; I have a thing for you.
Iago. A thing for me? it is a common thing—
Emilia. Ha!
Iago. To have a foolish wife.
Emilia. O, is that all? What will you give me now
For that same handkerchief?
Iago.   What handkerchief?
Emilia. What handkerchief!
310 Why, that the Moor first gave to Desdemona;
That which so often you did bid me steal.
Iago. Hast stole it from her?
Emilia. No, faith; she let it drop by negligence,
And, to th'advantage, I being here took't up.
Look, here it is.
Iago.   A good wench; give it me.
Emilia. What will you do with't, that you've been
     so earnest
To have me filch it?
Iago [*snatching it*].   Why, what's that to you?
Emilia. If't be not for some purpose of import,
Give't me again. Poor lady, she'll run mad
320 When she shall lack it.
Iago. Be not acknown on't; I have use for it.
Go, leave me.   [*Emilia goes*
I will in Cassio's lodging lose this napkin,

And let him find it. Trifles light as air
Are to the jealous confirmations strong
As proofs of Holy Writ: this may do something.
The Moor already changes with my poison:
Dangerous conceits are in their natures poisons
Which at the first are scarce found to distaste
But, with a little act upon the blood,　　　　　330
Burn like the mines of sulphur.

Re-enter OTHELLO

　　　　　　　　　　I did say so:
Look where he comes! Not poppy, nor mandragora,
Nor all the drowsy syrups of the world,
Shall ever medicine thee to that sweet sleep
Which thou owedst yesterday.

Othello.　　　　　　　Ha! Ha! false to me?

Iago. Why, how now, general! no more of that.

Othello. Avaunt! be gone! thou hast set me on
　　the rack:
I swear 'tis better to be much abused
Than but to know't a little.

Iago.　　　　　　　How now, my lord!

Othello. What sense had I of her stolen hours
　　of lust?　　　　　　　　　　　　　340
I saw't not, thought it not, it harmed not me:
I slept the next night well, fed well, was merry;
I found not Cassio's kisses on her lips.
He that is robbed, not wanting what is stolen,
Let him not know't, and he's not robbed at all.

Iago. I am sorry to hear this.

Othello. I had been happy, if the general camp,
Pioneers and all, had tasted her sweet body,
So I had nothing known. O, now for ever
Farewell the tranquil mind! farewell content!　　350

5

Farewell the pluméd troops, and the big wars
That make ambition virtue—O, farewell!
Farewell the neighing steed and the shrill trump,
The spirit-stirring drum, th'ear-piercing fife,
The royal banner, and all quality,
Pride, pomp, and circumstance, of glorious war!
And, O you mortal engines, whose rude throats
Th'immortal Jove's dread clamours counterfeit,
Farewell! Othello's occupation's gone!

360 *Iago.* Is't possible, my lord?

Othello. Villain, be sure thou prove my love
    a whore;
Be sure of it; give me the ocular proof;

                         [takes him by the throat

Or, by the worth of mine eternal soul,
Thou hadst been better have been born a dog
Than answer my waked wrath!

    Iago.   Is't come to this?

Othello. Make me to see't; or, at the least, so
    prove it,
That the probation bear no hinge nor loop
To hang a doubt on; or woe upon thy life!

    Iago. My noble lord—

370 *Othello.* If thou dost slander her and torture me,
Never pray more; abandon all remorse;
On horror's head horrors accumulate;
Do deeds to make heaven weep, all earth amazed;
For nothing canst thou to damnation add
Greater than that.

    Iago.   O grace! O heaven forgive me!
Are you a man? have you a soul, or sense?
God bu'y you; take mine office. O wretched fool,
That liv'st to make thine honesty a vice!
O monstrous world! Take note, take note, O world,

To be direct and honest is not safe.   380
I thank you for this profit, and from hence
I'll love no friend sith love breeds such offence.
  Othello. Nay, stay; thou shouldst be honest.
  Iago. I should be wise; for honesty's a fool,
And loses that it works for.
  Othello.   By the world,
I think my wife be honest, and think she is not;
I think that thou art just, and think thou art not:
I'll have some proof. Her name, that was as fresh
As Dian's visage, is now begrimed and black
As mine own face. If there be cords, or knives,   390
Poison, or fire, or suffocating streams,
I'll not endure it. Would I were satisfied!
  Iago. I see, sir, you are eaten up with passion:
I do repent me that I put it to you.
You would be satisfied?
  Othello.   Would! nay, and will.
  Iago. And may; but how? how satisfied, my lord?
Would you, the supervisor, grossly gape on—
Behold her topped?
  Othello.   Death and damnation! O!
  Iago. It were a tedious difficulty, I think,
To bring them to that prospect: damn them then,   400
If ever mortal eyes do see them bolster
More than their own! What then? how then?
What shall I say? Where's satisfaction?
It is impossible you should see this,
Were they as prime as goats, as hot as monkeys,
As salt as wolves in pride, and fools as gross
As ignorance made drunk. But yet, I say,
If imputation and strong circumstance,
Which lead directly to the door of truth,
Will give you satisfaction, you might have't.   410

Othello. Give me a living reason she's disloyal.

Iago. I do not like the office;
But sith I am entered in this cause so far,
Pricked to't by foolish honesty and love,
I will go on. I lay with Cassio lately,
And being troubled with a raging tooth,
I could not sleep.
There are a kind of men so loose of soul,
That in their sleeps will mutter their affairs:
420 One of this kind is Cassio.
In sleep I heard him say 'Sweet Desdemona,
Let us be wary, let us hide our loves';
And then, sir, would he gripe and wring my hand,
Cry 'O sweet creature!' and then kiss me hard,
As if he plucked up kisses by the roots,
That grew upon my lips; then laid his leg
Over my thigh, and sighed, and kissed, and then
Cried 'Curséd fate that gave thee to the Moor!'

Othello. O monstrous! monstrous!

Iago.   Nay, this was but his dream.

430 *Othello.* But this denoted a foregone conclusion:
'Tis a shrewd doubt, though it be but a dream.

Iago. And this may help to thicken other proofs
That do demonstrate thinly.

Othello.   I'll tear her all to pieces.

Iago. Nay, but be wise: yet we see nothing done;
She may be honest yet. Tell me but this:
Have you not sometimes seen a handkerchief
Spotted with strawberries in your wife's hand?

Othello. I gave her such a one; 'twas my first gift.

Iago. I know not that; but such a handkerchief—
440 I am sure it was your wife's—did I today
See Cassio wipe his beard with.

Othello.   If it be that—

Iago. If it be that, or any that was hers,
It speaks against her with the other proofs.

Othello. O, that the slave had forty thousand lives!
One is too poor, too weak for my revenge.
Now do I see 'tis true. Look: here, Iago,
All my fond love thus do I blow to heaven—
'Tis gone.
Arise, black vengeance, from thy hollow cell!
Yield up, O love, thy crown and hearted throne   450
To tyrannous hate! Swell, bosom, with thy fraught,
For 'tis of aspics' tongues!

Iago.   Yet be content.

Othello. O, blood, blood, blood!

Iago. Patience, I say; your mind perhaps may change.

Othello. Never, Iago: like to the Pontic sea,
Whose icy current and compulsive course
Ne'er feels retiring ebb, but keeps due on
To the Propontic and the Hellespont;
Even so my bloody thoughts, with violent pace,
Shall ne'er look back, ne'er ebb to humble love,   460
Till that a capable and wide revenge
Swallow them up. Now, by yond marble heaven,
In the due reverence of a sacred vow   [*kneels*
I here engage my words.

Iago.   Do not rise yet.   [*kneels*
Witness you ever-burning lights above,
You elements that clip us round about,
Witness that here Iago doth give up
The execution of his wit, hands, heart,
To wronged Othello's service! Let him command,
And to obey shall be without remorse,   470
What bloody business ever.   [*they rise*

Othello.   I greet thy love,
Not with vain thanks, but with acceptance bounteous,

And will upon the instant put thee to't:
Within these three days let me hear thee say
That Cassio's not alive.

    Iago.   My friend is dead;
'Tis done at your request. But let her live.

    Othello. Damn her, lewd minx! O, damn her!
    damn her!
Come, go with me apart; I will withdraw,
To furnish me with some swift means of death
480 For the fair devil. Now art thou my lieutenant.

    Iago. I am your own for ever.   *[they go*

[3. 4.]   *The same*

Enter DESDEMONA, EMILIA, *and Clown*

    Desdemona. Do you know, sirrah, where Lieutenant
Cassio lies?

    Clown. I dare not say he lies anywhere.

    Desdemona. Why, man?

    Clown. He's a soldier; and for one to say a soldier
lies, is stabbing.

    Desdemona. Go to: where lodges he?

    Clown. To tell you where he lodges, is to tell you
where I lie.

10   *Desdemona.* Can anything be made of this?

    Clown. I know not where he lodges; and for me to
devise a lodging, and say he lies here or he lies there,
were to lie in mine own throat.

    Desdemona. Can you inquire him out, and be edified
by report?

    Clown. I will catechize the world for him: that is,
make questions and by them answer.

Desdemona. Seek him; bid him come hither. Tell him
I have moved my lord on his behalf, and hope all will
be well.　　　　　　　　　　　　　　　　　　　　　20

Clown. To do this is within the compass of man's wit,
and therefore I will attempt the doing it.　　　[*goes*

Desdemona. Where should I lose that
　　　handkerchief, Emilia?
Emilia. I know not, madam.
Desdemona. Believe me, I had rather lose
　　　my purse
Full of crusadoes; and but my noble Moor
Is true of mind and made of no such baseness
As jealous creatures are, it were enough
To put him to ill thinking.
Emilia.　　　　　　　　Is he not jealous?
Desdemona. Who, he! I think the sun where he
　　　was born　　　　　　　　　　　　　　　　　30
Drew all such humours from him.
Emilia.　　　　　　　　Look where he comes!
Desdemona. I will not leave him now till Cassio
Be called to him.

　　　　　　　　Enter OTHELLO

　　　　　　　　How is't with you, my lord?
Othello. Well, my good lady. [*aside*] O, hardness
　　　to dissemble!
How do you, Desdemona?
Desdemona.　　　　　　　Well, my good lord.
Othello. Give me your hand: this hand is moist,
　　　my lady.
Desdemona. It yet hath felt no age nor known
　　　no sorrow.
Othello. This argues fruitfulness and liberal heart:
Hot, hot, and moist. This hand of yours requires

40 A sequester from liberty, fasting and prayer,
Much castigation, exercise devout;
For there's a young and sweating devil here
That commonly rebels. 'Tis a good hand,
A frank one.

Desdemona. You may, indeed, say so;
For 'twas that hand that gave away my heart.

Othello. A liberal hand: the hearts of old
gave hands;
But our new heraldry is hands, not hearts.

Desdemona. I cannot speak of this. Come now,
your promise.

Othello. What promise, chuck?

50 *Desdemona.* I have sent to bid Cassio come speak
with you.

Othello. I have a salt and sorry rheum offends me;
Lend me thy handkerchief.

Desdemona. Here, my lord.

Othello. That which I gave you.

Desdemona. I have it not about me.

Othello. Not?

Desdemona. No, indeed, my lord.

Othello. That's a fault. That handkerchief
Did an Egyptian to my mother give;

60 She was a charmer, and could almost read
The thoughts of people: she told her, while she
kept it
'Twould make her amiable and subdue my father
Entirely to her love; but if she lost it
Or made a gift of it, my father's eye
Should hold her loathéd and his spirits should hunt
After new fancies. She dying gave it me,
And bid me, when my fate would have me wive,
To give it her. I did so; and take heed on't:

Make it a darling like your precious eye;
To lose't or give't away were such perdition   70
As nothing else could match.

  Desdemona.   Is't possible?
  Othello. 'Tis true. There's magic in the web of it:
A sibyl, that had numbered in the world
The sun to course two hundred compasses,
In her prophetic fury sewed the work;
The worms were hallowed that did breed the silk;
And it was dyed in mummy which the skilful
Conserved of maidens' hearts.

  Desdemona.   Indeed! is't true?
  Othello. Most veritable; therefore look to't well.
  Desdemona. Then would to God that I had
      never seen't!   80
  Othello. Ha! wherefore?
  Desdemona. Why do you speak so startingly and rash?
  Othello. Is't lost? is't gone? speak, is it out o'th'way?
  Desdemona. Heaven bless us!
  Othello. Say you?
  Desdemona. It is not lost; but what an if it were?
  Othello. How!
  Desdemona. I say it is not lost.
  Othello. Fetch't; let me see't.
  Desdemona. Why, so I can, sir, but I will not now.   90
This is a trick to put me from my suit:
Pray you, let Cassio be received again.
  Othello. Fetch me the handkerchief: my
     mind misgives.
  Desdemona. Come, come;
You'll never meet a more sufficient man.
  Othello. The handkerchief!
  Desdemona.   I pray, talk me of Cassio.
  Othello. The handkerchief!

Desdemona.   A man that all his time
Hath founded his good fortunes on your love,
Shared dangers with you—

100 *Othello.* The handkerchief!

Desdemona. In sooth, you are to blame.

Othello. Away!   [*he goes*

Emilia. Is not this man jealous?

Desdemona. I ne'er saw this before.
Sure there's some wonder in this handkerchief:
I am most unhappy in the loss of it.

Emilia. 'Tis not a year or two shows us a man:
They are all but stomachs and we all but food;
They eat us hungerly, and when they are full

110 They belch us. Look you, Cassio and my husband.

Enter CASSIO and IAGO

Iago. There is no other way: 'tis she must do't;
And, lo, the happiness! go and importune her.

Desdemona. How now, good Cassio! what's the
    news with you?

Cassio. Madam, my former suit: I do beseech you
That, by your virtuous means, I may again
Exist and be a member of his love
Whom I with all the office of my heart
Entirely honour. I would not be delayed:
If my offence be of such mortal kind

120 That nor my service past nor present sorrow,
Nor purposed merit in futurity,
Can ransom me into his love again,
But to know so must be my benefit;
So shall I clothe me in a forced content
And shut myself up in some other course
To fortune's alms.

Desdemona.   Alas, thrice-gentle Cassio!

My advocation is not now in tune;
My lord is not my lord, nor should I know him
Were he in favour as in humour altered.
So help me every spirit sanctified,   130
As I have spoken for you all my best
And stood within the blank of his displeasure
For my free speech! You must awhile be patient:
What I can do I will; and more I will
Than for myself I dare—let that suffice you.

   Iago. Is my lord angry?

   Emilia.   He went hence but now,
And certainly in strange unquietness.

   Iago. Can he be angry? I have seen the cannon
When it hath blown his ranks into the air
And, like the devil, from his very arm   140
Puffed his own brother; and is he angry?
Something of moment then: I will go meet him;
There's matter in't indeed if he be angry.

   Desdemona. I prithee, do so.   [*Iago goes*
                  Something sure of state,
Either from Venice, or some unhatched practice
Made demonstrable here in Cyprus to him,
Hath puddled his clear spirit; and in such cases
Men's natures wrangle with inferior things,
Though great ones are their object. 'Tis even so;
For let our finger ache, and it indues   150
Our other healthful members to a sense
Of pain. Nay, we must think men are not gods,
Nor of them look for such observancy
As fits the bridal. Beshrew me much, Emilia,
I was, unhandsome warrior as I am,
Arraigning his unkindness with my soul;
But now I find I had suborned the witness,
And he's indicted falsely.

Emilia. Pray heaven it be state matters, as you think,
160 And no conception nor no jealous toy
Concerning you.
    Desdemona. Alas the day, I never gave him cause!
    Emilia. But jealous souls will not be answered so;
They are not ever jealous for the cause,
But jealous for they're jealous: 'tis a monster
Begot upon itself, born on itself.
    Desdemona. Heaven keep that monster from
        Othello's mind!
    Emilia. Lady, amen.
    Desdemona. I will go seek him. Cassio,
        walk hereabout:
170 If I do find him fit, I'll move your suit,
And seek to effect it to my uttermost.
    Cassio. I humbly thank your ladyship.
                   [Desdemona and Emilia depart

Enter BIANCA

    Bianca. 'Save you, friend Cassio!
    Cassio.   What make you from home?
How is it with you, my most fair Bianca?
In faith, sweet love, I was coming to your house.
    Bianca. And I was going to your lodging, Cassio.
What, keep a week away? seven days and nights?
Eight score eight hours? and lovers' absent hours,
More tedious than the dial eight score times?
180 O weary reckoning!
    Cassio.   Pardon me, Bianca:
I have this while with leaden thoughts been pressed;
But I shall in a more continuate time
Strike off this score of absence. Sweet Bianca,
                  [giving Desdemona's handkerchief
Take me this work out.

Bianca.　　　　　　　O Cassio, whence came this?
This is some token from a newer friend:
To the felt absence now I feel a cause;
Is't come to this? Well, well.
　Cassio.　　　　　　Go to, woman!
Throw your vile guesses in the devil's teeth,
From whence you have them. You are jealous now
That this is from some mistress, some remembrance:　　190
No, by my faith, Bianca.
　Bianca.　　　　　　Why, whose is it?
　Cassio. I know not neither. I found it in
　　my chamber.
I like the work well. Ere it be demanded—
As like enough it will—I'ld have it copied:
Take it, and do't; and leave me for this time.
　Bianca. Leave you! wherefore?
　Cassio. I do attend here on the general;
And think it no addition, nor my wish,
To have him see me womaned.
　Bianca.　　　　　　Why, I pray you?
　Cassio. Not that I love you not.
　Bianca.　　　　　　But that you do not love me.　200
I pray you, bring me on the way a little;
And say if I shall see you soon at night.
　Cassio. 'Tis but a little way that I can bring you,
For I attend here; but I'll see you soon.
　Bianca. 'Tis very good; I must be circumstanced.
　　　　　　　　　　　　　　[they go

[4 . 1.]   *The same*

Enter OTHELLO *and* IAGO

Iago. Will you think so?
Othello.   Think so, Iago!
Iago.   What,
To kiss in private?
Othello.   An unauthorized kiss.
Iago. Or to be naked with her friend in bed
An hour or more, not meaning any harm?
Othello. Naked in bed, Iago, and not mean harm!
It is hypocrisy against the devil:
They that mean virtuously and yet do so,
The devil their virtue tempts and they tempt heaven.
Iago. So they do nothing, 'tis a venial slip:
10 But if I give my wife a handkerchief—
Othello. What then?
Iago. Why, then, 'tis hers, my lord; and
         being hers,
She may, I think, bestow't on any man.
Othello. She is protectress of her honour too:
May she give that?
Iago. Her honour is an essence that's not seen;
They have it very oft that have it not:
But for the handkerchief—
Othello. By heaven, I would most gladly have
         forgot it.
20 Thou said'st—O, it comes o'er my memory,
As doth the raven o'er the infected house,
Boding to all—he had my handkerchief.
Iago. Ay, what of that?
Othello.   That's not so good now.
Iago.   What

If I had said I had seen him do you wrong?
Or heard him say—as knaves be such abroad,
Who having, by their own importunate suit,
Or voluntary dotage of some mistress,
Convincéd or supplied them, cannot choose
But they must blab—

Othello.   Hath he said anything?

Iago. He hath, my lord; but, be you well assured,   30
No more than he'll unswear.

Othello.   What hath he said?

Iago. Faith, that he did—I know not what he did.

Othello. What? what?

Iago. Lie—

Othello.   With her?

Iago.   With her, on her; what you will.

Othello. Lie with her! lie on her!—We say lie on her,
when they belie her.—Lie with her! 'Zounds, that's
fulsome!   Handkerchief—confessions—handkerchief!
To confess and be hanged for his labour; first, to be
hanged; and then to confess. I tremble at it. Nature
would not invest herself in such shadowing passion   40
without some instruction. It is not words that shakes
me thus. Pish! Noses, ears, and lips. Is't possible?—
Confess?—Handkerchief?—O devil!

                              [*falls in a trance*

Iago. Work on,
My medicine, work! Thus credulous fools are caught;
And many worthy and chaste dames even thus,
All guiltless, meet reproach. What, ho! my lord!
My lord, I say! Othello!

                    Enter CASSIO

                    How now, Cassio!

Cassio. What's the matter?

50   *Iago.* My lord is fallen into an epilepsy.
This is his second fit; he had one yesterday.
    Cassio. Rub him about the temples.
    Iago.   No, forbear;
The lethargy must have his quiet course;
If not, he foams at mouth, and by and by
Breaks out to savage madness. Look, he stirs.
Do you withdraw yourself a little while.
He will recover straight; when he is gone,
I would on great occasion speak with you.
                              [*Cassio goes*
How is it, general? have you not hurt your head?
60   *Othello.* Dost thou mock me?
    Iago.   I mock you! no, by heaven.
Would you would bear your fortune like a man!
    Othello. A hornéd man's a monster and a beast.
    Iago. There's many a beast then in a
            populous city,
And many a civil monster.
    Othello. Did he confess it?
    Iago.   Good sir, be a man:
Think every bearded fellow that's but yoked
May draw with you. There's millions now alive
That nightly lie in those unproper beds
Which they dare swear peculiar; your case is better.
70 O, 'tis the spite of hell, the fiend's arch-mock,
To lip a wanton in a secure couch,
And to suppose her chaste! No, let me know;
And knowing what I am, know what shall be.
    Othello. O, thou art wise; 'tis certain.
    Iago.   Stand you awhile apart;
Confine yourself but in a patient list.
Whilst you were here o'erwhelméd with your grief—
A passion most unsuiting such a man—

Cassio came hither; I shifted him away,
And laid good scuse upon your ecstasy;
Bade him anon return and speak with me;   80
The which he promised. Do but encave yourself,
And mark the fleers, the gibes, and notable scorns,
That dwell in every region of his face;
For I will make him tell the tale anew,
Where, how, how oft, how long ago and when
He hath and is again to cope your wife.
I say, but mark his gestures. Marry, patience;
Or I shall say you're all in all a spleen,
And nothing of a man.
    Othello.   Dost thou hear, Iago?
I will be found most cunning in my patience;   90
But—dost thou hear?—most bloody.
    Iago.   That's not amiss;
But yet keep time in all. Will you withdraw?
                    [*Othello retires*
Now will I question Cassio of Bianca,
A hussy that by selling her desires
Buys herself bread and clothes: it is a creature
That dotes on Cassio; as 'tis the strumpet's plague
To beguile many and be beguiled by one.
He, when he hears of her, cannot refrain
From the excess of laughter. Here he comes.

          Re-enter CASSIO

As he shall smile, Othello shall go mad;   100
And his unbookish jealousy must construe
Poor Cassio's smiles, gestures, and light behaviours,
Quite in the wrong. How do you now, lieutenant?
    Cassio. The worser that you give me the addition
Whose want even kills me.
    Iago. Ply Desdemona well, and you are sure on't.

Now, if this suit lay in Bianca's power,
How quickly should you speed!

    Cassio.   Alas, poor caitiff!

    (*Othello.* Look how he laughs already!

110   *Iago.* I never knew a woman love man so.

    Cassio. Alas, poor rogue! I think, in faith, she loves me.

    (*Othello.* Now he denies it faintly, and laughs it out.

    Iago. Do you hear, Cassio?

    (*Othello.* Now he importunes him to tell it o'er.
Go to; well said, well said.

    Iago. She gives it out that you shall marry her.
Do you intend it?

    Cassio. Ha, ha, ha!

    (*Othello.* Do you triumph, Roman? do you triumph?

120   *Cassio.* I marry her! what, a customer! I prithee, bear
some charity to my wit; do not think it so unwholesome.
Ha, ha, ha!

    (*Othello.* So, so, so, so; they laugh that win.

    Iago. Faith, the cry goes that you marry her.

    Cassio. Prithee, say true.

    Iago. I am a very villain else.

    (*Othello.* Have you scored me? Well.

    Cassio. This is the monkey's own giving out: she is
persuaded I will marry her, out of her own love and
130 flattery, not out of my promise.

    (*Othello.* Iago beckons me; now he begins the story.

    Cassio. She was here even now; she haunts me in
every place. I was the other day talking on the sea-bank
with certain Venetians; and thither comes the bauble,
and, by this hand, falls me thus about my neck—

    (*Othello.* Crying 'O dear Cassio!' as it were: his
gesture imports it.

    Cassio. So hangs, and lolls, and weeps upon me; so
shakes, and pulls me: ha, ha, ha!

(*Othello*. Now he tells how she plucked him to my 140
chamber. O, I see that nose of yours, but not that dog
I shall throw it to.

Cassio. Well, I must leave her company.

Iago. Before me! look where she comes!

Cassio. 'Tis such another fitchew! marry, a perfumed
one.

Enter BIANCA

What do you mean by this haunting of me?

Bianca. Let the devil and his dam haunt you! What
did you mean by that same handkerchief you gave me
even now? I was a fine fool to take it. I must take out 150
the work? A likely piece of work that you should find
it in your chamber and not know who left it there!
This is some minx's token, and I must take out the
work? There; give it your hobby-horse. Wheresoever
you had it, I'll take out no work on't.

Cassio. How now, my sweet Bianca! how now! how
now!

(*Othello*. By heaven, that should be my handkerchief!

Bianca. An you'll come to supper tonight, you may;
an you will not, come when you are next prepared for. 160
                                      [*goes*

Iago. After her, after her.

Cassio. Faith, I must; she'll rail in the street else.

Iago. Will you sup there?

Cassio. Faith, I intend so.

Iago. Well, I may chance to see you; for I would very
fain speak with you.

Cassio. Prithee, come; will you?

Iago. Go to; say no more.   [*Cassio goes*

Othello [*comes forward*]. How shall I murder him, Iago?

Iago. Did you perceive how he laughed at his vice? 170

Othello. O Iago!

Iago. And did you see the handkerchief?

Othello. Was that mine?

Iago. Yours, by this hand—and to see how he prizes the foolish woman your wife! She gave it him, and he hath given it his whore.

Othello. I would have him nine years a-killing. A fine woman! a fair woman! a sweet woman!

Iago. Nay, you must forget that.

180 *Othello.* Ay, let her rot, and perish, and be damned tonight; for she shall not live. No, my heart is turned to stone: I strike it, and it hurts my hand. O, the world hath not a sweeter creature: she might lie by an emperor's side and command him tasks.

Iago. Nay, that's not your way.

Othello. Hang her! I do but say what she is: so delicate with her needle, an admirable musician— O, she will sing the savageness out of a bear—of so high and plenteous wit and invention—

190 *Iago.* She's the worse for all this.

Othello. O, a thousand, thousand times—and then, of so gentle a condition!

Iago. Ay, too gentle.

Othello. Nay, that's certain; but yet the pity of it, Iago! O Iago, the pity of it, Iago!

Iago. If you be so fond over her iniquity, give her patent to offend; for, if it touch not you, it comes near nobody.

Othello. I will chop her into messes—cuckold me!

200 *Iago.* O, 'tis foul in her.

Othello. With mine officer!

Iago. That's fouler.

Othello. Get me some poison, Iago—this night. I'll not expostulate with her, lest her body and beauty unprovide my mind again—this night, Iago.

Iago. Do it not with poison: strangle her in her bed, even the bed she hath contaminated.

Othello. Good, good: the justice of it pleases; very good.

Iago. And for Cassio, let me be his undertaker: you 210 shall hear more by midnight.

Othello. Excellent good. [*a trumpet sounds*] What trumpet is that same?

Iago. I warrant, something from Venice.

Enter LODOVICO, DESDEMONA, *and Attendants*

      'Tis Lodovico!
This comes from the Duke; and see, your wife is
  with him.

Lodovico. God save you, worthy general!

Othello.   With all my heart, sir.

Lodovico. The Duke and senators of Venice
  greet you.   [*gives him a letter*

Othello. I kiss the instrument of their pleasures.
         [*opens and reads*

Desdemona. And what's the news, good
  cousin Lodovico?

Iago. I am very glad to see you, signior;
Welcome to Cyprus.   220

Lodovico. I thank you. How does Lieutenant Cassio?

Iago. Lives, sir.

Desdemona. Cousin, there's fallen between him and
  my lord
An unkind breach; but you shall make all well.

(*Othello.* Are you sure of that?

Desdemona. My lord?

Othello [*reads*]. 'This fail you not to do, as you will—'

Lodovico. He did not call; he's busy in the paper.
Is there division 'twixt my lord and Cassio?

230 *Desdemona.* A most unhappy one; I would do much
T'atone them, for the love I bear to Cassio.
    (*Othello.* Fire and brimstone!
    Desdemona. My lord?
    (*Othello.* Are you wise?
    Desdemona. What, is he angry?
    Lodovico.   May be the letter moved him;
For, as I think, they do command him home,
Deputing Cassio in his government.
    Desdemona. By my troth, I am glad on't.
    (*Othello.*   Indeed!
    Desdemona.   My lord?
    Othello. I am glad to see you mad.
    Desdemona.   Why, sweet Othello!
240   *Othello.* Devil!   [*striking her*
    Desdemona. I have not deserved this.
    Lodovico. My lord, this would not be believed in Venice,
Though I should swear I saw't. 'Tis very much.
Make her amends; she weeps.
    Othello.   O devil, devil!
If that the earth could teem with woman's tears,
Each drop she falls would prove a crocodile.
Out of my sight!
    Desdemona.   I will not stay to offend you.   [*going*
    Lodovico. Truly, an obedient lady.
I do beseech your lordship, call her back.
250   *Othello.* Mistress!
    Desdemona. My lord?
    Othello. What would you with her, sir?
    Lodovico.   Who, I, my lord?
    Othello. Ay; you did wish that I would make her turn.
Sir, she can turn and turn, and yet go on
And turn again; and she can weep, sir, weep;
And she's obedient, as you say, obedient,

Very obedient. Proceed you in your tears.—
Concerning this, sir,—O well-painted passion!—
I am commanded home.—Get you away;
I'll send for you anon.—Sir, I obey the mandate,   260
And will return to Venice.—Hence, avaunt!—

                              [*Desdemona goes*

Cassio shall have my place. And, sir, tonight,
I do entreat that we may sup together.
You are welcome, sir, to Cyprus.—Goats and monkeys!

                              [*he goes*

  Lodovico. Is this the noble Moor whom our full senate
Call all in all sufficient? Is this the nature
Whom passion could not shake? whose solid virtue
The shot of accident nor dart of chance
Could neither graze nor pierce?
  Iago.   He is much changed.
  Lodovico. Are his wits safe? is he not light of brain?   270
  Iago. He's that he is. I may not breathe my censure
What he might be; if what he might he is not,
I would to heaven he were!
  Lodovico.   What, strike his wife!
  Iago. Faith, that was not so well; yet would I knew
That stroke would prove the worst!
  Lodovico.   Is it his use?
Or did the letters work upon his blood,
And new-create this fault?
  Iago.   Alas, alas!
It is not honesty in me to speak
What I have seen and known. You shall observe him,
And his own courses will denote him so   280
That I may save my speech; do but go after,
And mark how he continues.
  Lodovico. I am sorry that I am deceived in him.

                              [*they go*

[4. 2.]   *A room in the citadel*

Enter OTHELLO *and* EMILIA

Othello. You have seen nothing, then?
Emilia. Nor ever heard, nor ever did suspect.
Othello. Yes, you have seen Cassio and she together.
Emilia. But then I saw no harm, and then I heard
Each syllable that breath made up between them.
Othello. What, did they never whisper?
Emilia.   Never, my lord.
Othello. Nor send you out o'th'way?
Emilia. Never.
Othello. To fetch her fan, her gloves, her mask,
      nor nothing?
10 *Emilia.* Never, my lord.
Othello. That's strange.
Emilia. I durst, my lord, to wager she is honest,
Lay down my soul at stake. If you think other,
Remove your thought: it doth abuse your bosom.
If any wretch have put this in your head,
Let heaven requite it with the serpent's curse!
For if she be not honest, chaste, and true,
There's no man happy: the purest of their wives
Is foul as slander.
Othello.   Bid her come hither; go. [*Emilia goes*
20 She says enough; yet she's a simple bawd
That cannot say as much. This is a subtle whore,
A closet lock and key of villanous secrets;
And yet she'll kneel and pray; I have seen her do't.

Enter DESDEMONA *with* EMILIA

Desdemona. My lord, what is your will?
Othello.   Pray, chuck, come hither.

Desdemona. What is your pleasure?

Othello.   Let me see your eyes;
Look in my face.

Desdemona.   What horrible fancy's this?

Othello [*to Emilia*]. Some of your
    function, mistress:
Leave procreants alone and shut the door;
Cough, or cry hem, if anybody come—
Your mystery, your mystery; nay, dispatch.   30

                              [*Emilia goes out*

Desdemona. Upon my knees, what doth your
    speech import?
I understand a fury in your words,
But not the words.

Othello. Why, what art thou?

Desdemona. Your wife, my lord; your true and
    loyal wife.

Othello. Come, swear it, damn thyself;
Lest, being like one of heaven, the devils themselves
Should fear to seize thee. Therefore be
    double-damned:
Swear thou art honest.

Desdemona.   Heaven doth truly know it.

Othello. Heaven truly knows that thou art false
    as hell.   40

Desdemona. To whom, my lord? with whom? how
    am I false?

Othello. Ah, Desdemon! Away! away! away!

Desdemona. Alas the heavy day! Why do you weep?
Am I the motive of these tears, my lord?
If haply you my father do suspect
An instrument of this your calling back,
Lay not your blame on me; if you have lost him,
Why, I have lost him too.

Othello.   Had it pleased **heaven**
To try me with affliction; had they rained
50 All kind of sores and shames on my bare head,
Steeped me in poverty to the very lips,
Given to captivity me and my utmost hopes,
I should have found in some place of my soul
A drop of patience; but, alas, to make me
A fixéd figure for the time of scorn
To point his slow unmoving finger at!
Yet could I bear that too; well, very well;
But there, where I have garnered up my heart,
Where either I must live or bear no life,
60 The fountain from the which my current runs,
Or else dries up—to be discarded thence!
Or keep it as a cistern for foul toads
To knot and gender in! Turn thy complexion there,
Patience, thou young and rose-lipped cherubin,
Ay, there, look grim as hell!

   Desdemona. I hope my noble lord esteems
    me honest.

   Othello. O, ay; as summer flies are in the shambles,
That quicken even with blowing. O thou weed,
Who art so lovely fair and smell'st so sweet
70 That the sense aches at thee, would thou hadst ne'er
    been born!

   Desdemona. Alas, what ignorant sin have
    I committed?

   Othello. Was this fair paper, this most goodly book,
Made to write 'whore' upon? What committed!
Committed! O thou public commoner!
I should make very forges of my cheeks,
That would to cinders burn up modesty,
Did I but speak thy deeds. What committed!
Heaven stops the nose at it, and the moon winks;

The bawdy wind, that kisses all it meets,
Is hushed within the hollow mine of earth,   80
And will not hear it. What committed!
Impudent strumpet!

  Desdemona.   By heaven, you do me wrong.

  Othello. Are not you a strumpet?

  Desdemona.   No, as I am a Christian.
If to preserve this vessel for my lord
From any other foul unlawful touch
Be not to be a strumpet, I am none.

  Othello. What, not a whore?

  Desdemona.   No, as I shall be saved.

  Othello. Is't possible?

  Desdemona. O, heaven forgive us!

  Othello.   I cry you mercy then:
I took you for that cunning whore of Venice   90
That married with Othello. [*raising his voice*]
     You, mistress,
That have the office opposite to Saint Peter,
And keep the gate of hell!

Re-enter EMILIA

            You, you, ay, you!
We've done our course; there's money for your pains:
I pray you, turn the key, and keep our counsel. [*goes*

  Emilia. Alas, what does this gentleman conceive?
How do you, madam? how do you, my good lady?

  Desdemona. Faith, half asleep.

  Emilia. Good madam, what's the matter with
    my lord?

  Desdemona. With who?   100

  Emilia. Why, with my lord, madam.

  Desdemona. Who is thy lord?

  Emilia.   He that is yours, sweet lady.

Desdemona. I have none: do not talk to me, Emilia;
I cannot weep, nor answers have I none
But what should go by water. Prithee, tonight
Lay on my bed my wedding sheets—remember;
And call thy husband hither.
    Emilia.   Here's a change indeed!   [*goes*
    Desdemona. 'Tis meet I should be used so, very meet.
How have I been behaved, that he might stick
110 The small'st opinion on my least misuse?

Re-enter EMILIA with IAGO

    Iago. What is your pleasure, madam? How is't
      with you?
    Desdemona. I cannot tell. Those that do teach
      young babes
Do it with gentle means and easy tasks:
He might have chid me so; for, in good faith,
I am a child to chiding.
    Iago.   What's the matter, lady?
    Emilia. Alas, Iago, my lord hath so bewhored her,
Thrown such despite and heavy terms upon her,
As true heart cannot bear.
    Desdemona. Am I that name, Iago?
    Iago.   What name, fair lady?
120 *Desdemona.* Such as she said my lord did say I was.
    Emilia. He called her whore: a beggar in his drink
Could not have laid such terms upon his callet.
    Iago. Why did he so?
    Desdemona. I do not know; I am sure I am
      none such.
    Iago. Do not weep, do not weep. Alas the day!
    Emilia. Hath she forsook so many noble matches,
Her father, and her country, and her friends,
To be called whore? Would it not make one weep?

Desdemona. It is my wretched fortune.

Iago.   Beshrew him for't!
How comes this trick upon him?

Desdemona.   Nay, heaven doth know. 130

Emilia. I will be hanged, if some eternal villain,
Some busy and insinuating rogue,
Some cogging, cozening slave, to get some office,
Have not devised this slander; I'll be hanged else.

Iago. Fie, there is no such man; it is impossible.

Desdemona. If any such there be, heaven
      pardon him!

Emilia. A halter pardon him! and hell gnaw
      his bones!
Why should he call her whore? who keeps
      her company?
What place? what time? what form?
      what likelihood?
The Moor's abused by some most villanous knave,   140
Some base notorious knave, some scurvy fellow.
O heaven, that such companions thou'ldst unfold,
And put in every honest hand a whip
To lash the rascals naked through the world
Even from the east to th'west!

Iago.   Speak within door.

Emilia. O, fie upon them! Some such squire he was
That turned your wit the seamy side without,
And made you to suspect me with the Moor.

Iago. You are a fool; go to.

Desdemona.   Alas, Iago,
What shall I do to win my lord again?   150
Good friend, go to him; for, by this light of heaven,
I know not how I lost him. Here I kneel:
If e'er my will did trespass 'gainst his love
Either in discourse of thought or actual deed,

Or that mine eyes, mine ears, or any sense,
Delighted them in any other form,
Or that I do not yet, and ever did,
And ever will, though he do shake me off
To beggarly divorcement, love him dearly,
160 Comfort forswear me! Unkindness may do much;
And his unkindness may defeat my life,
But never taint my love. I cannot say 'whore':
It does abhor me now I speak the word;
To do the act that might the addition earn
Not the world's mass of vanity could make me.

   Iago. I pray you, be content; 'tis but his humour:
The business of the state does him offence,
And he does chide with you.

   Desdemona.   If 'twere no other!

   Iago. 'Tis but so, I warrant.   *[trumpets sound*
170 Hark how these instruments summon to supper!
The messengers of Venice stay the meat:
Go in, and weep not; all things shall be well.

                      [Desdemona and Emilia go

Enter RODERIGO

How now, Roderigo!

   Roderigo. I do not find that thou deal'st justly with me.

   Iago. What in the contrary?

   Roderigo. Every day thou daff'st me with some device,
Iago; and rather, as it seems to me now, keep'st from me
all conveniency than suppliest me with the least
advantage of hope. I will indeed no longer endure it;
180 nor am I yet persuaded to put up in peace what
already I have foolishly suffered.

   Iago. Will you hear me, Roderigo?

   Roderigo. Faith, I have heard too much; for your
words and performances are no kin together.

Iago. You charge me most unjustly.

Roderigo. With nought but truth. I have wasted myself out of my means. The jewels you have had from me to deliver to Desdemona would half have corrupted a votarist. You have told me she hath received them and returned me expectations and comforts of sudden 190 respect and acquaintance; but I find none.

Iago. Well; go to; very well.

Roderigo. Very well! go to! I cannot go to, man; nor 'tis not very well. By this hand, I think 'tis very scurvy, and begin to find myself fopped in it.

Iago. Very well.

Roderigo. I tell you 'tis not very well. I will make myself known to Desdemona. If she will return me my jewels, I will give over my suit and repent my unlawful solicitation; if not, assure yourself I will seek satisfaction 200 of you.

Iago. You have said now.

Roderigo. Ay, and said nothing but what I protest intendment of doing.

Iago. Why, now I see there's mettle in thee; and even from this instant do build on thee a better opinion than ever before. Give me thy hand, Roderigo: thou hast taken against me a most just exception; but yet, I protest, I have dealt most directly in thy affair.

Roderigo. It hath not appeared. 210

Iago. I grant indeed it hath not appeared, and your suspicion is not without wit and judgement. But, Roderigo, if thou hast that in thee indeed, which I have greater reason to believe now than ever—I mean purpose, courage, and valour—this night show it: if thou the next night following enjoy not Desdemona, take me from this world with treachery and devise engines for my life.

Roderigo. Well, what is it? is it within reason and
220 compass?

Iago. Sir, there is especial commission come from
Venice to depute Cassio in Othello's place.

Roderigo. Is that true? why then, Othello and
Desdemona return again to Venice.

Iago. O, no; he goes into Mauritania, and takes away
with him the fair Desdemona, unless his abode be
lingered here by some accident: wherein none can be
so determinate as the removing of Cassio.

Roderigo. How do you mean removing of him?

230 *Iago.* Why, by making him uncapable of Othello's
place; knocking out his brains.

Roderigo. And that you would have me do?

Iago. Ay, if you dare do yourself a profit and a right.
He sups tonight with a harlotry, and thither will I go
to him: he knows not yet of his honourable fortune.
If you will watch his going thence, which I will fashion
to fall out between twelve and one, you may take him
at your pleasure. I will be near to second your attempt,
and he shall fall between us. Come, stand not amazed
240 at it, but go along with me; I will show you such a
necessity in his death that you shall think yourself bound
to put it on him. It is now high supper-time, and the
night grows to waste. About it.

Roderigo. I will hear further reason for this.

Iago. And you shall be satisfied.   [*they go*

[4. 3.]   *Another room in the citadel*

Enter OTHELLO, LODOVICO, DESDEMONA, EMILIA,
        and Attendants

Lodovico. I do beseech you, sir, trouble yourself
    no further.
Othello. O, pardon me; 'twill do me good to walk.
Lodovico. Madam, good night; I humbly thank
    your ladyship.
Desdemona. Your honour is most welcome.
Othello.   Will you walk, sir?
O, Desdemona!
Desdemona. My lord?
Othello. Get you to bed on th'instant; I will be
returned forthwith. Dismiss your attendant there:
look't be done.
Desdemona. I will, my lord.   10
                [*Othello, Lodovico, and Attendants go*
Emilia. How goes it now? he looks gentler than
    he did.
Desdemona. He says he will return incontinent:
He hath commanded me to go to bed,
And bade me to dismiss you.
Emilia.   Dismiss me!
Desdemona. It was his bidding; therefore,
    good Emilia,
Give me my nightly wearing, and adieu:
We must not now displease him.
Emilia. I would you had never seen him!
Desdemona. So would not I: my love doth so
    approve him,
That even his stubbornness, his checks, his frowns—   20
Prithee, unpin me—have grace and favour in them.

Emilia. I have laid those sheets you bade me on
    the bed.
Desdemona. All's one. Good faith, how foolish are
    our minds!
If I do die before thee, prithee, shroud me
In one of those same sheets.
Emilia.   Come, come, you talk.
Desdemona. My mother had a maid called Barbara.
She was in love; and he she loved proved mad
And did forsake her. She had a song of 'willow'—
An old thing 'twas, but it expressed her fortune,
30 And she died singing it. That song tonight
Will not go from my mind. I have much to do
But to go hang my head all at one side
And sing it like poor Barbara. Prithee, dispatch.
  Emilia. Shall I go fetch your night-gown?
  Desdemona.   No, unpin me here.
This Lodovico is a proper man.
  Emilia. A very handsome man.
  Desdemona. He speaks well.
  Emilia. I know a lady in Venice would have walked
barefoot to Palestine for a touch of his nether lip.
40   *Desdemona* [*sings*].

    The poor soul sat sighing by a sycamore tree,
      Sing all a green willow;
    Her hand on her bosom, her head on her knee,
      Sing willow, willow, willow:
    The fresh streams ran by her, and murmured
        her moans;
      Sing willow, willow, willow;
    Her salt tears fell from her, and softened
        the stones—
  Lay by these—
      Sing willow, willow, willow;

Prithee, hie thee; he'll come anon—
   Sing all a green willow must be my garland.   50
   Let nobody blame him; his scorn I approve—
Nay, that's not next. Hark! who is't that knocks?
  Emilia. It's the wind.
  Desdemona [*sings*].
   I called my love false love; but what said he then?
   Sing willow, willow, willow;
   If I court moe women, you'll couch with moe men.
So, get thee gone; good night. Mine eyes do itch;
Does that bode weeping?
  Emilia.   'Tis neither here nor there.
  Desdemona. I have heard it said so. O, these men,
    these men!
Dost thou in conscience think—tell me, Emilia—   60
That there be women do abuse their husbands
In such gross kind?
  Emilia.   There be some such, no question.
  Desdemona. Wouldst thou do such a deed for all
    the world?
  Emilia. Why, would not you?
  Desdemona.   No, by this heavenly light!
  Emilia. Nor I neither by this heavenly light: I might
do't as well i'th'dark.
  Desdemona. Wouldst thou do such a deed for all the
world?
  Emilia. The world's a huge thing: it is a great prize
for a small vice.   70
  Desdemona. In troth, I think thou wouldst not.
  Emilia. In troth, I think I should; and undo't when
I had done't. Marry, I would not do such a thing for
a joint-ring, nor for measures of lawn, nor for gowns,
petticoats, nor caps, nor any petty exhibition. But for
all the whole world—ud's pity, who would not make

her husband a cuckold to make him a monarch?
I should venture purgatory for't.

Desdemona. Beshrew me, if I would do such a wrong
80 for the whole world.

Emilia. Why, the wrong is but a wrong i'th'world;
and having the world for your labour, 'tis a wrong in
your own world, and you might quickly make it right.

Desdemona. I do not think there is any such woman.

Emilia. Yes, a dozen; and as many to th'vantage as
would store the world they played for.
But I do think it is their husbands' faults
If wives do fall. Say that they slack their duties
And pour our treasures into foreign laps,
90 Or else break out in peevish jealousies,
Throwing restraint upon us; or say they strike us,
Or scant our former having in despite—
Why, we have galls, and though we have some grace,
Yet have we some revenge. Let husbands know
Their wives have sense like them: they see, and smell,
And have their palates both for sweet and sour,
As husbands have. What is it that they do
When they change us for others? Is it sport?
I think it is. And doth affection breed it?
100 I think it doth. Is't frailty that thus errs?
It is so too. And have not we affections,
Desires for sport, and frailty, as men have?
Then let them use us well: else let them know,
The ills we do, their ills instruct us so.

Desdemona. Good night, good night.   [*Emilia goes*
                    Heaven me such uses send,
Not to pick bad from bad, but by bad mend!   [*goes*

[5. 1.]   *A street*

Enter IAGO and RODERIGO

Iago. Here, stand behind this bulk; straight will
    he come.
Wear thy good rapier bare, and put it home;
Quick, quick; fear nothing; I'll be at thy elbow.
It makes us, or it mars us; think on that,
And fix most firm thy resolution.
Roderigo. Be near at hand; I may miscarry in't.
Iago. Here, at thy hand. Be bold, and take
    thy stand.   [*retires*
Roderigo. I have no great devotion to the deed;
And yet he hath given me satisfying reasons.
'Tis but a man gone. Forth, my sword: he dies.   10
Iago. I have rubbed this young quat almost to
    the sense,
And he grows angry. Now, whether he kill Cassio,
Or Cassio him, or each do kill the other,
Every way makes my gain: live Roderigo,
He calls me to a restitution large
Of gold and jewels that I bobbed from him,
As gifts to Desdemona—
It must not be; if Cassio do remain,
He hath a daily beauty in his life
That makes me ugly; and besides, the Moor   20
May unfold me to him—there stand I in much peril.
No, he must die. Be't so. I hear him coming.

Enter CASSIO

Roderigo. I know his gait; 'tis he. Villain,
    thou diest!   [*makes a pass at Cassio*
Cassio. That thrust had been mine enemy indeed,

But that my coat is better than thou think'st.
I will make proof of thine.

[draws, and wounds Roderigo

Roderigo.   O, I am slain!

[Iago from behind strikes at Cassio's legs, and hurries off

Cassio. I am maimed for ever. Help, ho!
   murder! murder!   *[falls*

Enter OTHELLO

Othello. The voice of Cassio: Iago keeps his word.
Roderigo. O, villain that I am!
Othello.   It is even so.
30 *Cassio.* O, help, ho! light! a surgeon!
Othello. 'Tis he. O brave Iago, honest and just,
That hast such noble sense of thy friend's wrong!
Thou teachest me: minion, your dear lies dead,
And your unblest fate hies. Strumpet, I come!
Forth of my heart, those charms, thine eyes,
   are blotted;
Thy bed lust-stained shall with lust's blood
   be spotted.   *[he goes*

Enter LODOVICO and GRATIANO

Cassio. What, ho! no watch? no passage?
   murder! murder!
Gratiano. 'Tis some mischance; the voice is
   very direful.
Cassio. O, help!
40 *Lodovico.* Hark!
Roderigo. O wretched villain!
Lodovico. Two or three groan. It is a heavy night;
These may be counterfeits: let's think't unsafe
To come in to the cry without more help.

[they stand aside

Roderigo. Nobody come? then shall I bleed to death.
Lodovico. Hark!

Re-enter IAGO, with a light

Gratiano. Here's one comes in his shirt, with light
    and weapons.
Iago. Who's there? whose noise is this that cries
    on murder?
Lodovico. We do not know.
Iago.   Did not you hear a cry?
Cassio. Here, here! for heaven's sake, help me!
Iago.   What's the matter? 50
Gratiano. This is Othello's ancient, as I take it.
Lodovico. The same indeed; a very valiant fellow.
Iago. What are you here that cry so grievously?
Cassio. Iago? O, I am spoiled, undone by villains!
Give me some help.
Iago. O me, lieutenant! what villains have
    done this?
Cassio. I think that one of them is hereabout,
And cannot make away.
Iago.   O treacherous villains!
What are you there? [*spies Lodovico and Gratiano*].
    Come in and give some help.
Roderigo. O, help me here!   60
Cassio. That's one of them.
Iago.   O murderous slave! O villain!
                 [*stabs Roderigo*
Roderigo. O damned Iago! O inhuman dog!
Iago. Kill men i'th'dark! Where be these
    bloody thieves?
How silent is this town! Ho! murder! murder!
             [*Lodovico and Gratiano come forward*
What may you be? are you of good or evil?

Lodovico. As you shall prove us, praise us.

Iago. Signior Lodovico?

Lodovico. He, sir.

Iago. I cry you mercy. Here's Cassio hurt
    by villains.

70 *Gratiano.* Cassio!

Iago. How is't, brother?

Cassio. My leg is cut in two.

Iago.   Marry, heaven forbid!
Light, gentlemen: I'll bind it with my shirt.

Enter BIANCA

Bianca. What is the matter, ho? who is't
    that cried?

Iago. Who is't that cried!

Bianca. O my dear Cassio! my sweet Cassio! O Cassio,
Cassio, Cassio!

Iago. O notable strumpet! Cassio, may you suspect
Who they should be that have thus mangled you?

80 *Cassio.* No.

Gratiano. I am sorry to find you thus: I have been
    to seek you.

Iago. Lend me a garter. So. O, for a chair,
To bear him easily hence!

Bianca. Alas, he faints! O Cassio, Cassio, Cassio!

Iago. Gentlemen all, I do suspect this trash
To be a party in this injury.
Patience awhile, good Cassio. Come, come;
Lend me a light. Know we this face or no?
Alas, my friend and my dear countryman

90 Roderigo? No—yes, sure; 'tis Roderigo.

Gratiano. What, of Venice?

Iago. Even he, sir. Did you know him?

Gratiano.   Know him! ay.

Iago. Signior Gratiano? I cry your gentle pardon:
These bloody accidents must excuse my manners,
That so neglected you.
  Gratiano.   I am glad to see you.
  Iago. How do you, Cassio? O, a chair, a chair!
  Gratiano. Roderigo!
  Iago. He, he, 'tis he. [*a chair brought*] O, that's well
    said; the chair.
Some good man bear him carefully from hence;
I'll fetch the general's surgeon. [*to Bianca*] For
    you, mistress,   100
Save you your labour. He that lies slain here, Cassio,
Was my dear friend: what malice was between you?
  Cassio. None in the world; nor do I know the man.
  Iago [*to Bianca*]. What, look you pale? O, bear him
    out o'th'air.
  [*Cassio is borne in, and the body of Roderigo removed*
Stay you, good gentlemen. Look you pale, mistress?
Do you perceive the gastness of her eye?
Nay, if you stare, we shall hear more anon.
Behold her well; I pray you, look upon her:
Do you see, gentlemen? nay, guiltiness will speak,
Though tongues were out of use.   110

Enter EMILIA

  Emilia. 'Las, what's the matter? what's the
    matter, husband?
  Iago. Cassio hath here been set on in the dark
By Roderigo, and fellows that are scaped:
He's almost slain, and Roderigo dead.
  Emilia. Alas, good gentleman! alas, good Cassio!
  Iago. This is the fruits of whoring. Prithee, Emilia,
Go know of Cassio where he supped tonight.
What, do you shake at that?

Bianca. He supped at my house; but I therefore
  shake not.
120 *Iago.* O, did he so? I charge you, go with me.
  Emilia. O, fie upon thee, strumpet!
  Bianca. I am no strumpet; but of life as honest
As you that thus abuse me.
  Emilia.   As I! foh! fie upon thee!
  Iago. Kind gentlemen, let's see poor Cassio dressed.
Come, mistress, you must tell's another tale.
Emilia, run you to the citadel,
And tell my lord and lady what hath happed.
Will you go on afore? [*aside*] This is the night
That either makes me or fordoes me quite.   [*they go*

[5. 2.] *A chamber in the citadel; DESDEMONA
asleep in her bed*

Enter OTHELLO *with a light; he locks the door*

Othello. It is the cause, it is the cause, my soul.
Let me not name it to you, you chaste stars!
It is the cause. Yet I'll not shed her blood,
Nor scar that whiter skin of hers than snow
And smooth as monumental alabaster—
Yet she must die, else she'll betray more men.
Put out the light, and then put out the light:
If I quench thee, thou flaming minister,
I can again thy former light restore
10 Should I repent me; but once put out thy light,
Thou cunning'st pattern of excelling nature,
I know not where is that Promethean heat
That can thy light relume.   [*sets down the taper*
                    When I have plucked the rose,

I cannot give it vital growth again,
It needs must wither: I'll smell it on the tree.

                [*kisses her*

O balmy breath, that dost almost persuade
Justice to break her sword! One more, one more.
Be thus when thou art dead, and I will kill thee,
And love thee after. One more, and that's the last.
So sweet was ne'er so fatal. I must weep,   20
But they are cruel tears; this sorrow's heavenly:
It strikes where it doth love. She wakes.

  Desdemona. Who's there? Othello?

  Othello. Ay, Desdemona.

  Desdemona. Will you come to bed, my lord?

  Othello. Have you prayed tonight, Desdemona?

  Desdemona.   Ay, my lord.

  Othello. If you bethink yourself of any crime
Unreconciled as yet to heaven and grace,
Solicit for it straight.

  Desdemona. Alack, my lord, what may you mean
       by that?   30

  Othello. Well, do it, and be brief; I will walk by:
I would not kill thy unpreparéd spirit;
No—heaven forfend!—I would not kill thy soul.

  Desdemona. Talk you of killing?

  Othello. Ay, I do.

  Desdemona. Then heaven have mercy on me!

  Othello. Amen, with all my heart!

  Desdemona. If you say so, I hope you will not kill me.

  Othello. Hum!

  Desdemona. And yet I fear you; for you're fatal then   40
When your eyes roll so. Why I should fear I know not,
Since guiltiness I know not; but yet I feel I fear.

  Othello. Think on thy sins.

  Desdemona.   They are loves I bear to you.

Othello. Ay, and for that thou diest.

Desdemona. That death's unnatural that kills
 for loving.

Alas, why gnaw you so your nether lip?

Some bloody passion shakes your very frame:

These are portents; but yet I hope, I hope,

They do not point on me.

Othello.   Peace, and be still!

50 *Desdemona.* I will so. What's the matter?

Othello. That handkerchief which I so loved and
 gave thee,

Thou gav'st to Cassio.

Desdemona.   No, by my life and soul!

Send for the man, and ask him.

Othello.   Sweet soul, take heed,

Take heed of perjury: thou art on thy death-bed.

Desdemona. Ay, but not yet to die.

Othello.   Yes, presently:

Therefore confess thee freely of thy sin;

For to deny each article with oath

Cannot remove nor choke the strong conception

That I do groan withal. Thou art to die.

60 *Desdemona.* O Lord have mercy on me!

Othello.   I say, amen.

Desdemona. And have you mercy too! I never did

Offend you in my life; never loved Cassio

But with such general warranty of heaven

As I might love. I never gave him token.

Othello. By heaven, I saw my handkerchief in's hand.

O perjured woman! thou dost stone my heart,

And mak'st me call what I intend to do

A murder, which I thought a sacrifice.

I saw the handkerchief.

Desdemona.   He found it then;

I never gave it him. Send for him hither: 70
Let him confess a truth.

  Othello.   He hath confessed.

  Desdemona. What, my lord?

  Othello. That he hath used thee.

  Desdemona.   How? unlawfully?

  Othello. Ay.

  Desdemona. He will not say so.

  Othello.   No, his mouth is stopped;
Honest Iago hath ta'en order for't.

  Desdemona. O, my fear interprets! what, is he dead?

  Othello. Had all his hairs been lives, my
    great revenge
Had stomach for them all.

  Desdemona. Alas, he is betrayed, and I undone!   80

  Othello. Out, strumpet! weep'st thou for him to
    my face?

  Desdemona. O, banish me, my lord, but kill me not!

  Othello. Down, strumpet!

  Desdemona. Kill me tomorrow; let me live tonight!

  Othello. Nay, if you strive—

  Desdemona. But half an hour!

  Othello.   Being done, there is no pause.

  Desdemona. But while I say one prayer!

  Othello.   It is too late. [*he smothers her*

  Emilia [*at the door without*]. My lord, my lord!
    what, ho! my lord, my lord!

  Othello. What noise is this?—Not dead? not yet
    quite dead?
I that am cruel am yet merciful;   90
I would not have thee linger in thy pain.
So, so.

  Emilia [*without*].   What, ho! my lord, my lord!

  Othello.   Who's there?

    Emilia [*without*]. O, good my lord, I'ld speak
      a word with you!
    Othello. Yes: 'tis Emilia.—By and by.—She's dead.
'Tis like she comes to speak of Cassio's death;
The noise was high. Ha! no more moving?
Still as the grave. Shall she come in? were't good?
I think she stirs again. No. What's best to do?
If she come in, she'll sure speak to my wife—
100 My wife! my wife! what wife? I have no wife.
O, insupportable! O heavy hour!
Methinks it should be now a huge eclipse
Of sun and moon, and that th'affrighted globe
Should yawn at alteration.
    Emilia [*without*].   I do beseech
That I may speak with you. O, good my lord!
    Othello. I had forgot thee: O, come in, Emilia.
Soft; by and by. Let me the curtains draw.
Where art thou?   [*unlocks the door*

          Enter EMILIA

          What's the matter with thee now?
    Emilia. O, my good lord, yonder's foul murder done!
110   *Othello.* What, now?
    Emilia. But now, my lord.
    Othello. It is the very error of the moon;
She comes more nearer earth than she was wont
And makes men mad.
    Emilia. Cassio, my lord, hath killed a young Venetian
Called Roderigo.
    Othello.   Roderigo killed!
And Cassio killed!
    Emilia.   No, Cassio is not killed.
    Othello. Not Cassio killed! then murder's out of tune,
And sweet revenge grows harsh.
    Desdemona. O, falsely, falsely murdered!

Emilia.   Alas, what cry is that? 120
Othello. That! what?
Emilia. Out, and alas! that was my lady's voice.
                              [*she draws back the curtain*
Help! help, ho! help! O lady, speak again!
Sweet Desdemona! O sweet mistress, speak!
Desdemona. A guiltless death I die.
Emilia. O, who hath done this deed?
Desdemona. Nobody: I myself. Farewell;
Commend me to my kind lord: O, farewell!   [*dies*
Othello. Why, how should she be murdered?
Emilia.   Alas, who knows?
Othello. You heard her say herself, it was not I.   130
Emilia. She said so: I must needs report the truth.
Othello. She's like a liar gone to burning hell:
'Twas I that killed her.
Emilia.   O, the more angel she,
And you the blacker devil!
Othello. She turned to folly, and she was a whore.
Emilia. Thou dost belie her, and thou art a devil.
Othello. She was false as water.
Emilia.   Thou art rash as fire to say
That she was false: O, she was heavenly true!
Othello. Cassio did top her: ask thy husband else;
O, I were damned beneath all depth in hell   140
But that I did proceed upon just grounds
To this extremity. Thy husband knew it all.
Emilia. My husband!
Othello. Thy husband.
Emilia. That she was false to wedlock?
Othello. Ay, with Cassio. Nay, had she been true,
If heaven would make me such another world
Of one entire and perfect chrysolite,
I'ld not have sold her for it.

150   *Emilia.* My husband!

    Othello.   Ay, 'twas he that told me on her first;
An honest man he is, and hates the slime
That sticks on filthy deeds.

    Emilia.   My husband!

    Othello. What needs this iterance, woman? I say
      thy husband.

    Emilia. O mistress, villany hath made mocks
      with love!
My husband say that she was false!

    Othello.   He, woman:
I say thy husband; dost understand the word?
My friend, thy husband, honest, honest Iago.

    Emilia. If he say so, may his pernicious soul
Rot half a grain a day! He lies to th'heart.
160 She was too fond of her most filthy bargain.

    Othello. Ha!

    Emilia. Do thy worst:
This deed of thine is no more worthy heaven
Than thou wast worthy her.

    Othello.   Peace, you were best.

    Emilia. Thou hast not half that power to do
      me harm
As I have to be hurt. O gull! O dolt!
As ignorant as dirt! thou hast done a deed—
I care not for thy sword; I'll make thee known,
Though I lost twenty lives. Help! help, ho! help!
170 The Moor hath killed my mistress! Murder! murder!

Enter MONTANO, GRATIANO, IAGO, *and others*

    Montano. What is the matter? How now, general!

    Emilia. O, are you come, Iago? You have done well,
That men must lay their murders on your neck.

    Gratiano. What is the matter?

   Emilia. Disprove this villain, if thou be'st a man:
He says thou told'st him that his wife was false.
I know thou didst not, thou'rt not such a villain.
Speak, for my heart is full.
   Iago. I told him what I thought, and told no more
Than what he found himself was apt and true.   180
   Emilia. But did you ever tell him she was false?
   Iago. I did.
   Emilia. You told a lie, an odious, damnéd lie;
Upon my soul, a lie, a wicked lie!
She false with Cassio! Did you say with Cassio?
   Iago. With Cassio, mistress. Go to, charm
      your tongue.
   Emilia. I will not charm my tongue; I am bound
      to speak:
My mistress here lies murdered in her bed—
   All. O heavens forfend!
   Emilia. And your reports have set the murder on.   190
   Othello. Nay, stare not, masters: it is true indeed.
   Gratiano. 'Tis a strange truth.
   Montano. O monstrous act!
   Emilia.   Villany, villany, villany!
I think upon't; I think—I smell't: O villany!
I thought so then; I'll kill myself for grief:
O villany, villany!
   Iago. What, are you mad? I charge you, get
      you home.
Emilia. Good gentlemen, let me have leave to speak:
'Tis proper I obey him, but not now.
Perchance, Iago, I will ne'er go home.   200
   Othello. O! O! O!   [*falls on the bed*
   Emilia.   Nay, lay thee down and roar;
For thou hast killed the sweetest innocent
That e'er did lift up eye.

Othello [*rising*].   O, she was foul!
I scarce did know you, uncle. There lies your niece,
Whose breath indeed these hands have newly stopped.
I know this act shows horrible and grim.
   Gratiano. Poor Desdemon! I am glad thy
      father's dead.
Thy match was mortal to him, and pure grief
Shore his old thread in twain. Did he live now,
210 This sight would make him do a desperate turn,
Yea, curse his better angel from his side,
And fall to reprobance.
   Othello. 'Tis pitiful; but yet Iago knows
That she with Cassio hath the act of shame
A thousand times committed. Cassio confessed it;
And she did gratify his amorous works
With that recognizance and pledge of love
Which I first gave her—I saw it in his hand:
It was a handkerchief, an antique token
220 My father gave my mother.
   Emilia. O God! O heavenly God!
   Iago. 'Zounds! hold your peace.
   Emilia.   'Twill out, 'twill out. I peace!
No, I will speak as liberal as the north;
Let heaven and men and devils, let them all,
All, all, cry shame against me, yet I'll speak.
   Iago. Be wise, and get you home.
   Emilia.   I will not.
                      [*Iago offers to stab her*
   Gratiano.   Fie!
Your sword upon a woman!
   Emilia. O thou dull Moor! that handkerchief
      thou speak'st of
I found by fortune, and did give my husband;
230 For often with a solemn earnestness,

More than indeed belonged to such a trifle,
He begged of me to steal it.

 Iago.   Villanous whore!

 Emilia. She give it Cassio! no, alas, I found it,
And I did give't my husband.

 Iago.   Filth, thou liest!

 Emilia. By heaven, I do not, I do not, gentlemen.
O murderous coxcomb! what should such a fool
Do with so good a wife?

 Othello.   Are there no stones in heaven
But what serve for the thunder? Precious villain!

[*he runs at Iago, but Montano disarms him; in the confusion, Iago stabs Emilia from behind and escapes*

 Gratiano. The woman falls; sure, he hath killed his wife.

 Emilia. Ay, ay. O, lay me by my mistress' side. 240

 Gratiano. He's gone, but his wife's killed.

 Montano. 'Tis a notorious villain. Take you
  this weapon,
Which I have here recovered from the Moor.
Come, guard the door without; let him not pass,
But kill him rather. I'll after that same villain,
For 'tis a damnéd slave.

      [*all but Othello and Emilia depart*

 Othello.   I am not valiant neither,
But every puny whipster gets my sword.
But why should honour outlive honesty?
Let it go all.

 Emilia. What did thy song bode, lady?
Hark, canst thou hear me? I will play the swan, 250
And die in music. [*singing*] Willow, willow, willow.
Moor, she was chaste; she loved thee, cruel Moor;
So come my soul to bliss, as I speak true;
So speaking as I think, alas, I die.   [*dies*

 Othello. I have another weapon in this chamber:

It was a sword of Spain, the ice brook's temper—
O, here it is. Uncle, I must come forth.
    Gratiano [*at the door*]. If thou attempt it, it will
      cost thee dear:
Thou hast no weapon, and perforce must suffer.
260   *Othello*. Look in upon me then, and speak with me,
Or, naked as I am, I will assault thee.

Re-enter GRATIANO

    Gratiano. What is the matter?
    Othello.   Behold, I have a weapon:
A better never did itself sustain
Upon a soldier's thigh. I have seen the day
That with this little arm and this good sword
I have made my way through more impediments
Than twenty times your stop—but, O vain boast!
Who can control his fate?—'tis not so now.
Be not afraid, though you do see me weaponed:
270 Here is my journey's end, here is my butt
And very sea-mark of my utmost sail.
Do you go back dismayed? 'tis a lost fear:
Man but a rush against Othello's breast,
And he retires. Where should Othello go?
Now, [*he turns to the bed*] how dost thou look now?
    O ill-starred wench!
Pale as thy smock! When we shall meet at compt,
This look of thine will hurl my soul from heaven,
And fiends will snatch at it. Cold, cold, my girl!
Even like thy chastity.
280 O curséd, curséd slave! Whip me, ye devils,
From the possession of this heavenly sight!
Blow me about in winds! roast me in sulphur!
Wash me in steep-down gulfs of liquid fire!
O Desdemon! dead Desdemon! dead! O! O!

Enter LODOVICO, MONTANO, CASSIO *carried in
a chair, and Officers with* IAGO, *prisoner*

Lodovico. Where is this rash and most
     unfortunate man?
Othello. That's he that was Othello: here I am.
Lodovico. Where is that viper? Bring the
     villain forth.
Othello. I look down towards his feet: but that's
     a fable;
If that thou be'st a devil, I cannot kill thee.

                                  [*wounds Iago*
Lodovico. Wrench his sword from him.
Iago.   I bleed, sir, but not killed. 290
Othello. I am not sorry neither: I'ld have thee live;
For, in my sense, 'tis happiness to die.
Lodovico. O thou Othello, that wert once so good,
Fallen in the practice of a damnéd slave
What shall be said to thee?
Othello.   Why, anything:
An honourable murderer, if you will;
For nought did I in hate, but all in honour.
Lodovico. This wretch hath part confessed his villany.
Did you and he consent in Cassio's death?
Othello. Ay.   300
Cassio. Dear general, I never gave you cause.
Othello. I do believe it, and I ask your pardon.
Will you, I pray, demand that demi-devil
Why he hath thus ensnared my soul and body?
Iago. Demand me nothing: what you know,
     you know;
From this time forth I never will speak word.
Lodovico. What, not to pray?
Gratiano.   Torments will ope your lips.

Othello. Well, thou dost best.

Lodovico. Sir, you shall understand what
  hath befallen,
310 Which, as I think, you know not. Here is a letter,
Found in the pocket of the slain Roderigo,
And here another: the one of them imports
The death of Cassio to be undertook
By Roderigo.

  Othello. O villain!

  Cassio.   Most heathenish and most gross!

  Lodovico. Now here's another discontented paper,
Found in his pocket too: and this, it seems,
Roderigo meant t'have sent this damnéd villain;
But that, belike, Iago in the nick
320 Came in and satisfied him.

  Othello.   O the pernicious caitiff!
How came you, Cassio, by that handkerchief
That was my wife's?

  Cassio.   I found it in my chamber:
And he himself confessed but even now
That there he dropped it for a special purpose
Which wrought to his desire.

  Othello.   O fool! fool! fool!

  Cassio. There is besides, in Roderigo's letter,
How he upbraids Iago that he made him
Brave me upon the watch; whereon it came
That I was cast; and even but now he spake—
330 After long seeming dead—Iago hurt him,
Iago set him on.

  Lodovico. You must forsake this room, and go
  with us;
Your power and your command is taken off,
And Cassio rules in Cyprus. For this slave,
If there be any cunning cruelty

That can torment him much and hold him long,
It shall be his. You shall close prisoner rest,
Till that the nature of your fault be known
To the Venetian state. Come, bring away.

Othello. Soft you; a word or two before you go.　　340
I have done the state some service, and they know't.
No more of that. I pray you, in your letters,
When you shall these unlucky deeds relate,
Speak of me as I am; nothing extenuate,
Nor set down aught in malice. Then must you speak
Of one that loved not wisely but too well;
Of one not easily jealous but, being wrought,
Perplexed in the extreme; of one whose hand,
Like the base Indian, threw a pearl away
Richer than all his tribe; of one whose subdued eyes,　　350
Albeit unuséd to the melting mood,
Drop tears as fast as the Arabian trees
Their medicinable gum—Set you down this;
And say besides, that in Aleppo once,
Where a malignant and a turbaned Turk
Beat a Venetian and traduced the state,
I took by th'throat the circumciséd dog
And smote him—thus.　　　　　　*[he stabs himself*

Lodovico. O bloody period!

Gratiano.　　　　　　　　All that's spoke is marred.

Othello. I kissed thee ere I killed thee: no way
　　but this,　　　　　　　　　　　　　　360
Killing myself, to die upon a kiss.
　　　　　　　　　　　[falls on the bed, and dies

Cassio. This did I fear, but thought he had
　　no weapon;
For he was great of heart.

Lodovico [to Iago].　　　O Spartan dog,
More fell than anguish, hunger, or the sea!

Look on the tragic loading of this bed—
This is thy work. The object poisons sight;
Let it be hid. [*they draw the curtains*]. Gratiano,
    keep the house,
And seize upon the fortunes of the Moor,
For they succeed on you. To you, lord governor,
370 Remains the censure of this hellish villain,
The time, the place, the torture: O, enforce it!
Myself will straight aboard, and to the state
This heavy act with heavy heart relate   [*they go*

THE COPY FOR *OTHELLO*,
1622 AND 1623

We have two substantive texts of *Othello*: the first quarto (Q.) of 1622 and the First Folio text (F.). Q2 (1630), printed from an example of Q1 which had been edited in the light of F., is a derivative, eclectic text without independent authority.[1]

That F. preserves the better text has never been seriously in doubt, but until recently the relationship between Q. and F. was obscured by the belief that both were set up from manuscript. What their readings, on the contrary, suggest is that Jaggard's copy for F. was an example of Q. which had been hand-corrected by collation with an authoritative manuscript.[2] The editorial position is, therefore, much like that in *Richard III*: namely, an editor must expect to find that now the one text and now the other preserves the truth and that sometimes, through oversights on the part of the collator or compositor, F. will have reproduced a Q. error.

THE QUARTO, 1622

Q. (1622) was printed by Nicholas Okes for Thomas Walkley, whose copyright was entered in the Stationers' Register on 6 October 1621. The Q. title-leaf is followed by a short preface from 'The Stationer to the

---

[1] See C. K. Hinman, 'The "Copy" for the Second Quarto of *Othello*' (in *Joseph Quincy Adams Memorial Studies*, Folger Shakespeare Library (1948), pp. 373–89).

[2] See A. Walker, 'The 1622 Quarto and the First Folio texts of *Othello*' (in *Shakespeare Survey* 5 (1952), pp. 16–24) and *Textual Problems of the First Folio* (1953), pp. 153–6.

Reader', which unfortunately gives no information about the provenance of his manuscript:

To set forth a booke without an Epistle, were like to the old English prouerbe, *A blew coat without a badge*, & the Author being dead, I thought good to take that piece of worke vpon mee: To commend it, I will not, for that which is good, I hope euery man will commend, without intreaty: and I am the bolder, because the Authors name is sufficient to vent his worke. Thus leauing euery one to the liberty of iudgement: I haue ventered to print this Play, and leaue it to the generall censure.   Yours,
                                        Thomas Walkley.

It would have been helpful if Walkley had been more communicative about the history of his copy, though fortunately what matters, from an editorial point of view, is the character of his text and not the channels through which he acquired it.

On the evidence of Q.'s readings, Walkley's manuscript seems to have been a careless transcript of the play as cut for acting. Q. is shorter than F. by about 160 lines. Some of its lacunae were undoubtedly due to negligence in its printing. At the foot of K1^r, for instance, the compositor set up the correct catchword ('*Iag.*') but resumed, at the head of K1^v, with Othello's reply to Iago's omitted speech (4. 1. 174–6). A similar omission of seven lines at the head of N1^r (5. 2. 269–75), although the catchword is correct for the text as it stands, makes havoc of the sense, since 'Pale as thy smock' is consequently addressed to Gratiano. There is nothing to show who was responsible for the omissions at 3. 4. 8–10, 4. 2. 74–7, 4. 2. 102, 4. 3. 59–62, 5. 2. 154–7, but as all look like cases of eye-skip, picking up the right word (mostly a speech prefix) ahead of the matter, they are more likely due to accidents in transmission than deliberate excision.

The bulk of the omitted matter, however, fairly certainly represented cuts for performance, motivated, like those of the F. *Lear*, by practical rather than artistic considerations.[1] Minor characters are relieved: Roderigo of seventeen lines (1. 1. 122–38), Brabantio of eight (1. 2. 72–7), the First Senator of seven (1. 3. 24–30), and Emilia of eighteen (4. 3. 87–104). Othello's Pontic Sea simile (3. 3. 455–62) seems to have been cut and, more lamentable still from a dramatic standpoint, Desdemona's 'Here I kneel...' (4. 2. 152–65), a moving counterpoise to the vows of Othello and Iago at the close of 3. 3. The Willow Song is omitted in 4. 3. and Emilia's reference to it in 5. 2. As Chambers argued,[2] the integration of the Willow theme in the dialogue makes it unlikely that the song was interpolated; and, as it seems equally unlikely that Shakespeare would have introduced a song in the first instance for a boy actor who could not sing, it looks as if this cut at least was necessitated by a change in casting. Probably, therefore, Q. does not fully represent the original acting version of *Othello*.

Q. also differs from F. in about 1000 substantive readings. About two out of every five variants look like printing-house errors, and we may not be far wrong if we reckon that Okes's and Jaggard's compositor[3] contributed about 200 errors apiece, mainly through negligence. Although there is nothing to suggest that the handwriting of Walkley's manuscript presented exceptional difficulties, many of Q.'s blunders

---

[1] The cuts are sometimes accompanied by changes in wording, bridging a gap left in the sense: e.g. 'Such' is substituted for 'For' at 1. 2. 78.

[2] *William Shakespeare* (1930), i. 460.

[3] For the Q. compositor, see Hinman, *Library*, XXI (1940), pp. 78–94. The F. text was set throughout by compositor B. Cf. p. 132 n. 1.

were certainly due to misreading: e.g. 'resterine' for
're-stem' (1. 3. 37), 'by' for 'high' (2. 1. 68), 'enscerped' for 'ensteeped' (2. 1. 70), 'calmenesse' for
'calmes' (2. 1. 182), 'Loue lines' for 'loveliness'
(2. 1. 226),[1] 'art' for 'act' (3. 3. 330), 'merry' for
'wary' (3. 3. 422), 'returne' for 'relume' (5. 2. 13),
and often a little more attention to the meaning would
have shown that something was wrong. But negligence
in the printing of Q. will not explain its persistent
blurring of the sense by vulgarization: 'utmost pleasure'
for 'very quality' (1. 3. 251), 'concern' for 'import'
(1. 3. 283), 'know' for 'warrant' (3. 3. 3), 'denotements' for 'dilations' (3. 3. 126), 'duty' for 'office'
(3. 4. 117), 'her sex' for 'their wives' (4. 2. 18),
'conceit' for 'conception' (5. 2. 58), 'woman' for 'wife'
(5. 2. 237), and many similar substitutions that blunt
the edge of the matter,[2] cannot have been due to misreading at any stage in Q.'s transmission, and they are
too persistent a feature of Q. to represent no more than
the kind of verbal substitution to which compositors
were sometimes prone. Nor are they, in the main,
sensible enough to have originated in any reputable
manuscript. Chambers (*loc. cit.*) suspected perversion
in Q.; Granville-Barker[3] thought that it contained some
actors' interpolations; and what many of Q.'s inferior

[1] From a number of Q.'s misreadings it is possible to
deduce some of the spelling habits of the scribe responsible
for Walkley's manuscript: that he was, for instance, a 'nes'
speller, used contractions freely (for 'the', 'that', 'which'),
'tho' for 'though', 'ha' for 'have'; but we know too little
about the idiosyncrasies of scribes to be able to identify the
hand.

[2] For further examples, see *Shakespeare Survey* 5 (1952),
pp. 22–3, and *Textual Problems of the First Folio*, pp. 138–42.

[3] Prefaces to Shakespeare, 4th series, *Othello* (1945),
p. 59 n. 1.

readings suggest is contamination of Walkley's manuscript by a transcriber, familiar with the play, who
tended to rely on what he remembered, or thought he
remembered, of the matter. Only memorial error will
explain, for instance, Q.'s use of dramatically objection-
able oaths as stop-gaps (e.g. the substitution of 'Zouns'
for Othello's 'What dost thou mean?' at 3. 3. 157),[1] its
anticipation of 'feeds well' at 3. 3. 186 (see note), and
some inept interpolations (like 'O thou blacke weede'
at 4. 2. 68). On the evidence of its readings, Q. seems,
in short, to represent a licentious transcript of a late
acting version of *Othello* further mangled in its printing.
Consequently we must expect to find that both kinds
of corruption (the vulgarization of memorial contamination and printing-house errors) will have seeped
into F.[2]

[1] Q.'s perversions in 3. 3 are especially damaging to
dramatic nuances and alter the character of Othello very
crudely. See Introduction, p. xxxv.

[2] Greg (*The Shakespeare First Folio* (1955), pp. 357–74),
while recognizing the general superiority of F. and the
licentiousness of Q., offers a different interpretation: that
Walkley's manuscript was a scribal copy of 'much and
carelessly altered foul papers' and that the scribe was
familiar with the play only to the extent that he knew the
Willow Song was not sung in the current stage version (but
see note to 3. 3. 186). Q.'s inferior readings (apart from
errors introduced in printing) were therefore due, he thinks,
partly to the scribe's having arbitrarily altered the wording
and partly to his having sometimes adopted a reading which
Shakespeare later rejected. He also suggests the possibility
of a second layer of authoritative corrections (made by
Shakespeare or with his consent) subsequent to the preparation of the prompt book. If this is correct, chaos is
indeed come again. What seems partly to have suggested
that foul papers, and not a prompt book, lie behind
Walkley's manuscript is the Q. direction 'Exit two or

That the majority of the Q. variants are perversions is evident from F., on balance the sounder text, and editors of literary discrimination have traditionally steered a steady course between Okes's Scylla and Jaggard's Charybdis, giving the former the wider berth. Some indication of their comparative merits can be derived from the texts of the Old Cambridge editors, Craig (in his Oxford edition), Kittredge, Alexander and Sisson, who are unanimous in rejecting about 170 F. readings against about 500 of Q.; and the most informative small-scale picture of the superiority of F. is the text of 3. 4. 97 (head of p. 74 above) to 3. 4. 166 and 4. 1. 22 to 4. 1. 92. This matter occupied Inner I of Q., and since this is the only Q. forme known to have been carefully proof-corrected with reference to copy,[1] it provides the best objective evidence we have for assuming that most of Q.'s errors were derived from Walkley's manuscript. So far as is known, no such

---

three' (om. F.) at 1. 3. 120 and 'and the rest' ('Attendants', F.) at 1. 3. 170—directions which are not necessarily authorial (as Greg argues) but, in fact, of a type fairly common in bad quartos (especially 1 *Contention*). One of the fundamental weaknesses of his theory is the assumption that a scribe would arbitrarily substitute 'know' (Q.) for 'warrant' at 3. 3. 3 and then alter 'I know't' to 'O sir' (Q.) seven lines later. If we explain variants of this kind as memorial errors when we find them in bad quartos or Q. *Richard III*, we must be consistent in our assumptions and explain the numerous variants of this kind in Q. *Othello* in the same way. For fuller discussion of some of the readings examined by Greg, see notes to 1. 1. 122 ff., 1. 2. 19–21, 1. 3. 145, 1. 3. 277–8, 2. 1. 51 S.D.[1], 5. 2. 222–3.

[1] Hinman's article in *J.Q.A. Memorial Studies* (see above, p. 121 n. 1) gives a general account (though not details) of Okes's press-corrections, mentioning that six formes were subject to stop-press correction and that the proof-correction of Inner I was exceptionally fastidious.

systematic proof-correction is exemplified in F.,[1] but
the readings of the above five editions will make clear
where the higher authority appears to be. Readings
unanimously preferred are distinguished by an asterisk
and sigla are attached to readings over which opinion
is divided (C standing for the Cambridge, O for Craig's
Oxford Text). The readings of the two states of Q.
agree unless a variant is cited.

	Q. (uncorrected)[2]	Q. (corrected)[3]		F.[4]	
3.4.101		Ifaith	A	Insooth	COKS
3.4.102		Zouns	AS	Away	COK
3.4.106	this losse	the losse		*the losse of it	
3.4.117		duty		*Office	
3.4.120		neither	K	nor my	COAS
3.4.125		shoote		*shut	
3.4.141		can he be angry	COK	is he angry	AS
3.4.149		the obiect		*their obiect	
3.4.151		that sence	COK	a sense	AS

[1] See Hinman, 'A Proof-Sheet in the First Folio of
Shakespeare' (in *Library*, XXIII (1942), pp. 101–7) for an
account of the variants on vv3^r and vv4^v and of the former
page in the Jonas copy, one of four known Folio pages with
the proof-reader's manuscript corrections. A later article,
'New Light on the Proof-Reading for the First Folio of
Shakespeare' (in *Studies in Bibliography*, University of
Virginia, III (1950–1), pp. 145–53) makes special reference
to *Othello*. Hinman's collation of the text of *Othello* in the
Folger First Folios was completed some years ago and forms
part of the much more considerable and important undertaking of which he gives an account (again with special
reference to *Othello*) in *Shakespeare Quarterly* (July 1953),
pp. 279–88.

[2] Exemplified in Capell's copy. I am indebted to the
kindness of the Librarian of Trinity College, Cambridge,
for photostats of the relevant pages.

[3] Exemplified in the Praetorius Facsimile.

[4] I disregard insignificant variants.

	Q. (uncorrected)	Q. (corrected)	F.
3.4.153		obseruances	*obseruancie
4.1.27		Or by the voluntaty	*Or voluntary
4.1.28	Coniured	*Conuinced =	*Conuinced
4.1.32		*Faith	Why
4.1.33		But what?	*What? What?
4.1.36		Zouns, that's CAK	that's OS
4.1.37		handkerchers (bis)	*Handkerchiefe (bis)
4.1.37		Confession	*Confessions
4.1.38–43		omits	*To... O diuell
4.1.43	S.D. omitted	He fals downe	*Falls in a Traunce
4.1.45		*my medicine, worke	My Medicine workes
4.1.52		*No, forbeare,	omits
4.1.54	he he	*he =	*he
4.1.60		*I mocke you? no	I mocke you not,
4.1.61		fortunes	*Fortune
4.1.65		confesse?	*confesse it?
4.1.65	God sir	*Good sir =	*Good Sir
4.1.71		Coach	*Cowch
4.1.76		ere while, mad	*o're-whelmed
4.1.77	vnfitting K	vnsuting COAS	resulting
4.1.79		scuse, vpon COKA	scuses vpon S
4.1.80		retire	*returne
4.1.81		but	*Do but
4.1.82	geeres	Ieeres	*Fleeres

In addition to making the above alterations, the
Q. proof-reader corrected most of Q.'s literal errors
and made a number of pernickety changes in spelling
(as at 4. 1. 82) and punctuation; and although fussiness
is no guarantee of sustained attention or comprehension
(e.g. the errors 'voluntaty', 'shoote' and 'Coach'
escaped notice), we must suppose on the above evidence
that, by and large, the inferiority of Q. was due to
inaccuracies in the copy.

THE FOLIO TEXT

The main virtue of F. seems to derive from the
collation of an example of Q. with a reputable manuscript. What was missing from Q. was seemingly
restored and its errors were, for the most part, cor-

rected. That this manuscript stood at no more than one remove from Shakespeare's foul papers seems likely, though the type of transcript to which it belonged is not clear. F.'s speech prefixes (like Q.'s) are uniform—as they are not, for instance, in the Folio *Richard III*, where quarto copy was collated with author's manuscript. The stage directions are also businesslike in the main and usually less graphic than those of Q., which exhibit, by contrast, a lively interest in stage business.[1] If we make some allowance for omissions on the part of the F. compositor, either through negligence or for typographical convenience, F.'s stage directions, like its speech prefixes, suggest something more like a fair copy or prompt-book basis than foul papers. So too do its dialogue readings, since F.'s cruxes and errors have nothing in common with the unresolved tangles, false starts and duplications which the collator recovered from foul papers in preparing F. copy for *Troilus and Cressida*. We must therefore suppose that, if an example of Q. was corrected by reference to characteristically Shakespearian foul papers, the collator or a later editor did an unusual amount of tidying up. Possibly, therefore, it is more reasonable to postulate that a transcript was used—either fair copy (much like that from which the *1 Henry IV* quarto was printed) or the prompt book. In the latter event, this was presumably the manuscript from which Walkley's transcript was made and, unlikely as this might seem at first sight, it is not beyond the bounds of possibility, if we suppose that a careless transcriber, in preparing Walkley's manuscript, cut and altered in

[1] In Q.'s 1. 1., for instance, Brabantio appears 'at a window' and 'in his night gowne'; in 2. 1. there are directions for 'Trumpets within' and 'they kisse'; in 2. 3. 'they fight', etc. Some of this commentary may have been supplied for the reader's benefit.

accordance with representation *c.* 1620, whereas the collator punctiliously followed the script. But if Q. and F. indeed go back to the prompt book, what the texts between them preserve may fall short of what Shakespeare wrote by anything from about 50 to 200 lines. What befogs the issue is that we can trust neither the scribe of Walkley's manuscript nor the F. compositor to have reproduced exactly the wording of his copy. Since the former perverted the wording of the dialogue (substituting 'duty' for 'office', 'utmost pleasure' for 'very quality', etc.), he may similarly have improvised in the wording of stage directions; and, on the evidence of *1 Henry IV*,[1] the F. compositor is as little to be trusted. Hence, the variant stage directions at 4. 1. 43 (see table above p. 128) would be poor witnesses for any argument that different manuscripts lay behind Walkley's transcript and the copy for F. Like many other problems of transmission, the question may defy solution, but that the manuscript available for collation was vastly better than Walkley's is evident from the way in which F. restored the Shakespearian edge so often blunted in Q.[2]

That F. is not an entirely trustworthy text is, however, only too clear from its numerous manifest errors, but the main source of its corruption is not far to seek. On the evidence of the F. compositor's work in *1 Henry IV*, we should be prepared to find at least 200 substantive errors in the dialogue—words omitted, substituted or altered, sometimes through the addition, omission, or change of a letter, sometimes by anticipation, recollection or loose memorization, as well as for

[1] See A. Walker, 'The Folio Text of *1 Henry IV*' (in *Studies in Bibliography*, VI (1954), pp. 45–59).

[2] I still incline to the conclusion that the MS. used for collation was a fair copy, anterior to the prompt book. (A.W.)

typographical convenience. What is manifest in Compositor B's work in *1 Henry IV* comes out just as clearly in *Othello* and his far more numerous slips of an obvious kind (like 'Siginor' for 'Signior', 'Forune' for 'Fortune')[1] give no confidence that he was working with greater accuracy. The chances are, in fact, otherwise and, since we now know that Jaggard's proof-correction of *Othello* was not, as a rule, made with reference to copy, the number of F. blunders attributable to the compositor can only be gauged from what other plays reveal about his failings. These make it reasonably certain that he was largely responsible for the corruption in F. Consequently, whereas the corruption in Q. must be laid mainly to the charge of the copy, that in F., on the contrary, can be more plausibly laid to the charge of the compositor.

Apart from the compositor, there is probably only one other serious falsifier of the wording of this text to be reckoned with—the expurgator. The same kind of purge of oaths and asseverations was made in this play as in the Folio *2 Henry IV* and, since the *Othello* quarto serving as F. copy was a memorially contaminated text, it is sometimes difficult to determine whether a variant in F. was due to his hand or not. The cynical wit of Iago's 'bi' the masse tis morning' (Q., 2. 3. 370), after a night of mischief-making, establishes the Q. reading

---

[1] Further examples from the Oxford Facsimile are 'populus' (1. 1. 78), 'apines' (= paines, 1. 1. 155), '*Roderigoc?* Cme' (1. 2. 58), '*Antropophague*' (1. 3. 144), 'Alacartie' (1. 3. 232), 'Grcaious' (1. 3. 243), 'Snpe' (= Snipe, 1. 3. 383), 'authorithy' (2. 1. 145), 'famillar' (2. 3. 302), 'stonger' (= stronger, 2. 3. 317), 'Handkerchikfe' (3. 4. 105), 'deonte' (= 'denote' 4. 1. 280), 'May' (= Nay 4. 2. 30). We shall, of course, be better able to judge of the care (or lack of care) with which this text was set when Hinman's account of the press corrections is published.

as authentic and F.'s 'Introth' as editorial, but it is much less easy to discriminate between F's 'Insooth' and Q.'s 'Ifaith' from Desdemona at 3. 4. 101. The problem is much like that in the Folio *Richard III*, but aggravated in so far as the expurgating of *Othello* was much more thorough. There are fifty-two variants of this kind. The Old Cambridge editors rejected nineteen of these Q. variants, mostly in the speeches of Othello and Desdemona, and this is where Q.'s oaths and asseverations are most open to criticism. Until Iago's poison has done its work (towards the end of Act 3), any oath from Othello implies a lack of control that is out of character. The discrimination exercised by the Old Cambridge editors seems therefore justified both on dramatic grounds and in view of the many vulgarizations of Q.

These two agents, Jaggard's compositor[1] and the expurgator, seem to have been responsible for most of the falsification in F., and although we have also to reckon on the erratic corrections of Jaggard's proof-reader as well as on the collator's having sometimes misread his manuscript, it seems very doubtful whether either materially contributed to the number of F.'s substantive errors. There is also some sophistication in F., though this has mainly affected accidentals.

More serious and far more numerous than the collator's miscorrections are the Q. errors which escaped

---

[1] In a forthcoming article, which I have had the privilege of seeing in typescript, Dr Hinman concludes that most of Act I was set by an apprentice. His evidence fails to convince me, as it is based on too narrow a range of spellings. In any case, his conclusion does not affect the editing of *Othello*, since the kinds of error that occur in what he believes to be apprentice work in the Tragedies are indistinguishable from those which are commonest in the work of B.

correction through oversights. We have no means of determining objectively what this margin of error was, but if we assume, on the evidence of *Richard III* and *Lear*, that one error in every ten escaped correction and that there were 500 errors in Q. (see p. 126 above), we must expect to find about fifty-five errors common to Q. and F.; and the number will be nearer eighty if Q.'s errors are (as most editors have supposed them to be) in the region of 700.

THE PRESENT TEXT

In view of what the readings of Q. and F. suggest about their transmission and the manifest superiority of F., our principle has been to give precedence to what is, in general, the better text (F.) whenever the merits of variants seem evenly matched and whenever we have failed to agree over the choice of variant; but whenever Q. appears to have preserved a reading more consonant with Shakespeare's style and dramatic intentions we have not hesitated to adopt it. On these principles, we have rejected 280 of F.'s substantive variants, of which we suppose thirty-five to have been due to the expurgator and the rest (except for an occasional misreading on the part of the collator) to have been due to the compositor. Since he was responsible for 113 errors in fourteen and a half pages of *1 Henry IV*, when we find rather more than twice this number of errors running true to type in the twenty-nine pages of *Othello*, we must accept them as his. We have rejected a further seven readings in matter peculiar to F.—one more than is customary (1. 1. 129).

The eclectic editing of *Othello* is, of course, inevitable, since neither text preserves the whole truth. Where we part company with recent practice is in emending

readings common to Q. and F. which we believe to be Q. errors reproduced by F. through oversight.[1] We make forty-six emendations of this kind in substantive readings, of which eight only are now usual, though most of the rest were either current or proposed in the eighteenth century. These new readings are distinguished in the notes by a following 'A.W.' or 'J.D.W.' (as the case may be) 'after Rowe' etc. and in the following lists an asterisk:

1. 3. *42, *58, *89, *114, *179, *219, 234, *263, *264, *322, *331
2. 1. *50, *205
2. 3. *135, *148, *150, 163, *164, 214, *223, *249, *302, 310, *330, 377
3. 1. *48
3. 3. 67, *80, *88, *121, *184, *186, *210, *408, 442
3. 4. *42, *120, *151
4. 1. *73, *80, *87, *88
4. 2. 65
5. 1. *124
5. 2. *104, *109

We further emend fourteen F. readings which seem clearly (or very probably) imperfectly executed corrections of Q. readings (nine more than is customary):

1. 3. 230, *326
2. 1. 297

[1] These common errors have been emended in accordance with what an analysis of the variants suggests about the kinds of corruption in Q.—errors of misreading, confusion in number, word substitution of an explicable kind (e.g. through repetition or anticipation), and interpolation. What may have been lost through the more serious kind of memorial error or omission (since it is hardly likely that, when two texts independently omitted so much, they lost nothing between them) is presumably beyond recovery.

2. 2. 6.
2. 3. *247–8
3. 3. *151, *172, *182, *342, *395, *470
4. 1. 101
5. 1. *90
5. 2. 323

It follows, of course, that since we assume that the manuscript used in preparing copy for F. was either the prompt book underlying Walkley's transcript or fair copy immediately antecedent to the prompt book, a few of the errors common to Q. and F. may have originated in this common ancestor, for it is hardly to be supposed that any transcript was impeccable. All the same, only a much debased transcript would have perpetrated some of the errors common to the two texts of *Othello* and we should, therefore, postulate no remoter source for most of them than Walkley's manuscript.

ACCIDENTALS

In the main we follow F., the more reputable authority, though we have not hesitated to accept Q. readings where they seem preferable for metre or euphony. Neither text suggests closeness to autograph. F. is, for instance, bookish in its avoidance of Q.'s colloquial 'em' and 'ha', but seems to preserve a more authentic touch in eliding the 'e' of the definite article before both vowels and consonants. When we have adopted a Q. reading, we have, of course, translated it into the idiom of F. and then modernized in the usual way. Thus Q.'s 'Ifaith' (=F. 'Infaith') appears (at 3. 3. 217, for instance) as 'In faith'. We have also silently substituted the modern 'you're' for the obsolete 'y'are'. Emendations of what we take to be common errors are, of course, noted.

NOTES

All significant departures from F. are recorded and only its insignificant errors and irregularities in verse lining have been silently disregarded. Q.'s readings are cited only when they seem to merit discussion or have some bearing on the F. reading. Readings common to Q. and F. are cited in F. spelling. As explained above (p. 134), 'A.W. after Rowe' etc. draws attention to the emendations of earlier editors or critics which we adopt, contrary to the practice of most recent editions. Line numbers for plays not yet issued in this edition are those of Bartlett's *Concordance* (based on the 1891 Globe edition).

Q. stands for Q 1 (except when there is need to distinguish a Q 1 reading from that of Q 2) and F. for the First Folio. F. readings are cited from the Oxford Facsimile.

The following is a list of abridged titles etc.:

Abbott=*A Shakespearian Grammar*, by E. A. Abbott, 1889.

Al.=ed. of Sh. by Peter Alexander, 1951.

Baldwin=*William Shakspere's Small Latine & Lesse Greeke*, by T. W. Baldwin, 2 vols., Univ. of Illinois, 1944.

Barker=(*Prefaces to Shakespeare*, (4th ser.), 'Othello', by Harley Granville-Barker, 1945.

Bradley=*Shakespearean Tragedy*, by A. C. Bradley, 1904.

Camb.=*The Cambridge Sh.* (3rd ed. 1891–3).

Cap.=ed. of Sh. by Edward Capell, 1768.

D.D.=*The English Dialect Dictionary*, ed. Joseph Wright.

Delius = ed. by Nicholas Delius, 3rd ed. 1872.

Dyce = ed. of Sh. by Alexander Dyce, 5th ed. 1886.

Furness = The *Variorum* ed. of *Othello*, by H. H. Furness, 1886.

G. = Glossary.

Greg, *Sh.F.F.* = *The Shakespeare First Folio* by W. W. Greg, 1955.

Hanmer = ed. of Sh. by Thomas Hanmer, 1743–4.

Hart = ed. by H. C. Hart (Arden Sh.), (2nd ed. 1917).

J. = ed. of Sh. by Samuel Johnson, 1765.

J.C.M. = J. C. Maxwell (private communications).

Kittredge = ed. of Sh. by G. L. Kittredge, 1936.

Linthicum = *Costume in the Drama of Shakespeare and his Contemporaries*, by M. C. Linthicum, 1936.

M.L.R. = *Modern Language Review*.

Madden = D. H. Madden, *The Diary of Master William Silence*, 1907.

Mal. = James Boswell's Variorum ed. of *Malone's Sh.*, 1821.

Noble = *Shakespeare's Biblical Knowledge*, by Richmond Noble, 1935.

O.E.D. = *The Oxford English Dictionary*.

On. = *A Shakespeare Glossary*, by C. T. Onions, 1911.

Pope = ed. of Sh. by Alexander Pope, 1723–5.

R.E.S. = *The Review of English Studies*.

Rowe = ed. of Sh. by Nicholas Rowe, 1709 (3rd ed. 1714).

S.D. = Stage Direction.

S.N. = Speaker's Name.

Schmidt = *Shakespeare-Lexicon*, by Alexander Schmidt, 1874.

Sh. Eng. = *Shakespeare's England*, 2 vols. 1917.

Sprague = *Shakespeare and the Actors*, by A. C. Sprague, Harvard University Press, 1944.

Steev. = ed. of J.'s Sh., by George Steevens, 1773.

Theob. = ed. of Sh. by Lewis Theobald, 1733.

Tilley = *A Dictionary of the Proverbs in England in the Sixteenth and Seventeenth Centuries,* by M. P. Tilley, Univ. of Michigan, 1950.

S. Walker = *A Critical Examination of the text of Shakespeare,* by William Sidney Walker, 1860.

Warb. = ed. of Sh. by William Warburton, 1747.

Names of the Characters. Othello is one of seven First Folio plays with an appended list of Dramatis Personae. The two other lists in the Histories and Tragedies, following *2 Henry IV* and *Timon of Athens,* were clearly inserted to provide matter for what would otherwise have been blank space (a page in the former case, a leaf in the latter). Hence, we must infer that they were drawn up in the printing house. That there were only seven lines of type to the column on the last page of *Othello* in all likelihood therefore explains why a list was similarly provided for this play. It is as follows:

The Names of the Actors

Othello, *the Moore*
Brabantio, *Father to Desdemona*
Cassio, *an Honourable Lieutenant*
Iago, *a Villaine*
Rodorigo, *a gull'd Gentleman*
Duke of Venice
Senators
Montano, *Gouernour of Cyprus*
Gentlemen of Cyprus
Lodouico *and* Gratiano, *two Noble Venetians*
Saylors
Clowne
Desdemona, *Wife to Othello*
Æmilia, *Wife to Iago*
Bianca, *a Curtezan*

Since Montano is nowhere described as 'Governor of

Cyprus' in F., we must infer that this description was derived from Q. (see note to 2. 1. S.D.) and may have no authority. The name of Desdemona came from the *novella* (cf. Introduction, pp. xvii–xviii). Q. has 'Roderigo', 'Emilia' (or 'Emillia') and 'Montanio' (generally) against F.'s 'Rodorigo', 'Æmilia' (generally) and 'Montano'. It is useless to guess to what extent these differences were due to the compositors. The F. compositor was certainly apt to back his own fancy (as witness his persistent 'Auffidious' in *Coriolanus*, aa3ʳ, aa3ᵛ). We follow, therefore, the now customary spelling of these names.

Acts and Scenes. Q. has headings for '*Actus* 2. *Scæna* 1.', '*Actus*. 4.' and '*Actus*. 5.' and presumably failed to indicate the beginning of Act 3 through an oversight. F. has all the now customary act and scene divisions apart from 2. 3, where a change of scene was first indicated by Theobald.

Locality. There are no indications of locality in Q. and F. except such as occur in the dialogue, though the Duke and Senators are 'set at a Table' in Q.'s heading to 1. 3. and Desdemona is 'in her bed' in F.'s heading to 5. 2. We adopt the customary locality headings save that we follow Alexander in substituting the 'Citadel', for the 'Castle' of earlier editors, and, like Alexander (following Capell), suppose no change of scene in 3. 4 and 4.1.

Punctuation. Both texts show, in general, an adequate comprehension of the matter (Q. contrasting very favourably, for instance, with Okes's *Lear* quarto, and F. with *Coriolanus*). F.'s pointing is much heavier than Q.'s and is rhythmical rather than syntactical, both in prose and verse. There is a small legacy of errors from Q. and there are, of course, blunders—due sometimes probably to foul case and at other times to negligence in setting (e.g. 2. 1. 229–30, 'heaue the,

gorge,'). It is impossible to guess what the collator or
compositor respectively contributed, though it seems
likely that the former was responsible for the brackets
which distinguish Brabantio's apostrophes to Desdemona from his remarks to Roderigo in 1. 1. 164–7 and
Desdemona's remarks to Emilia from the Willow song
in 4. 3 (see note to 4. 3. 47–8). These brackets serve
a more dramatic purpose than the kind which the Folio
compositor normally introduced on his own account
and the type differentiation in 4. 3 made them, in fact,
unnecessary in print.

The present text has been punctuated throughout
in accordance with modern practice and the F. pointing
is recorded only when it seriously suggests a different
interpretation of the matter from ours.

Stage Directions. We record all significant variants
of this kind, since in spite of the possibility that some
of Q.'s commentary on the action may be just as much
invention as some of its readings, the unusually early
placing of some of its entries suggests a book-keeper's
hand either in or behind the manuscript from which
it was printed. In Q., for instance, Cassio's entry
for 1. 2. 33 appears at 1. 2. 28, and the entry for
Othello, Desdemona, Lodovico and Emilia etc. at
the beginning of 4. 3. appears two lines before
the close of 4. 2. and therefore before Iago and
Roderigo have left the stage. F. sometimes follows
Q.'s lead and sometimes delays the entry for a few
lines.

Verse Lining. In general, we silently follow the
arrangement of the 1891–3 Cambridge edition. In
both Q. and F. the verse lining is often erroneous and
to have recorded their arrangement would have occupied space out of all proportion to its usefulness.
It is evident that one of the disturbing factors in F.
was the need to 'justify' the page and this is a matter

which cannot be profitably considered until we know
in what order formes were set (see Hinman, 'Cast-Off
Copy for the First Folio of Shakespeare', *Shakespeare
Quarterly* (Summer 1955), pp. 259–73).

I. I

Head Title F. 'The Tragedie of Othello, the Moore
of Venice.' (and Q. substantially).

S.D. *Loc.* (Cap. after Theob.) *Entry* (F.) Q. 'Enter
Iago and *Roderigo.*'

1. *Tush,* (Q.) F. omits. Q. is given the benefit of
the doubt, since Roderigo's impatient ejaculation, like
Iago's oath at l. 4, underlines their difference in
character.

never tell me 'expressing incredulity or impatience'
(O.E.D. 'tell', 20); cf. *2 H. IV,* 2. 4. 79, 'Tilly-fally,
Sir John, ne'er tell me'. Iago has presumably just
denied all earlier knowledge of Othello's marriage and
reaffirms his denial in l. 5.

4. *'Sblood,* (Q.) F. omits.

13. *bombast   circumstance* = pompous   rigmarole;
'stuffed' (l. 14) carries on the metaphor of 'bombast'.

15. *And, in conclusion,* (Q.) F. omits. The phrase
is perhaps more than a conjunctive tag for 'and
finally': 'conclusion' (= a binding act) was a legal
term (O.E.D. 13). The *fait accompli* of Cassio's
appointment put solicitation on Iago's behalf out of
court.

16. *for, 'Certes,' says he* (Steev. 1773) Neither Q.
nor F. indicates where the reported speech begins and
some editors print 'for' as the opening word. Since
the stress is on 'Certes', it seems to make the more
natural start.

Certes Generally dissyllabic but, from *c.* 1300,
occasionally monosyllabic (as probably here; cf.
H. VIII, 1. 1. 48).

19. *arithmetician* With allusion to (i) a student of 'the bookish theoric' (l. 24), i.e. of books on tactics, full of numerals representing the arrangement of troops; (ii) a mere clerk or official—the usual sneer of an old ranker for a brass-hat from the War Office promoted over him. 'Nobody has ever sat in an army mess for long without hearing this complaint repeated' (Duff Cooper, *Sergeant Shakespeare* (1949), p. 64). The sneer is repeated in l. 31 ('debitor-and-creditor', 'counter-caster').

20. *a Florentine* i.e. not even a Venetian; for Iago's Venetian nationality, see 3. 3. 203–4, 5. 1. 88–90.

21. *almost...wife* Much debated: some see an anticipation of Cassio's liaison with Bianca (cf. 4. 1); Barker (p. 3, n. 1) thought that Shakespeare's first intention was to follow the *novella*, where Cassio's counterpart is married. The Italian proverb 'L'hai tolta bella? Tuo danno' (cited by Hart; see Florio, *Giardino di recreatione* (1591), p. 140), or a current English version of it (cf. Tilley, H 657, W 377), explains the general allusion.

23. *division* The emphasis is on 'battle'; Cassio's knowledge of 'division' may qualify him as an arithmetician but not as a soldier.

25. *togéd* (Q.) F. 'Tongued'; cf. the error of 'tongue' for 'toge', *Cor.* 2. 3. 122.

26. *as he* (Q. F.) The words are redundant and should perhaps (as Steev. suggested) be omitted.

29. *other* (Q.) F. 'others'.

30. *Christian* (Q.) F. 'Christen'd', which looks like a blunder for 'christen', the obsolescent form of 'christian' (cf. *1 H. IV*, 2. 1. 17, *Ham.* 5. 1. 29). The dissyllabic pronunciation is, of course, wanted here.

31. *debitor-and-creditor* (hyphens Staunton) See G. and l. 19 n.

counter-caster See G. To 'cast' counters (token

discs of metal, etc.) was the means of reckoning before the general use of arabic numerals; 'counter' is used contemptuously (cf. *A.Y.L.* 2. 7. 63, *J.C.* 4. 3. 80), since it was a substitute for the real thing (like Cassio's 'bookish theoric').

33. *God* (Q.) F. omits.

Moorship's With play on Worship's (Delius).

36. *letter and affection* = graft and favouritism.

37. *old gradation* = customary promotion according to seniority. The image is of orderly progress up a ladder. With this approving use of 'old', cf. the depreciatory use of 'modern' at 1. 3. 109.

39. *term* (Q. F.) The singular = 'manner', 'respect', is rare and may be a common error for 'terms'.

48. *when he's* (Q. F.) Possibly a common error for 'when's' (which A.W. thinks would improve the line).

49. *Whip me* O.E.D. 11 *b* cites as the first instance of a mild execration (= confound, hang), but a literal interpretation is here more forceful; 'me' is an 'ethic' dative.

50. *trimmed...duty* = plausibly obsequious in manners and mien.

53. *they've* (Pope) Q. F. 'they haue'.

57–8. *It is...Iago* i.e. (with a typical double edge) 'you can be as certain of my duplicity as you are of your own simplicity'. Cf. 'I am not what I am', l. 66.

60. *I* Pleonastic, recalling the subject of the main sentence after a parenthesis.

62–4. *For...extern* i.e. for when the obsequiousness ('compliment extern') of my behaviour ('outward action') manifests my heart's real motive ('native act') and design ('figure').

65. *But* = that (O.E.D. 15 *c*).

upon my sleeve A usual place for the badges of servingmen.

67. *full...thick-lips* (Q.) F. 'fall...Thicks-lips'.

68–9. *father, Rouse him,* (Q.) F. 'Father: Rowse him,'. The 'him' throughout is Othello.

71–2. *And...flies* i.e. and, although his good fortune is assured, pester him with petty annoyances.

72. *joy be joy* (Q. F.) The repetition suggests the possibility of common error; Iago characteristically glosses his figurative language in ll. 71–2 (cf. 3.3.327–8).

73. *changes* (Q.) F. 'chances'. A.W. finds both readings an anti-climax and suspects 'charges' was intended. J.D.W. notes that in Shakespeare 'change' often contextually = change for the worse—as here.

80. *thieves* (thrice Q.) F. twice (full line).

82. S.D. Q. 'Brabantio *at a window*.' F. omits, but prefixes l. 83 '*Bra.Aboue*'.

87. *'Zounds,* (Q.) F. omits.

for shame...gown = it's disgraceful to be abed when such things are happening. Up and dress! 'Gown' (see G.) is his everyday coat, perhaps his senator's robe, not a dressing-gown; cf. l. 160 S.D.[2] n.

101. *knavery* (F.) Q. 'brauery'. Roderigo's 'in simple and pure soul' (l. 108) replies to this charge.

104. *spirit...them* (Q.) F. 'spirits...their'. F. is clumsy in construction.

108. *In simple...soul* = from disinterested and honest motives.

109. *'Zounds,* (Q.) F. omits.

117. *now* (Q.) F. omits.

119. *are a* (Q. F.) Cap. +most editors 'are—a'. To suppose Iago suppresses something uncomplimentary is unnecessary; he is seriously (if ironically) reminding Brabantio of his status and duty.

120. *thou* Emphatic: Brabantio holds Roderigo answerable for his unknown companion (Delius).

122 ff. Greg (*Sh.F.F.* pp. 372–3) finds the speech inconsistent, but the line of thought is clear: if Desde-

mona has gone to Othello with Brabantio's consent, they owe him an apology for disturbing him; if she has secretly eloped, he should apologize to them for taking the news so uncivilly (ll. 122–31). Roderigo reiterates ('I say again ...') the gist of ll. 122–7 and, if a search of the house proves him a liar, he is prepared to take the consequences. The only difficulty is that the syntax of ll. 122–7 is cluttered with subordinate clauses, resulting in anacoluthon, but the thread is picked up by the recapitulation of l. 128—a common phenomenon after a parenthesis (cf. 1. 3. 19–30, where a similar recapitulation occurs at l. 26). Roderigo is not baiting Brabantio, but putting his case in a mannerly way.

124. *odd-even* (hyphen Mal.) See G. Q. omits ll. 122–38.

126. *But*=than; see Abbott, §127.

129. *saucy wrong* (A.W.) F. 'saucie wrongs'. The style requires the singular, to balance 'wrong rebuke' in l. 131.

132. *from ...civility*=contrary to all consideration for good manners.

133. *your reverence* A respectful style of address.

137. *an extravagant ...stranger*=a gadabout and restless foreigner.

145. S.D. F. '*Exit.*' Q. omits.

147. *produced* (Q.) F. 'producted'. In contemporary usage 'product' (frequent in texts printed by Jaggard)=to bring forth young, beget.

149. *gall ...check* Iago is probably still thinking in terms of the 'Barbary horse' (l. 112), chafed and checked with a bridle or bit.

152. *stand* (Pope) Q. F. 'stands'. Although 'wars' was often singular in meaning (O.E.D. 1 *c*), we accept the usual emendation here, and also at 1. 3. 234, 3. 3. 67, 352.

153. *fathom* Originally what could be embraced in

the arms, thence a measure of length (about 6 ft.) or depth; here fig. (with nautical allusion) = capability.

155. *hell-pains* (hyphen Dyce).

157. *flag and sign* With allusion to his rank as ensign.

159. *the Sagittary* i.e. a house, = the Centaur (cf. the addresses in *Err.*: the Phoenix, the Centaur, the Tiger, etc.).

160. S.D.¹ Q. F. '*Exit.*'

S.D.² (Mal.) Q. '*Enter* Barbantio *in his night gowne, and seruants with Torches.*' F. '*Enter Brabantio, with Seruants and Torches.*' Q.'s 'night gowne' = gown (see G.). 'Night gowns' were worn for warmth indoors and out; see Linthicum, pp. 183–5.

167. *more* (Q.) F. 'moe' (full line).

176. *that you* (Q.) F. 'would you'. The stresses in Q. fall more naturally.

183. *special officers of night* (Q.) F. '...might'. The F. reading is plainly a blunder. Mal. cited Lewkenor's translation of Contarini's *Venice* (1599) in support of Q., but cf. the officer of night in Shakespeare's Messina (*Ado*, 3. 3. 82–3), 'An there be any matter of weight chances, call up me'.

184. *I'll* (Q.) F. 'I will'.

1. 2

S.D. *Loc.* (Camb.) *Entry* (Q.) F. omits '*and*'.

2. *stuff* Carrying on the metaphor of 'trade'.

4. *Sometimes* (Q.) F. 'Sometime'.

5. *jerked* Q. ('ierk'd') F. 'yerk'd'. The now obsolete 'yerk' appeared first as a term in shoemaking (= to twitch stitches tightly) and was used, like the surviving variant 'jerk', for any quick movement—here, almost certainly, for a sword thrust; cf. *L.L.L.* 4. 2. 132,

'the jerks of invention' (Q. 'ierkes') and *H.V*, 4. 7. 79, where F. 'yerke' (a spelling of compositor B) is used for a horse's kick.

him = Roderigo; cf. Iago's pretence at l. 58.

10. *pray* (Q.) F. 'pray you'.

11. *For be sure* (Q.) F. 'Be assur'd'. Q.'s is the more natural reading and F.'s 'Be assur'd' may be merely a typical F. perversion (cf. 'You'le be asham'd' at 2. 3. 159).

14. *double* See G.; i.e. his voice in council is, like the Duke's, equal to that of two others.

15. *restraint and grievance* (Q.) F. 'restraint or ...'. Iago tactfully glosses his 'gall him with some check' (1. 1. 149).

19–21. *'Tis yet ...promulgate* Greg finds difficulty here (*Sh.F.F.* pp. 368–9), but the sense seems straight-forward: 'it is still unknown (and, when I know that boasting is an honour, I shall make it common know-ledge) that I am of royal birth'. The relative pronoun 'which' refers, of course, to the following noun clause ('I fetch ...siege'); cf. Abbott, §271.

21. *promulgate* (F.) The stress fell on the second syllable. We follow the more modern form, but Q.'s (rarer) 'provulgate', which Greg (*Sh.F.F.* p. 365, n. 28) notes as 'most unlikely to have been introduced by the transcriber' may well be Shakespeare's (J.D.W.).

23. *unbonneted* (Q. F.) The sense required is plainly 'as an equal', an interpretation not precluded by 'off-capped' (1. 1. 10), since 'bonnet' in *Cor.* 2. 2. 30 = to take the cap *off*. J.D.W. favours Hanmer's emendation 'e'en bonneted' (copy-spelling 'in bon-neted'), 'in' being a not impossible spelling for 'e'en'; see *Ant.* (N.S.), p. 124; *M.V.* 3. 5. 20; *Rom.* 5. 1. 24; *Err.* 2. 2. 101; *All's*, 3. 2. 18.

26. *unhousèd* The nomad speaks.

28. *sea's* (Theob.) Q. F. 'Seas'. The riches of the

sea were proverbially inestimable (cf. *R. III*, 1. 4. 26–8;
Erasmus, *Adagia*, Bonae Fortunae, *mare bonorum*); hence
'the sea's worth' = untold wealth.

look...yond (punct. Al., following Q. 'looke...
yonder.') F. 'looke, ...yond?' (full line). F.'s 'yond'
is metrically smoother, while Q.'s pointing gives a freer
and lighter run, as well as better idiom.

31–2. *My parts...rightly* i.e. my personal qualities
(character), my legal right, and my clear conscience
will vindicate me. His marriage is naturally uppermost
in Othello's mind when Brabantio appears and 'title'
refers to his legal position as Desdemona's husband;
cf. *Ant.* 5. 2. 286–7, 'Husband, I come: Now to that
name my courage prove my title !'.

33. *Janus* Iago's deity (Warb.).

S.D. (Camb.) F. '*Enter Cassio, with Torches.*' (after
l. 28); Q. '*Enter* Cassio *with lights, Officers, and torches.*'
(opposite l. 28).

34. *duke* (Q.) F. 'Dukes'.

37. *haste-post-haste* (Steev.) Q. 'hast, post hast';
F. 'haste, Post-haste'.

46. *quests* Abstract noun for collective (=search
parties); cf. the similar metonymy 'the raiséd search'
(1. 1. 159).

48. *here in the house* The 'word' is with Desdemona.

49. S.D. (after Rowe) Q. F. omit.

Ancient Cassio puts Iago in his place at once.

50–1. *he...boarded* etc. A characteristic comment
on 'for the sea's worth' (l. 28); Iago represents Othello's
marriage as a lucrative act of piracy (see G. 'carack',
'prize').

52. S.D. (after Rowe) Q. F. omit.

56. S.D. (Collier) F.'*Enter Brabantio, Rodorigo,
with Officers, and Torches.*' (after l. 54); Q. '*Enters*
Brabantio, Roderigo, *and others with lights and weapons.*'
(after l. 52).

57. S.D. (Rowe) Q. F. omit.

59. *for the dew* (Q. F.) S. Walker's conj. 'or the dew' is plausible, but the meaning is, in either case, 'there will be no fighting'.

62. *foul* A frequent epithet for the Devil, implying 'black' (cf. the 'foul fiend', *Lr.* 3. 4. 46 etc.), and 'devilish' is the implication here. Cf. 2. 1. 223 n. and Introduction, p. xi, n. 1.

stowed=placed, lodged; more dignified in associations than now, as in *Lucr.* 119.

68. *darlings* (Q.) F. 'Deareling'.

72. *me* 'ethic' dative.

gross in sense=palpable.

75. *weaken* (Rowe) F. 'weakens'; Q. omits ll. 72–7.

motion=mental or spiritual inclinations or impulses (good or bad); a fairly precise term in Elizabethan psycho-physiology, explained by Sherrington, *Man on his Nature* (1940), p. 21.

78. *an abuser of the world*=a devilish malefactor.

79. *arts...warrant*=prohibited and unlawful practises (i.e. black magic).

84. *Where* (Q.) F. 'Whether'.

87. *I* (Q.) F. omits.

91. S.N. (Cap.) Q. F. '*Officer.*'

98–9. *For...be* i.e. if deeds like this go unpunished, it will be the undoing of our free, Christian state.

1. 3

S.D. *Loc.* (Cap.) *Entry* (Camb.) F. '*Enter Duke, Senators, and Officers.*' Q. '*Enter Duke and Senators, set at a Table with lights and Attendants.*'

1. *There is* (Q.) F. 'There's'.

1–2. *composition...disproportioned* See G. The use of both words as technical terms (e.g. in music and rhetoric) made them preciser in meaning than now.

1. *these news* (Q.) F. 'this Newes'. 'News' was still used as a plural, though F. was apt to alter to the singular (cf. *R. II*, 3. 4. 100).

4. *hundred and forty* (Q.) F. 'Hundred fortie'.

6. *where the aim reports* (F.+most editors) Q. 'where they aym'd reports'. F.'s reading is explained as = 'where conjecture reports' (and so, 'when reports are based on conjecture'). A.W. finds this loose and unidiomatic, suspects that 'reports' is Q.'s anticipation of 'report' in l. 15, and would emend (with Anon. in Camb.) to 'accords' (carrying on the musical associations of 'composition' and 'disproportioned' in ll. 1–2); 'aim' then = 'general intention'. The sense then is that although the numbers don't tally (just as you often find discrepancies in detail with agreement in general intention), they all confirm that the Turkish fleet is making for Cyprus; common experience warns them, in brief, not to be side-tracked by minor matters—a judgment to which the Duke assents in his following speech.

10. *I...error* = 'I do not lay aside anxiety on account of the discrepancy' (Purnell, cited Furness).

11–12. *But...sense* = But I believe the main item of news gives cause for alarm.

12. S.N. and S.D. (J.D.W.) F. '*Saylor within.*' Q. '*One within.*'

13. S.N. (Dyce) F. '*Officer.*' Q. '*Sailor.*' S.D. As in Dyce. F. places after l. 12; Q. '*Enter a Messenger.*' (after 'sense' in l. 12).

18–19. *a pageant...gaze* = a put up show to distract our attention.

19–20. F. 'gaze, ...Turke;'.

22–3. *as...So* = not only...but also.

23. *question* Onions queries his gloss 'trial', but 'question', usually an abstract noun, associated closely with judicial procedure, is merely used figuratively and

concretely here for trial by force; hence 'with … bear it' = 'take it with less trouble' (cf. 'an attempt of ease', l. 29, and 'rebuke', 2. 3. 205, where again the use of force is implicit).

24. *brace* See G.—the part for the whole and concrete for abstract; hence = preparedness.

25. *abilities* = capacity to act, and here (concretely) = equipment, thus carrying on, with 'dressed in', the personification begun in l. 24.

26. *if … this* Recapitulates the foregoing considerations with a change in construction (cf. 'When we consider …', l. 19).

32. S.N. (Dyce) Q. F. '*Officer.*'

35. *injointed* (Q.) F. 'inioynted them'. The F. line seems too cumbrous for the urgency of the matter.

41. *With his free duty* Presumably a complimentary phrase = 'in willing service'.

42. *relieve* (A.W. after T. Clark and Cap. conj.) Q. F. 'beleeue'. The Q. F. reading seems an anticlimax and 'relieve' (= aid) is in accordance with the action taken. It is surely undignified, if not absurd, to ask them to believe his words, and a request for assistance in the defence of Cyprus comes naturally after F.'s account (ll. 24–30, omitted Q.) of its unpreparedness.

44. *Luccicos* (Q. F.) Possibly a common error—for 'Lucchese' (as Cap. thought) or 'Luccicus'. For a 'Marco Lucchese', resident in London and master of an Italian ordinary in the early seventeenth century, see J. S. Smart in *M.L.R.* xi (1916), p. 339.

in town i.e. in Venice. We may suppose Marcus to be an important Cypriot whom the Duke wishes to consult at this crisis. But the reference is perhaps purposely left vague: it suggests urgency and state business—that is all.

46. *from us to him;* (Camb.) F. 'from vs,/To him,')

Q. (+Al.) 'from vs, wish him'. J.D.W. prefers Q.; i.e. 'the letter bids him hurry back to Cyprus'.

post-post-haste dispatch (Steev.) Q. 'post, post hast dispatch'; F. 'Post, Post-haste, dispatch'.

47. *Here ...Moor* (Q. F.) We suspect interpolation and that 'Here comes the Moor' (J.D.W.) may be correct, as it would not only obviate the Duke's repetition of 'valiant' and failure to notice Brabantio's entry but would also make a flabby line more dramatic.

S.D. (after Cap.) F. '...*Othello, Cassio, Iago* ...'; Q. '...Othello, Roderigo, Iago, Cassio, Desdemona...'.

50 S.D. (Theob.) Q. F. omit.

56. *flood-gate* Used for both the gate that controlled the water and (as here) for the spate of water itself; hence, 'torrential', 'overwhelming'.

58. *yet* (J.D.W. after Rowe) Q. F. 'it'—possibly Q.'s repetition of 'it' in l. 57.

59. S.N. All. (Q.) F. '*Sen.*'

70. *Stood in your action* = faced your charge.

74. S.D. (Theob.) Q. F. omit.

80. *head and front* See G. 'head'.

87. *broil* (Q.) F. 'Broiles'.

89. *patience* (A.W. after Pope) Q. F. 'gratious patience'. The Q. F. reading seems obsequiously out of character and is awkward after 'grace' in l. 88.

91–4. *what drugs ...I won* For this construction, see Abbott, §202.

93. *proceedings* (Q.) F. 'proceeding'.

95. *motion* Cf. 1. 2. 75 n.

96. *herself* = itself.

99. *maimed* (Q.) F. 'main'd', an obsolescent form; at 5. 1. 27 F. has the surviving form, Q. the obsolete.

105. *conjured* Stressed on the second syllable, and at 3. 3. 296.

106. S.N. Duke (Q.) F. omits.

107. *more wider* (F.) = fuller (to be associated with

the 'thin habits' of l. 108). Camb.+many editors read 'more certain' (Q.).

overt (Q.) F. 'ouer'.

108. *habits* Normally used by Shakespeare of external appearance (clothes, carriage, etc.); hence 'thin habits' are (fig.) 'flimsy pretexts'. Brabantio's case lacks substance; cf. 3. 3. 433 ('do demonstrate thinly').

poor likelihoods = unsubstantiated conjectures.

109. *modern* See G. What was untested by time and custom was depreciated; cf. 'old' (1. 1. 37).

110. S.N. 1 Senator. (Q.) F. '*Sen.*'

111. *indirect and forcéd courses* = foul means.

114. *beseech* (A.W. after Pope) Q. F. 'do beseech'; cf. l. 89 n.

121. S.D. (after Cap.) Q. '*Exit two or three.*' (after l. 120). F. omits.

122. *till* (Q.) F. 'tell'.

130. *battles...fortunes* (Q.) F. 'Battaile ... Fortune'.

134. *spake* (Q.) F. 'spoke'.

134–5. *of most...field* = of calamitous misfortunes, of exciting adventures by sea and land.

139. *travels'* (Globe) Q. 'trauells'; F. 'Trauellours'.

140 *antres vast* Cf. the 'ingens antrum' of the Sibyl in *Aen.* VI. 42.

idle (a word J. thought 'poetically beautiful') = either 'useless', 'unprofitable' or, more probably, 'solitary', 'unfrequented' (the original sense; O.E.D. 1); cf. Isa. xxxv. 1, 'the wilderness and the solitary place'.

141. *Rough quarries* = rugged precipices. As 'rough' (= both 'jagged' and 'in a state of nature') implies, the 'quarries' are potential rather than actual, though O.E.D. cites no example of 'quarry' in this sense before 1630.

and (Q.) F. omits (full line).

heads (Q.) F. 'head' (full line).

142. *the process* (Q.) F. 'my Processe'.

process i.e. the 'proceedings I am charged withal' (l. 93); cf. note to l. 156, 'beguile'. Onions's gloss ('story') misses the point.

143–5. *the Cannibals...shoulders*. Othello's 'history' (owing something directly or indirectly to Pliny) would not have seemed like armchair travel to Shakespeare's contemporaries. Anthropophagi (see G.) had been found in the Caribbean and Raleigh had heard in Guiana of men with eyes in their shoulders and mouths in their breasts (Pliny, vii, 2). What kind of fresh interest was infused into travellers' tales of the Old World by discoveries in the New is evident from *Tp.* where 'men whose heads stood in their breasts' (3.3.47) are again referred to. In an age avid for marvels, Shakespeare could count on a willing suspension of disbelief.

143. *other* (Q.) F. 'others'.

145. *Do grow...This* (Q.) F. 'Grew...These things'—a typical example of F. perversion at the beginning of the line and we may therefore legitimately suspect that the compositor was responsible for its flabby 'These things'; Q.'s 'This' (= 'the process', l. 142) says all that is needful more cogently (cf. l. 169). Greg (*Sh.F.F.* p. 369) defends 'Do grow...These things' as what Shakespeare wrote.

147. *thence* (Q.) F. 'hence'.

153. *pilgrimage* i.e. his travels' history.

155. *intentively* (Q.) F. 'instinctiuely'. Q.'s reading (see G.) gives the right antithesis to 'by parcels'.

156. *beguile* Used in its normal sense as a deliberate echo of the Duke's own words at l. 66 ('beguiled your daughter of herself'); cf. l. 169, 'This only is the witchcraft I have used'.

159. *sighs* (Q.) F. 'kisses'. The F. reading is an

example of the kind of inexplicable error liable to occur in this compositor's work (cf. F. 'merit' for Q.'s 'friends', *M.N.D.* 1. 1. 139).

163. *made her such a man* i.e. that she had been made a man of that kind.

170. S.D. F. '*Enter Desdemona, Iago, Attendants.*' Q. '…Iago, *and the rest.*'

173. *mangled* lit. 'mutilated', and so to be associated with the following 'broken weapons'.

179. *company* (A.W.) Q. F. 'Noble Companie'— a common error, anticipating 'noble father', l. 180. Desdemona's choice lay between father and husband, and Brabantio would have been the last to concede nobility to Othello.

189. *God bu'y* (Q.) F. 'God be with you' (cf. 3. 3. 377).

I've (A. W. after S. Walker conj.) Q. 'I ha' F. 'I haue'.

194. *hast* As Furness noted, the pronoun is not omitted but merged with the verb; cf. 'le't' (=let it), *Wint.* 2. 2. 53. Q. omits the line.

195. *For your sake*=on your account.

jewel (ironic)=my precious.

197. *escape*=running away; cf. G. 'clog'. Onions's gloss 'outrageous transgression' applies to '*foul* escape' (*Tit.* 4. 2. 113) but not here, and 'escape' (=escapade, slip; cf. *Wint.* 3. 3. 71) is irrelevant.

199. *like yourself*='as if I was in your position' (Hart) or=as you have done (i.e. on resignation).

201. *Into your favour* (Q.) F. omits.

207. *Patience…makes* i.e. Resignation to an inevitable loss makes it seem a trifle (cf. the proverb 'past cure, past care', *L.L.L.* 5. 2. 28); 'her'=Fortune's.

212–15. *He bears…borrow* Here 'sentence'=(i) a judicial verdict, and (ii) a maxim. Brabantio's meaning is: 'a sentence (in both senses) falls lightly on a man who

gets satisfaction at no cost, but it bears doubly hard on a man who is sentenced (in both senses) to bear the burden of his grief and to support it from his own small resources of fortitude'. The Duke's maxims add insult to injury.

218–19. Leonato (*Ado*, 5. 1. 15–32) was of the same opinion that grief was not patched with proverbs or wounds healed by words.

219. *piecéd* (J.C.M. after Theob.) Q. F. 'pierc'd'. The emendation gives far better sense; see G. 'bruised', 'piece'.

ear (Q.) F. 'eares'.

221–2. *preparation...fortitude* Concrete in meaning; 'fortitude' (=material strength) is simply a case of Council Chamber metonymy, like 'question' in l. 23 and 'abilities' in l. 25.

224–5. *opinion...effects* i.e. public opinion, so essential to morale, and therefore pithily personified as the 'mistress' dictating policy.

224. *a sovereign* (Q.) F. 'a more soueraigne'.

228. *boisterous* = 'rough', 'unpolished', thus carrying on, like 'stubborn' (=intractable, difficult to work), the image of 'gloss'.

230. *couch* (Pope) Q. 'Cooch'; F. 'Coach'.

233. *hardness* See G. The word looks back to both 'stubborn' (difficulty) and 'the flinty and steel couch of war' (hardship).

do (F.) Q. 'would'. J.D.W. prefers Q. and suspects F.'s 'do' was caught from l. 231.

234. *These* (Mal.) Q. F. 'This'. See 1. 1. 152 n.

239–40. *Why...father's* (A.W.) F. 'Why at her Fathers?' Q. (+most editors) 'If you please, bee't at her fathers.' The F. text is so abrupt that omission seems fairly certain.

240. *I'll* (Q.) F. 'I will'.

241. *Nor I; I would not* (Q.) F. 'Nor would I'.

245. *a charter in your voice* = 'let your favour privilege me' (J.).

248. *did* (Q.) F. omits.

249. *downright violence* = flagrant breach of filial duty (what Roderigo called her 'gross revolt', 1.1.135); 'Violence is not *violence suffered*, but *violence acted*. Breach of common rules and obligations' (J.).

scorn (Q., A.W.) F. (+most editors) 'storme': J. conj. 'scorn of fortune'. The lines are a challenge; Desdemona (as 1. 1. 136–7; 1. 3. 254; 4. 2. 126–8 emphasize) sacrifices all for Othello.

254. *soul and fortunes* = myself and my future.

256. *A moth of peace* i.e. an idle parasite.

257. *rights* (A.W. after Warb.) Q. F. spell (ambiguously) 'Rites', which most editors read, interpreting as = 'love-rites'; but the word must be associated with Othello's 'very quality' (cf. also l. 163 n.) and 'rights' = 'privileges' (sharing his life and dangers).

263. *and young* (J.D.W. after Steev. conj.) Q. F. 'the yong'. See next note.

264. *my distinct* (A.W. after Theob.) Q. F. 'my defunct'; Cap. (+most editors) 'me defunct'. F. prints ll. 263–4 thus:

> Nor to comply with heat the yong affects
> In my defunct, and proper satisfaction.

Q has the same words, with variant spellings and with commas after 'heat' and 'satisfaction'. Most modern editors accept Cap.'s 'me' for 'my' and read:

> Nor to comply with heat—the young affects
> In me defunct—and proper satisfaction.

This gives choppy metre and syntax, as well as poor sense in view of ll. 266 ff., while Theob.'s reading has the smoother style we expect of Othello. J.D.W. also finds Steev.'s 'and' in l. 263 necessary to the sense.

A.W. does not, since she believes 'comply' is transitive (=satisfy) and 'with heat' adverbial (=urgently).

266. *think*=should think.

268. *For* (Q.) F. 'When'.

269. *seel* See G.; with allusion to blind Cupid.

wanton dullness proleptic='dullness arising from wanton indulgences' (Mal.).

270. *My speculative…instruments* i.e. the eyes (as the metaphor 'seel' implies), but perhaps=all the faculties of vision and foresight of which the eye is the type and symbol.

instruments (Q.) F. 'Instrument'.

276. *her* (F.) Q. omits. J.D.W. defends Q., since the Senator's 'You' is emphatic.

277–8. *answer it…heart.* (F.) Q. 'answer, you must hence to night,/*Desd.* To night my Lord?/*Du.* This night./*Oth.* With all my heart.' Q. sentimentalizes (as at l. 251, where it substituted 'utmost pleasure' for 'very quality'). Further, Othello's 'With all my heart' would be impossibly brusque after such an exclamation from her.

278. S.N. F. '*Sen.*'

282. *With* (Q.) F. 'And'.

282–3. *such…you* i.e. things suitable for your rank and position.

288. S.D. (Cap.) Q. F. omit.

289–90. *If virtue…black* Steev. compared *Tw.N.* 3.4. 365 ff., 'In nature there's no blemish but the mind; None can be called deformed but the unkind: Virtue is beauty….'.

291. S.N. 1 Senator. (Q.) F. '*Sen.*'

294. S.D. (J.D.W. after Theob.) Q. '*Exeunt.*'; F. '*Exit.*' Q. F. (+most editors) place after l. 293.

299. *worldly* (Q.) F. 'wordly'.

300. F. 'the the'.

S.D. Q. '*Exit Moore and* Desdemona.' F. '*Exit.*'

309–10. *have we ...physician* i.e. we are entitled to commit suicide when death is the remedy.

313. *a man* (Q.+Al.) F. (+most editors) 'man'. We prefer Q. as more idiomatic.

320. *gardens* (Q.) F. 'our Gardens'.

322. *tine* (A.W.) Q. F. 'Time'; Pope (+editors) 'thyme'. The emendation gives the necessary antithesis: 'tine'=tare, wild vetch; 'thyme', an aromatic herb like hyssop, confuses the argument.

323. *distract* Glossed by Schmidt as 'parcel out', but the word generally implied confusion (as at 2. 3. 251).

326. *beam* (A.W. after Theob.) F. 'braine'; Q. (+most editors) 'ballance'. F.'s variant looks like a misreading of 'beame'; see G. and cf. *Tp.* 2. 1. 130.

330. *our unbitted* (Q.) F. 'or vnbitted'.

unbitted lusts Possibly a recollection of a passage in Cinthio's Introduction citing Plato's comparison of lust with an unbridled beast; cf. 3. 3. 186 n.

331. *set* (A.W. after J.) Q. F. 'Sect'. J. provides no comment, but 'set' (=scion) is wanted to carry on the garden metaphor.

339. *thou these* (A.W. after Rowe) F. 'thou the' (end of line); Q. 'these'. F. suggests trimming to suit the compositor's convenience; 'follow the wars' merely ='enlist'. A reference to the particular Cyprus wars is wanted.

340. *defeat ...beard* The words are characteristically double-edged (see G. 'defeat', 'favour', 'usurped') like the advice: 'disguise yourself by assuming a beard' or 'look like a man'.

341–2. *It ...long* (Q.) F. 'It cannot be long that *Desdemona* should'. Since the F. line ends after '*Desdemona*', the interchange of 'long' and 'should' looks as if it had been made for the compositor's convenience.

343–4. *commencement* (Q.) F. 'Commencement in her'. F.'s 'in her' (ruining the balanced style) looks like the compositor's interpolation, and 'commencement' may be a common error. J.'s conj. 'conjunction' is very attractive, especially as the word was used specifically for 'marriage' and (in a sense which would have appealed to Iago) for the copulation of animals. The 'answerable sequestration' presupposes a better antithesis than 'commencement'.

347. *locusts* Probably the fruit, not the insect. Hart cites Gerarde's *Herbal* on the cobs of the carob tree 'of some called St. John's bread, and thought to be that which is translated locusts whereon St. John did feed when he was in the wilderness' (see Matt. iii. 4). He also cites Gerarde as noting that coloquintida is found in the Sinaitic Desert and on the shores of the southern Mediterranean. Iago contemptuously mentions two products of the desert from which this 'erring barbarian' sprang.

348. *bitter as* (F.) Q. 'acerbe as the'. J.D.W. supports Q. since 'acerb' is (i) a rare word most unlikely to be invented by the transcriber, (ii) often occurs ('acerbo') in Cinthio, meaning 'bitter to the mind', (iii) meant also 'sour to the taste' in English (see O.E.D. 'acerbity') as it does in Latin, (iv) 'as acerbe as' provides a good mouthful of sibilants for the rasping sneer of Iago. Yet an actor might well stumble over it, and thus 'bitter' get into the prompt book, perhaps with Shakespeare's consent. A.W. thinks the commoner word (almost proverbially associated with coloquintida) appropriate to Iago.

350. *error* (Q.) F. 'errors'.
choice (F.) Q. 'choyce; shee must haue change, shee must'. Q.'s lapse in style suggests a memorial substitution for 'she must change for youth', which it omits.

352. *more delicate* The pleasanter way to be damned appears later—'to be hanged in compassing thy joy'.

354. *a supersubtle* (Q.) F. 'super-subtle'.

357. *'Tis* (Q.) F. 'it is'.

365–6. *against him* (Q. F.) Possibly an interpolation.

368. *Traverse* A military command (cf. *2 H. IV*, G.) = 'Quick march' or possibly 'Right about turn'; see G.

374–80. *Go to ... land* (Al.) F. reads:

> *Iago.* Go too, farewell. Do you heare *Rodorigo?*
> *Rod.* Ile sell all my Land. *Exit.*

This is clearly too abrupt. Q. reads:

> *Iag.* Go to, farewell:---doe you heare *Roderigo?*
> *Rod.* what say you?
> *Iag.* No more of drowning, doe you heare?
> *Rod.* I am chang'd.   *Exit Roderigo.*
> *Iag.* Goe to, farewell, put money enough in your purse:

Al.'s conflation postulates omission in both texts: '*Rod.* Ile sell all my Land' in Q. and that the F. compositor's eye jumped from 'Go to, farewell' opening l. 374 to the later line which also opens with 'Goe to, farewell', omitting the intervening words (Sisson, *New Readings in Shakespeare* (1956), ii. 249). Most editors, following Q 2, print:

> *Iago.* Go to; farewell. Do you hear, Roderigo?
> *Rod.* What say you?
> *Iago.* No more of drowning, do you hear?
> *Rod.* I am chang'd: I'll go sell all my land.

380. S.D. F. '*Exit.*' Q. '*Exit Roderigo.*' (see above).

383. *a snipe* (Q.) F. 'Snpe'.

386. *He's* (Q. 'Ha's') F. 'She ha's'.

387. *Yet* (Q.) F. 'But'.

391. *plume up* J.D.W. interprets as = 'crown' or 'set a crest on' (from the plumes on a warrior's helmet; cf. *1 H. IV*, 5.4.72, and Introduction to *3 H. VI*, p. xii); 'will' = 'purpose', 'scheme'. Hence 'plume ... knavery' = set a double crest on my knavish purposes. A.W. thinks that 'plum' (a variant of 'plump') = 'fatten' was intended, since it gives more point to 'double knavery'; Iago is enlarging his design (or thickening the plot) by double knavery. Q.'s variant 'make up' lends some support to this interpretation, since O.E.D. ('make' 96*h* (*e*)) records 'make up' = 'fatten' (especially of a horse), though citing no example before 1794.

393. *ear* (Q.) F. 'eares'.

396. *To be suspected* i.e. to excite suspicion.

399. *led* (Q.) F. 'lead'.

402. S.D. Q. '*Exit*.' F. omits (full line).

2. 1

S.D. *Loc.* (Globe) *Entry* (F.) Q. '*Enter* Montanio, *Gouernor of* Cypres, *with two other Gentlemen*.'

2. *a high-wrought flood* = an angry sea.

7. *ruffianed* carrying on the personification of 'spoke aloud'; cf. *2 H. IV*, 3. 1. 21 ff.:

> the winds,
> Who take the ruffian billows by the top,
> Curling their monstrous heads, and hanging them
> With deafing clamour in the slippery clouds.

11. *foaming* (F.) Q. 'banning'. J.D.W. strongly supports Q. on the grounds that no scribe or actor would have introduced this word and because it leads on to and explains the chidden billows; cf. *R. II*, 2. 1. 62–3, 'Whose rocky shore beats back the envious siege Of watery Neptune'. A.W. thinks the Q. reading was suggested by the chidden billows and 'chidden'

carries on the personification of the wind in 'spoke
aloud' and 'ruffianed'. It was the 'scolding' wind (as
in *J.C.* 1. 3. 5–8) which made the sea swell and foam,
scattering the Turkish fleet. The topic of interest is
the effects of the storm at sea.

14. *the burning Bear* See G. Baldwin (ii, 148)
notes that 'feritque ad sidera fluctus' was a textbook
example of hyperbole.

15. *ever-fixèd* Cf. *J.C.* 3. 1. 60–2.

16. *molestation* i.e. of the wind (=stormy
conditions).

19. *they bear* (Q.) F. 'to beare'. F. generalises (as
it proves, wrongly).

S.D. (Q.) F. '*Enter a Gentleman.*'

25–6. *in, A Veronesa* (Theob.) F. 'in : A*Verennessa*,'
(Q. 'in : A Veronessa,'). It seems generally agreed that
'Veronesa' refers to the ship (not Cassio) and that
(unless a common error has affected more than the
punctuation) the ship belongs to Verona.

33. *prays* (Q.) F. 'praye'.

34. *heaven* (Q.) F. 'Heauens'.

40. S.N. (Q.) F. '*Gent.*'

42. *arrivance* (Q.) F. 'Arriuancie'.

43. *this* (Q.) F. 'the'.

49. *Of...allowance* i.e. reputed as highly skilled
and experienced.

50. *hopes* (F 3) Q. F. 'hope's'.

forfeited (J.D.W. after J. conj.) Q. F. (+most
editors) 'surfetted'. We make nothing of Q. F.
The tenour of Cassio's speech suggests that there is
hope so long as there is no certainty of Othello's death.
A.W. suspects that 'certified' may be the true reading.

51. S.D.¹ (after Camb.) F. '*Within. A Saile...*'
(as dialogue); Q. '*Mess.* A saile...' (as dialogue, after
Messenger's entry). The cry is, of course, 'within' and
Q. suggests that the Messenger was responsible for the

cry *before* he entered—an economic disposition for stage purposes. Q.'s habit of placing entries early (see Note on the Copy, p. 140) gives the erroneous impression that the words were addressed to Cassio and the rest.

S.D.² (Dyce) Q. '*Enter a Messenger.*' (after 'cure'); F. omits.

53. S.N. (Cap.) F. '*Gent.*' Q. '*Mess.*'

55. S.D. (Cap.) Q. '*A shot.*' (after 'least' in l. 57); F. omits.

56, 59. S.N. (Q.) F. '*Gent.*'

56. *of courtesy*=in salute.

59. S.D. Q. F. '*Exit.*'

62. *paragons...fame*=matches panegyric and the most extravagant report. To equate the sense of 'paragons' with 'excels' (O.E.D., On.) robs the hyperbole of ll. 62–5 of an intended climax.

63. *quirks...pens* a metaphor from the art of the illuminator.

blazoning (see G.)—a compendious heraldic term: the blazoner, a skilled craftsman, 'blazoned' (=depicted) attested honours.

64. *th'essential...creation* The 'vesture of creation' is the human form (cf. *M.V.* 5. 1. 65) and 'essential' carries the full renaissance meaning of all that constituted *being*; hence='the quintessence of loveliness' (cf. 5. 2. 11, 'Thou cunning'st pattern of excelling nature').

65. *Does...ingener* (Steev.) F. 'Do's tyre the Ingeniuer'. The 'ingener'=the 'inventor' and hence (by metonymy)='invention', 'imagination'. The word would include all whom Enobarbus enumerates (*Ant.* 3. 2. 16–7)—'hearts, tongues, figures, scribes, bards, poets'; hence 'transcends imagination'. Cf. *Tp.* 4. 1. 10–11, 'For thou shalt find she will outstrip all praise, And make it halt behind her.'

S.D. (after Q.) F. '*Enter Gentleman.*'

66, 94. S.N. (Q.) F. '*Gent*.'

67. *He's* (Grant White; 'Ha's' F.).

69. *guttered ... sands* = reefs and sandbanks.

70. *insteeped* (F.) = submerged. Q.'s 'enscerped' is probably a misreading, though (since it is an odd word) it has recently been defended: 'congregated sands' can only be sandbanks, dangerous to navigation because they are hidden rather than because they are (somehow) 'scarped'.

clog (Q.) F. 'enclogge', which clutters the line and suggests assimilation to the preceding 'ensteep'd' (F.'s spelling).

82. *And ... comfort* (Q.) F. omits.

S.D. (Mal. after Cap.) F. '*Enter Desdemona, Iago, Rodorigo, and Æmilia.*' (after l. 81); Q. '*Enter Desdemona, Iago, Emillia, and Roderigo.*' (after l. 80).

83. *riches* (< French *richesse*) was used as a singular noun until well into the seventeenth century; cf. 3. 3. 175.

88. *me* (Q.) F. omits.

92. *the sea* (Q.) F. omits 'the'.

93. S.D. (after Camb.) F. '*Within.* A Saile, a Saile.' (as dialogue) Q. the same (as S.D. after l. 91).

94. *their* (Q.) F. 'this'.

95. S.D. (after Cap.) Q. F. omit.

96. S.D. (Rowe) Q. F. omit.

99. S. D. (J.) Q. F. omit.

102. *You'ld* (Q. 'You'd') F. 'You would'.

104. *list* (Q. + most editors) F. 'leaue'. F. may be due to assimilation of endings (cf. 'fatch paunch' for 'fat paunch', *1 H. IV*, 2. 4. 141), but 'had liefer sleep' may have been intended.

107. *And chides with thinking* i.e. only *thinks* her chiding. Emilia keeps a rein on her tongue before Desdemona.

109. *pictures* Hart took this to refer to painted faces, but what follows suggests that the silence of pictures was in mind (cf. *T.N.* 3. 4. 212, 'It hath no tongue to vex you'; also *M.V.* 1. 2. 68–9, *Macb.* 2. 2. 53–4). Cf. also preceding note.

109–10. *of doors* (Q. 'adores') F. 'of doore'.

110. *bells* i.e. pandemonium; comparison of a shrew's tongue with a bell was a commonplace, like Iago's satiric portrait of women.

wild-cats i.e. spitfires.

111. *in your injuries* = when malicious.

112. *housewifery* Implied originally a good (thrifty) manager, but the word was acquiring an uncomplimentary meaning as well (as in the latter part of this line, where the sense is 'hussy'; cf. 4. 1. 94).

hussies (Grant White conj.) F. 'Huswiues'; Q. 'houswiues'.

114. *or...Turk* = (as the Turks were infidels) 'on my faith'.

117. *wouldst thou* (Q.) F. omits 'thou'.

122. Aside (A.W. after Delius conj. and Schücking, *Character Problems in Shakespeare's Plays* (1922), p. 224). Desdemona disguises her anxiety by a pretence of willingness to be amused.

133. *white* 'punning on wight' (Schmidt).

hit (Q.) F. *fit*. The readings suggest much the same, but 'hit' seems to have been more commonly used in this indecent sense (cf. *L.L.L.* 4. 1. 117) and may allude to the black and white pieces of backgammon: 'to hit a blot' was to take an unguarded piece.

138. *paradoxes* Iago's paradoxes are of the type exemplified in Puttenham's *Arte of English Poesie*—jeux d'esprit combining word-play and paradox.

145–7. *one that...itself* i.e. one whose high qualities malice itself was rightly compelled to acknowledge.

155. *To change...tail* i.e. to solace herself with a handsome lover when married to a blockhead (see G. 'cod's head'). Salmon was a delicacy then as now.

158. *wight* (Q.) F. '*wightes*'.

160. *To suckle...beer* i.e. to live a life of foolish domesticity and trivial occupations—children and small chat.

164. *counsellor* Not a 'talker' (as Hart suggests) but a 'mentor', since Emilia has just been advised not to 'learn of him'.

166. *in the soldier*=as a (blunt) soldier; a home-truth which provokes the venomous retaliation of Iago's aside.

167. S.D. Aside first in Rowe.

172–3. *kissed your three fingers* 'Cassio's demeanour was that of an accomplished courtier' (Hart, citing parallels). This Italianate fashion was often ridiculed; cf. *L.L.L.* 4. 1. 145.

174. *an* (Q.) F. 'and'.

176. *clyster-pipes* (Q.) F. 'Cluster-pipes'. The filthiest thing he can think of.

S.D. (Q., after 'trumpet', l. 177) F. omits.

177–8. As verse (A.W.).

178 S.D. Q. places in l. 177.

179. *warrior* Cf. 1. 3. 250 ff., 3. 4. 155.

191. *loves and comforts* The plural of abstract nouns was usual when referring to two or more persons (hence='our love and comfort'); cf. 3. 3. 419, 'in their sleeps'.

195. S.D. (Q.) F. omits.

197. S.D. Aside first in Rowe.

199. *let's* (Rowe ii) Q. F. (+most editors) 'let us'. The words seem absurdly stilted and Rowe's change also helps the metre (A.W.).

202. *well desired*=very welcome.

204. *out of fashion* See G. 'fashion'; 'out of method,

without any settled order of discourse' (J.), hence = incoherently, monstrously. Othello's happiness has gone to his head and he is too excited to compose his thoughts; cf. *Tp*. 3. 1. 57–8, 'prattle Something too wildly'.

205. *comfort* (A.W. after Pope) Q. F. 'comforts' (cf. l. 189).

210. S.D. (Camb.) F. '*Exit Othello and Desdemona.*' Q. '*Exit.*'

211. *Do…harbour* It has generally been assumed that the words are addressed to Roderigo (and probably rightly), but Al. (< Delius) adds the S.D. '*To one leaving*', supposing they were spoken to an attendant.

212. *hither* (Q.) F. 'thither'.

212–14. *as they say…them* The saying has been traced to Plato, but Shakespeare might have come across it in the *Adagia* of Erasmus (Profusio, *Cupidinum crumena porri folio vincta est*) where the saying that love 'e sordido splendidum…e timido audacem reddit hominem' is attributed to Plutarch.

218. *Lay thy finger thus* hold your tongue and listen to a wiser man (J.) A French critic (cited by Furness) suggests that Iago here seizes Roderigo's finger and shuts his mouth with it (the mouth gaping with astonishment).

221. *lies…love* (Q.) F. 'lies. To loue'. F. must be rejected on grounds of style, but it may be that a correction of Q.'s reading was imperfectly carried out.

223. *the devil* i.e. the black Othello, black being the devil's colour and the 'badge of hell'; cf. 1. 2. 62 n.

225. *again* (Q.) F. 'a game'.

226. *appetite*—(after Theob.) Q. F. 'appetite.'

228. *conveniences* = compatibilities. Onions's gloss ('advantages') is unsatisfactory, since 'conveniences' = the 'sympathies' Iago has enumerated.

229. *delicate tenderness* Characteristically conceived in purely physical terms.

232–3. *pregnant…position* =valid and natural assumption.

234. *degree* With allusion to the 'degrees' (=rungs) of a ladder, and hence the associated 'eminent'.

237. *compassing* (Q.) F. 'compasse'.

239. *finder-out* (Q.) F. 'finder'.

occasions (Q.) F. 'occasion'.

has (Q.) F. 'he's'.

stamp =coin; 'counterfeit' and 'advantages' (with monetary associations = 'profit', as in *M.V.* 1. 3. 67) carry on the metaphor. Cassio has an eye to his own interests and can turn anything to account.

244. *found him* =seen what he is after; see G. 'find'.

256. *mutualities* (Q.) F. 'mutabilities'.

259–60. *for…you* = I shall give you your orders.

267. *haply may* (F.) Q. 'haply with his Truncheon may'. The truncheon, as a symbol of office, had more dignified associations than now, and since Iago would be particularly conscious of Cassio's carrying a truncheon as staff-officer, J.D.W. suspects accidental omission in F. A.W. thinks that the less said about the risk of bodily harm to Roderigo the better and that Q.'s reading is an interpolation, suggested by Roderigo's speaking of himself as having been 'exceedingly well cudgelled' at 2. 3. 358–9.

269. *whose qualification…taste again* The metaphor is of the palate. To 'qualify' was to change the strength or taste of a liquid, generally by dilution (cf. 2. 3. 38); hence = 'whose disaffection will not be remedied'.

275. *you* (F.) Q. 'I'. It seems more in character for Roderigo to thrust the responsibility on Iago, who gives consent in 'I warrant thee'.

279. S.D. Q. F. '*Exit.*'

290. *leaped into my seat* A characteristic image from horse riding.

293. *evened* (F.) Q. 'euen'. A.W. prefers Q.'s

more idiomatic expression and thinks F.'s reading a slip
like 'wift' at the end of the line.

wife (Q.) F. 'wift'.

297. *leash* (J.D.W. after Bailey conj. in Camb.)
Q. 'crush'; F. 'trace'. Steev.'s emendation 'trash'
(=check) is customary, but 'this poor trash...whom
I trash' is the reverse of Shakespearian in style and
'leash' (a recurring image with Shakespeare) suits the
context better, since it suggests holding in with a view
to slipping, thus looking forward to 'putting on'.
'Leash' and 'lease' (or 'leace') were variants of the
same word and would explain the divergent errors of
Q. and F.

300. *rank* (Q.) F. 'right'.

301. *night-cap* (Q.) F. 'Night-Cape'. The night-
cap would not fit over a cuckold's horns.

2. 2

S.D. *Loc.* (Cap.) *Entry* (Mal.) F. '*Enter Othello's,
Herald with a Proclamation.*'; Q. '*Enter a Gentleman
reading a Proclamation.*'

6. *addiction* (Q 2) F. 'addition'; Q 1, 'minde'.

10. *Heaven* (Q.) F. omits.

11. S.D. (J.D.W.) F. '*Exit.*' Q. omits.

2. 3

S.D. *Loc.* (after Cap. and Al.) *Entry* (F.) Q. '*Enter
Othello, Cassio, and Desdemona.*'

11. S.D.[1] (J.D.W.) Q. '*Exit* Othello *and* Desdemona.' F. '*Exit.*'

14. *o'clock* ('aclock' Q.) F. 'o'th'clocke'.

39. *unfortunate* (Q.) F. 'infortunate'.

45. S.D. Q. F. '*Exit.*'

48–9. *as full...dog* with allusion to dogs as the

spoilt pets of Elizabethan women and their proverbial quarrelsomeness—hence, Erasmus explains (*Adagia*, Rixosus, *Canina facundia*), 'r' was the dog's letter because it was the initial letter of *rixari*; cf. *Rom.* 2. 4. 202 n. For the common idiomatic use of 'my' (used without particular application) cf. *Ado*, 2. 1. 9, 'my lady's eldest son' (=a spoilt boy); hence 'my... mistress"=a young lady's.

53. *else* (F.) Q. 'lads'. For this quasi-adjectival use of 'else' (=other), cf. *Ham.* 1. 4. 33, 'His virtues else' (=all his other virtues). Iago uses 'three else' contemptuously=three nameless Cypriots who will further his ends. Q.'s 'lads' is too affectionate and familiar (cf. 2. 1. 20).

53–4. *noble swelling...distance*=high-spirited gallants who are quick to take offence; 'hold...distance' means that they are 'touchy' about their honour.

55. *elements...isle*=typically quarrelsome Cypriots.

58. *to put* (Q.) F. 'put to'.

61. S.D. (Camb.) F. '*Enter Cassio, Montano, and Gentlemen.*' (after l. 59); Q. '*Enter* Montanio, Cassio, *and others.*' (opposite l. 59).

62. *God* (Q.) F. 'heauen'.

67. S.D. (Rowe) Q. F. omit.

67 ff. *And let me...* 'Probably an old toping stave' (Hart, citing parallels).

70. *man's life's but a span* As Hart observed, an echo (almost proverbial) of the Prayer Book version of Ps. xxxix. 6, 'Behold thou hast made my days as it were a span long'.

73. *God* (Q.) F. 'Heauen'.

78. *Englishman* (Q.) F. 'Englishmen'.

exquisite (F.) Q. (+most editors) 'expert'. F.'s is the choicer word. It is not only more tricky for the tipsy Cassio (repeated at l. 97) but suggests, like what follows, a consummate ability to hold his own. There

may be an allusion to the old drinking song 'potatores exquisiti'.

85. *for it* Montano is seconding the toast; see G. 'justice'.

88. S.D. (Cap.) Q. F. omit.

88 ff. *King Stephen*... Lines from a popular song (cf. *Tp.* 4. 1. 222–3), later included in Percy's *Reliques* (no. 29 in the Oxford Book of English Verse).

88. *was and-a* Cf. *Tw.N.* 5. 1. 388. Abbott's explanation (§95–6) that the 'and' was emphatic is plausible.

95. *Then* (Q.) F. '*And*'.

101. *God's* (Q.) F. 'heau'ns'.

110. *God* (Q.) F. omits.

113. *left hand* (Q.) F. omits 'hand'. Since the maudlin Cassio is bent on showing himself capable of speech, we give him the maximum opportunity. There is little to show where the truth lies.

116. S.N. All. (Q.) F. '*Gent.*'

118. S.D. F. '*Exit.*'

122. *He is* (Q.) F. 'He's'.

124. *equinox* 'The force of the metaphor lies in equating the night of Cassio's vice to the daylight of his virtue' (Hart).

126. *puts him in* (Q. F.) Cap.'s inversion ('puts in him') is tempting.

127. *odd time*=chance occasion.

128. *island* (Q. F.) Possibly a common error for 'isle' (Seymour conj. in Camb.).

129. *the prologue* (Q.) F. 'his prologue'.

130. *watch...set*=be up twice the clock round (i.e. won't go to bed); see G. 'set'.

134–5. *virtue...evil* (A.W.) F. '...euills'; Q. 'vertues...euills'. There should be a just equinox and, as a particular evil was in mind (cf. ll. 123, 144), we emend accordingly.

136. S.D. Aside first in Cap.

137. S.D. (after Q.) F. omits.

144. S.D.¹ As in Al. Q. '*Helpe, helpe, within*' (after l. 143); F. omits.

S.D.² (after F.) Q. '*Enter* Cassio, *driuing in* Roderigo.'

145. '*Zounds*, (Q.) F. omits.

147–8. *A knave...bottle* Q. F. print as prose; editors generally divide after 'duty'.

148. *twiggen bottle* See G. Hart was probably right in thinking that Cassio's intention was not to beat Roderigo into sticks but to pursue him until he found a bolt-hole; 'Roderigo is running wildly, looking for any cranny to hide in...The first little aperture that occurs to Cassio's mind is the last one he looked at'. Cf. *1 H. IV*, 2.4. 260–1, 'what starting-hole canst thou now find out, to hide thee from this open...shame?'.

prate (A.W.) Q. F. 'thou prate'. Here, and in the next two speeches, speed and metre seem to be wanted. For what it is worth, the evidence of F. suggests that verse was intended, since Montano's 'Nay...hand' and Cassio's reply are divided after 'lieutenant' and 'sir' (as if verse). Many editors print as prose.

S.D. (Camb. after Cap.) Q. F. omit.

149. *pray sir* (Q.) F. 'I pray you Sir'.

150. *Let go* (A.W.) Q. F. 'Let me go'.

152. S.D. (Q.) F. omits.

153. S.D.¹ Aside first in Cap.

S.D.² (after Q2) Q1, F. omit.

154. S.D. Q. F. omit.

God's will (Q.) F. 'Alas'.

155. *sir —Montano —sir—* (Q. 'Sir *Montanio*, sir') F. 'Sir *Montano*'.

156. S.D. (Q. '*A bell rung.*' after l. 153) F. omits. The alarum bell of the town, rung in time of danger, and theatrically the large bell in the wooden tower

above the tiring-house (Adams, *Globe Theatre* (1943), pp. 371–2).

157. *that that* (Q.) F. 'that which'. The F. reading (like others hereabouts) loses pace.

158. *God's will* (Q.) F. 'Fie, fie'.
hold (Q.) F. omits.

159. *You…shamed* (Q.) F. 'You'le be asham'd'.
S.D. (after F.) Q. '*Enter* Othello, *and Gentlemen with weapons.*'

160. *'Zounds,* (Q.) F. omits.

161. *He dies.* (F.) Q. omits (but concludes the speech with a colon). As Cap. indicates, Montano rushes at Cassio again.
S.D. (Cap.) Q. F. omit.

162. Q. F. 'Sir *Montano*'.

163. *sense of place* (Hanmer) Q. F. 'place of sense'.

164. *The general* (A.W. after Pope) Q. F. 'Hold. The Generall'. 'Hold' at the beginning of the line breaks the thread of the sense.
hold, hold (Q.) F. 'hold'.

167. *heaven…Ottomites* By destroying their fleet.

173. *look'st* (Hanmer) Q. F. 'lookes' (a common form of the period).

174. *Speak…this;* (A.W.) Q. 'Speake, …this,'; F. 'Speake: …this?'. The more idiomatic construction with 'speak' = 'say' is in keeping with ll. 180–1.

178. *some planet* According to the Ptolemaic system, the planets (wandering stars, including the sun and moon) moved in their spheres round the earth and, if they came too close, popular superstition attributed to them disasters of all kinds; loss of wits was associated with the influence of the moon (cf. 5. 2. 112–14; *Wint.* 2. 1. 105–7).

179. *breast* (Q.) F. 'breastes'.

186. *be* (Q.) F. 'to be'.

190. *unlace* O.E.D. glosses (s.v. 5, citing) 'to undo',

'destroy', but the next line makes it clear that a metaphor is involved, and either 'unlace' has reference to
'cutting up', 'carving' (O.E.D. 3), as Hart suggested,
comparing l. 169, or the loosening of the purse strings.
The words 'spend your rich opinion' would carry
either line of thought, alluding to the 'spending' of
blood (cf. *R. III*, 1. 3. 125) or money. The metaphor
is probably ambivalent.

207. *approved…offence*=proved guilty; 'approved'
was neutral in meaning and Onions's somewhat loose
gloss ('convict') takes into account the qualifier both
here and in *Ado*, 4.1. 43.

212. *court and guard* Generally taken as a corruption of 'corps de garde' (see G. 'court of guard'), but
the expression is awkward; possibly 'court' is elliptical
(=court of guard) and 'guard of safety' a noun
phrase: i.e. at a time ('by night'), in a place ('on the
court' of guard), and in a capacity ('guard of safety')
calling for self-discipline. Cf. ll. 292–4.

214. *leagued* (Pope) Q. F. 'league'.

223. *following* (A.W. after Pope) Q. F. 'following
him'.

226–30. *Myself…swords* Iago gambles on the
chance that they may not have noticed his presence
during the fray—an unnecessary lie.

229. *the* (Q.) F. 'then'.

236. *can I not* (Q.) F. 'cannot I'.

245. S.D. (after F.) Q. '*Enter* Desdemona, *with
others*.'

247. *What's* (Q2) Q1, F. 'What is'.

matter? (Q.) F. 'matter (Deere?)'. The F. reading
does not keep decorum. This kind of affectionate
familiarity in public is more appropriate to Othello
than Desdemona (A.W.). See next note.

248. *dear sweeting* (A.W.) F. 'Sweeting'; Q. 'now
sweeting'. Unless F.'s 'Deere' in l. 247 was the

compositor's invention, this is where it belongs, especially as the F. line is metrically defective (A.W.).

248–9. As in Pope. Q. F. print as three lines (dividing after 'sweeting' and 'hurts', the third line ending 'Lead him off'). See next note.

249. *surgeon* This is followed in Q. and F. by 'Lead him off:', which most editors print as dialogue (adding a S.D. to cover the leading off). Mal.'s conj. that it was itself a S.D. was probably right. The speech is much better ordered without it.

S.D. (after Steev.) Q. F. omit.

253. S.D. (after Camb.) Q. '*Exit Moore*, Desdemona, *and attendants*.' (after l. 254). F. '*Exit.*'

256. *heaven* (F.) Q. 'God'. Iago's preceding light oath 'Marry' suggests that F. is here correct; cf. 5. 1. 72.

261. *thought* (Q.) F. 'had thought'.

264. *imposition*=attribution. Onions suggested that the germ of the later meaning 'imposture' was here, but as the phrase is 'false imposition' the noun must be neutral in sense. This 'false imposition' rises to the value of a jewel in 3. 3. 158–9.

267. *ways* (Q.) F. 'more wayes'.

269–70. *as one…lion* An old proverb (cf. Tilley, D 443) meaning 'to punish a mean man in the presence of, and for an example to, the mighty' (Cotgrave, cited Hart). Cf. Chaucer, *Squire's Tale*, 491.

273. *light* (Q.) F. 'slight'. Q. is not only more euphonious but also covers a wider range of meaning ('unsteady' as well as 'worthless').

281. *Is't possible?* Iago is thinking of his lie.

283. *O, that* (F.) Q. 'O God, that'. Q. mitigates by the use of an oath the sobriety and sincerity of Cassio's repentance.

301. *ingredience* (Q.) F. 'Ingredient'; see *Macb.* G.

302. *wine* (A.W.) Q. F. 'good wine', presumably

in anticipation of 'good familiar'; the quality of the wine is an irrelevance which confuses the argument.

306. *at a time* = on a (particular) occasion, once.

time (Q.) F. 'time man'. F.'s 'man' is too familiar for the ingratiating tactics Iago is now employing (cf. 'good lieutenant', l. 304) and looks as if it had been caught from earlier in the speech. Assured that Cassio is unsuspicious, Iago is obsequious and gives him the title he has forfeited at l. 304 and again at l. 326.

307. *I'll* (Q.) F. 'I'.

310. *denotement* (Q2) Q1, F. 'deuotement'.

325. *here* (Q.) F. omits.

328. S.D. F. '*Exit Cassio.*' Q. '*Exit.*'

330. *I give is free* (A.W.) Q. F. 'is free I giue'.

336. *were't* (Q.) F. 'were'.

342. *parallel* See G. The sting lies in the fact that parallel courses will not meet.

343. *Divinity of hell!* A favourite theme of Shakespeare's and other sixteenth-century writers, based on the Devil's citation of Scripture during the Temptation (Matt. iv. 6); cf. Tilley, D 230.

346. *while* (Q.) F. 'whiles'. Q. is preferable for euphony.

347. *fortunes* (Q.) F. 'Fortune'.

355. *enmesh* (Q.) F. 'en-mash'.

S.D. As in Q. F. places after l. 355.

357. *cry* See G.; i.e. one of the pack for his voice alone.

360. *pains* (F.) Q. 'paines, as that comes to'. A.W. takes Q.'s 'as...to' as an interpolation; J.D.W. thinks it makes the sense clearer.

362. *How...patience* Echoes the proverb 'He that has no patience has nothing' (Tilley, P 103).

367. *hast* (Q.) F. 'hath'.

368–9. *Though...ripe* This seems to puzzle critics. The things yet unripe which 'grow fair' are the designs

upon Desdemona and Othello; those now ripening are the subsidiary designs upon Cassio.

370. *By th'mass* (Q. 'bi'the masse') F. 'Introth'.

374. S.D. F. '*Exit Rodorigo*.' Q. omits (cf. l. 380 n.).

377. *the while* (Theob.) Q. F. 'a while'.

380. S.D. F. '*Exit*.' Q. '*Exeunt*.'

3. 1

S.D. *Loc.* (after Cap. and Al.) *Entry* (Camb.) F. '*Enter Cassio, Musitians, and Clowne*.' (Q. '...*with Musitians and the* ...').

2. *Good morrow* An aubade was a usual compliment on special occasions such as the morning after Othello's arrival in Cyprus. J.D.W. thinks the 'concert' was a 'hunts-up' (cf. *Rom.* 3. 5. 34), the 'morning Song for a new married Wife, the day after the Marriage' (Cotgrave's explanation of *Resveil*, cited Hart).

S.Ds. (Camb. after Q 2) Q 1, F. omit.

4. *Naples* A reference to the Neapolitan disease, a kind of syphilis, so called because of the reputation of Naples for immorality.

5, etc. S.N. (Cap.) F. '*Mus.*'; Q. '*Boy*.'

8. *thereby hangs a tail* Cf. Tilley, T 48.

19–20. *for I'll away* (Q. F.) Hart (p. xvii n.) suggests that this was the name of a tune.

20. S.D. F. '*Exit Mu.*'; Q. omits.

21. *hear,* (Theob.) Q. 'heare'; F. 'heare me'. Normalized pointing half spoils this simple joke, which the F. interpolation loses altogether.

my (Q.) F. 'mine'.

25. *general's wife* (Q.) F. 'Generall'.

27. *stirring...stir* A poor quibble on (i) to get up, (ii) to move about.

28. *I shall seem to notify* (Q. F.) A similar use of 'seem' from Lancelot in *M.V.* 2. 4. 11 ('it shall seem

to signify') and Bottom, *M.N.D.* 3. 1. 16 ('let the prologue seem to say'), suggests that a vulgarism gave more point to the Clown's words than is now apparent.

29. Cassio. *Do...friend.* (Q.) F. omits.

S.D.[1] F. '*Exit Clo.*' (after l. 28) Q. omits.

S.D.[2] Q. F. after l. 28.

31. *Why...parted* (as in Q. F. and Al.) Cap.'s arrangement, dividing after 'broke', breaks the sense in the wrong place.

32–5. *I...access* (as in Al.) Q. prints as three lines (dividing after 'her' and '*Desdemona*'); F. as three lines (dividing after 'wife:' and '*Desdemona*').

35. *to you* (Q. F.) Possibly an interpolation.

39. S.D. Q. F. '*Exit.*' (after l. 38).

39–40. *I...honest* As Cassio is of Florence (cf. 1. 1. 20) and Iago of Venice (cf. 3. 3. 203–5), editors interpret as 'I never found a man more kind in my own country'; possibly Shakespeare temporarily forgot his distinction.

42. *sure* (F.) Q. 'soone' (for which there is much to be said).

48. *liking* (A.W. after S. Walker conj.) Q. F. 'likings'.

49. *To...front* (Q.) F. omits.

safest (Q.) J. read 'first' (plausibly to A.W.).

by the front To seize opportunity by the forelock was a commonplace; cf. *The Distichs of Cato* (a popular schoolbook):

> Rem tibi quam noris aptam dimittere noli:
> Fronte capillata, post est Occasio calva.

See Baldwin, i, 352, 603, 640, and cf. Tilley, T 311.

53. *Desdemon* With the trisyllabic variant (peculiar to F.) cf. Prosper (Prospero), Isabel (Isabella), Helen (Helena), Cressid (Cressida), Dian (Diana) etc.

55. S.D. (after Q.) F. omits.

3.2

S.D. *Loc.* (after Cap. and Al.) *Entry* (F.) Q.
'...*and other Gentlemen.*'

4. S.D. (A.W.) Q. F. omit.

6. *We'll* (F2 'Weel') F. 'Well'.

3.3

S.D. *Loc.* (after Cap. and Al.) *Entry* (Q. F.)

4. *case* (Q.) F. 'cause'.

13. *a politic distance* = [such aloofness] as public
policy dictates.

15. *Or feed* (Q. F.) Possibly an error for 'And
feed'. The alternative seems to lie between the policy's
being deliberately or accidentally prolonged. The
alternative to 'either' (l. 14) is perhaps not presented
until 'Or' in l. 16.

15–16. *Or feed...circumstance* i.e. or be maintained
for such slight and insubstantial reasons, or be aggravated so fortuitously.

16. *circumstance* (Q.) F. 'Circumstances'.

28. S.D. (Theob.) F. '*Enter Othello, and Iago.*';
Q. '*Enter* Othello, Iago, *and Gentlemen.*'

34. S.D. Q. F. '*Exit Cassio.*'

41. *you* (Q.) F. 'your'.

61. *or* (Q.) F. 'on'.

67. *their* (Rowe) Q. F. 'her'. See 1. 1. 152 n.

79. *or keep* (Q. F.) 'keep' (J.C.M. conj.).

80. *peculiar* (A.W. after Pope) Q. F. 'a peculiar'.
The omission gives better sense and better metre.

83. *full...weight* = very weighty (see G. 'poise')
and momentous.

88. *come* (J.D.W. after Pope) Q. F. 'come to thee'.

90. S.D. Q. '*Exit* Desd. *and* Em.'; F. '*Exit.*'

92. *But* = if...not; see Abbott, § 126.

92–3. *But I...come again* i.e. 'if I do not love you, and if ever I do not love you, Chaos will have come again.' 'He has so totally forgotten Iago's "Ha! I like not that," that the tempter has to begin all over again' (Bradley, p. 435). Cf. Introduction, pp. xxxvi ff.

94–5. *Did...love?* (as in F.) Q. (+most editors) divides after 'lady,'.

95. *you* (Q.) F. 'he'.

109–10. *Alas, thou echo'st...thy* (F.) Q. (+most editors) 'By heauen he ecchoes...his'. A.W. finds Q.'s reading (necessarily an aside) a bad blunder on two scores: that its indirectness is out of character, and that it loses the dramatic irony of 'as if there were some monster...'; of the kind of monster Iago was indeed hatching Othello has no suspicion as yet.

111. *dost* (F. full line) Q. 'didst'. A.W. prefers Q. as giving a firmer link with l. 113, and suspects the F. compositor altered the reading for his convenience.

112. *likedst* (Pope) Q. F. 'lik'st'.

115. *In* (Q.) F. 'Of'.

121. *honest* (A.W.) Q. F. 'Honestie'; 'full of... honesty' is lame in expression and metre.

126. *dilations* (F.) Q. 'denotements'. J.'s conj. 'delations', accepted by most modern editors except Hart and Kittredge, misses the point: 'dilations' was used for (i) stops, delays, and (ii) = 'dilatations', physiologically used for expansion of the arteries (believed to be air-ducts and including the windpipe) and so '*working* from the heart'. The meaning is that 'in an honest man these stops are due to the hidden motions of a heart that cannot suppress its feelings'.

130. *would...none* i.e. 'would they might no longer seem, or bear the shape of men' (J.).

134–5. *speak...ruminate*=speak to me in the kind of language you use when debating with yourself (i.e. be frank).

138. *that all...free to* (Q.) F. 'that: All...free'.
that=that which.

141. *a* (Q.) F. 'that'.

142. *But*=but that; see Abbott, §120.

But some (Q.) F. 'Wherein'. F., which fails to
convey the negative implicit in Q.'s 'But', may be
either a deliberate effort to sophisticate Q.'s idiom or
simply the compositor's recollection of l. 140.

143. *session* (Q.) F. 'Sessions'.

147–53. *I do...notice* The passage lies under
suspicion, but the line of thought (which is what
principally matters) is coherent if Q1's 'then' (see
note below) is restored at the end of l. 151. Iago has
already said that his thoughts may be vile and false
(ll. 139–44) and now, after parenthetically reiterating
that he may be wrong and confessing a proneness to
baseless suspicions, he begs Othello *on that account*
('then') to take no notice of a man liable to untrust-
worthy fancies. Q.'s 'then' is wanted (apart from
metrical considerations) to explain *why* it would be
wisdom in Othello to give the matter no further
thought and in Iago to conceal what he thinks. The
difficulty lies in the syntax, since 'then' is linked with
the parenthesis ('As I...are not') and not the main
subordinate clause ('Though...guess'). Q2's 'yet'
(if='nonetheless') improves the syntax but not the
sense; 'yet' (if='as yet') improves neither the syntax
nor the sense, since 'as yet' does not enter into the
argument until Iago has been ostensibly persuaded that
Othello will not allow the matter to rest on suspicion
l. 181 ff.).

150. *oft* (Q.) F. 'of'.

151. *that...wisdom then* (A.W.) F. 'that...wis-
dome'; Q2 (+many editors) 'that...wisedome yet';
Q1 'I intreate you then'.

152. *conceits* (F.) Q. 'coniects'. A.W. links 'con-

ceits' (=fancies) with 'shapes faults that are not';
J.D.W., preferring Q., associates 'conjects' with
'vicious in my guess...are not' (ll. 148–51) and
'scattering and unsure observance' (l. 154).

156. *or* (Q.) F. 'and'.

160 ff. *Who steals*... Almost a commonplace, which
Baldwin (ii, 275–6) refers to Erasmus, *De Conscri-
bendis Epistolis.*

166. *while 'tis* (A.W.) Q. F. 'whil'st 'tis'. The
emendation is wanted for euphony.

168. *green-eyed monster* Cf. *M.V.* 3. 2. 110, 'green-
eyed jealousy'.

168–9. *doth mock...feeds on* The rest of the speech
makes it clear that jealousy feeds on love, since the
argument runs that where there is no love there is no
jealousy; 'mock'=torment.

172. *fondly* (A.W. after Knight) Q. 'strongly';
F. 'soundly'. All that can be said for Q. and F. is that
they give approximately the right sense and alliteration;
but 'dotes, yet doubts, suspects, yet—loves' suggests
that a chiasmus was intended and that what qualifies
'love' must make it synonymous with 'dotes'.

173. *O misery* 'Spoken without reference to
himself' (Booth, cited Furness); 'it expresses an
imagined feeling, as also the speech which elicits it
professes to do (for Iago would not have dared here
to apply the term 'cuckold' to Othello)' (Bradley,
p. 434).

178 ff. *Why, why is this?*... An important speech.
Othello now sees what Iago is insinuating and in
ll. 185–8 makes it clear that what he has adduced is
worthless as evidence.

182. *Is once* (A.W.) Q. (+most editors) 'Is once
to be'; F. 'Is to be'. If the F. compositor was intended
to delete anything in the line, 'to be' are the suspect
words, since their removal throws all the emphasis on

'once', meaning first 'on one occasion' ('once in doubt') and then here 'once for all'.

184. *exsufflicate* (Q. F. 'exufflicate') A word not known to occur elsewhere but clearly = full of air, insubstantial.

blown (Q.) F. 'blow'd'. The same unattractive variant occurs in the F. *R. III*, 4. 4. 10 (a page set by the *Othello* compositor).

surmise (A.W.) Q. F. 'Surmises'. This should match in number with 'inference'.

186. *fair* (A.W.) Q. F. 'faire, feeds well'. An irrelevant interpolation which F. should have deleted (cf. l. 342 for the relevant context). This enumeration of Desdemona's attractions gains in significance when it is related to the context where Shakespeare met it— a passage in Cinthio's Introduction where the company is warned against the snares of beautiful courtesans whose plausible accomplishments ('sembianze di virtù') conceal evil minds: singing, playing, dancing well ('leggiadramente'), pleasing talk ('dolcemente favellare') and composing amorous trifles are mentioned as the acquired graces which deceive simple men (see 1853 ed. (Torino), i, 49). It is not surprising that 'feeding well' is not mentioned. This is only referred to by Cinthio, in another context, as a male vice.

187. *well* (Q.) F. omits.

195. *it* (Q.) F. 'this'.

200. *eye* (Q.) F. 'eyes'. Though the *novella* has 'se terrete aperti gli occhi', the Q. reading is less prosaic and more idiomatic; 'thus' = therefore.

204–6. *In Venice...unknown* Apart from the particular relevance here, Venice was noted for its courtesans; cf. *Ado*, 1. 1. 255–6.

205 *best conscience* = highest conception of morality.

206. *keep't* (Q 2) F. 'kept'; Q 1, 'keepe'.

210. *Why then* (A.W.) Q. F. 'Why go too then'.

The extrametrical words are too familiar and, what is worse, break the thread of the argument. Iago is not dismissing the point Othello has made (which 'go to' implies) but, on the contrary, following it up.

212. *seel* See G. The *novella* has 'appannati gli occhi' (=hoodwink); with 'close' the metaphor shifts to the close grain of 'oak'.

214. *of* = for. Constructions with 'beseech' varied a great deal and 'of' here seems a natural choice since 'for' (=on account of) follows.

217. *In faith* (Q.) F. 'Trust me'.

219. *my* (Q.) F. 'your'.

220. *am to* The idiom expresses duty, obligation (=must).

221. *grosser ... larger* Equivocal; see G.

224. *success* Neutral in sense (=sequel).

225. *As* (Q.) F. 'Which' (a sophistication).

at (Q.) F. omits. O.E.D. ('aim' verb 4) accepts F.'s transitive use, citing a parallel *c.* 1400, but 'aim at' seems to have been the usual expression at this date in the sense of 'calculate' and 'aim' seems to have been used transitively only in the vaguer sense of 'guess', 'conjecture'.

227. *but* = but that; see Abbott, §120.

229. *nature* = (as usual) 'human nature'. 'And yet', broods Othello, 'our human nature often goes astray, departs from the norm'—a general reflection upon which Iago seizes to recall the scene (and Brabantio's words) of 1. 3. 62 ('For nature so preposterously to err') and 1. 3. 94–101. Cf. Introduction, p. xl.

234. *such* (pronominal) = persons of the fore-mentioned kind (ll. 231–2).

235. *disproportion* (Q.) F. 'disproportions'; 'foul disproportion' = deformity, depravity.

238–9. *recoiling ... forms* 'Iago is here deeply and designedly insulting' (Hart). Othello never takes

offence at reflections upon his race and colour; he seems
to accept them as inevitable, though we must ourselves suppose them to be exceedingly painful. Hence,
'form' = style of beauty, good looks (O.E.D. 1 *e*).

240. *happily* The common trisyllabic form of 'haply'.

243. S.D. (Rowe) Q. F. omit.

246. S.D. (after Cap.) Q. F. omit.

248. *Although 'tis* (F.) Q. 'Tho it be'. A.W.
suspects sophistication in F.

250. *hold* (Q.) F. omits.

252. *strain his entertainment* = presses for his reinstatement; see G. 'entertainment'.

259. S.D. Q. F. '*Exit.*'

261–2. *knows ...dealings* = has an expert knowledge
of all kinds of human affairs.

261. *qualities* (Q.) F. 'Quantities'.

263. *jesses ...heart-strings* Hawks were released
with the jesses (see G.) attached, and the 'heart-strings'
(see G.) were the vital strings.

264. *whistle ...wind* See G. 'down'. To whistle off
a falcon down the wind was to set it free and this was
done with a haggard that proved untamable (see
Madden, p. 192); see also Tilley, W 432; 'to go down
the wind' = 'to go to ruin'.

267. *chamberers* See G., but with particular
reference to 1. 2. 26 and 1. 3. 81–7, implying contrast
with 'unhousèd' and 'the tented field'. Iago has
shaken Othello's self-confidence and in this retro-
spective and introspective passage he has, of course,
a particular 'chamberer' (Cassio) in mind.

275. *of* (Q.) F. 'to'.

279. S.D. (after Q. F., Q. placing after l. 281).

280. *O, then* (Q.) F. omits.
mocks (Q.) F. 'mock'd'.

284–5. *Why ...well?* As in F. Q.'s arrangement
as one line is perhaps preferable.

284. *faintly* (F.) Possibly a sophistication, since 'faint' (=faintly) would be idiomatic; Q. reads 'Why is your speech so faint'.

286. *upon my forehead* Alludes to the cuckold's horns.

287. *Faith* (Q.) F. 'Why'.

289. S.D. (after Cap.) Q. F. omit.

291. S.D. (after Q., placing opposite ll. 292–3) F. '*Exit*.' (after l. 290).

292. *I've* (Elze conj.) Q. F. 'I haue'.

298–9. *I'll...Iago* See G. 'take (out)'. Such patterns were highly valued; see note to ll. 436–7.

301. *I nothing...fantasy* i.e. I only know how to humour his whim.

S.D. (after Q. F., Q. placing after l. 300).

304. *A thing* (Q.) F. 'You haue a thing'.

thing— Iago first insults her (see G. 'thing', 'common'; and cf. Falstaff to Quickly, *1 H. IV*, 3. 3. 116 ff.) and then warned by her 'Ha!' changes course.

312. *stole* (Q.) F. 'stolne'.

313. *No, faith* (Q.) F. 'No: but'.

315. *it is* (Q.) F. ''tis'.

316. *you've* (Hudson) Q. F. 'you haue'.

317. S.D. (Rowe) Q. F. omit.

what's (Q.) F. 'what is'.

318. *If't* (Q2) Q1, F. 'If it'.

322. S.D. Q. F. '*Exit Æmil.*' (Q. after l. 323).

327–8. *poison...poisons* The repetition has been suspected, but A.W. finds it plausible that Iago should use a metaphor and then laboriously explain it; J.D.W. would emend 'poison' in l. 327 (Q. omits) to 'potion' (S. Walker conj.): 'the similarity of the two words one under the other would readily lead to the F. misprint'.

331. S.D. (after Q. F.; Q. after l. 330, F. after l. 331).

332. *poppy, nor mandragora* opiates; see G.

335. *Ha! Ha!* ... Othello does not notice Iago's presence until he plucks him by the sleeve in l. 336 and even then scarcely heeds his words until he rounds upon him in l. 361.

337. *Avaunt!* (as to a devil); see G.

340. *of her* (Q.) F. 'in her'.

342. *fed well, was* (A.W.) F. 'fed well, was free, and'; Q. 'was free, and'. The F. correction seems to have been made without removing the Q. words it was intended to replace; cf. l. 186 n.

348. *Pioneers* Stressed on the first syllable and commonly spelt 'pioners', 'pyoners' at the time.

352. *make* (F 2) Q. F. 'makes'. See 1. 1. 152 n.
farewell! (Pope) Q. F. 'farewell,'.

362. *give me the ocular proof* Cf. Introduction, p. xvii.
S.D. (after Cap.) Q. F. omit. Rowe's 'Catching hold on him' probably follows an old tradition; see Sprague, pp. 197–200.

363. *mine* (F.) Q. 'mans'. The particularity of F.'s asseveration (the most solemn Othello could make) seems preferable to the Q. generalization.

371. *abandon all remorse* 'throw aside all restraints' (J.).

372. *horror's* (Hanmer) Q. F. 'Horrors'.

378. *liv'st* (Q.) F. 'lou'st'.

381. *profit* = 'profitable lesson' (On.), i.e. 'to be direct ... is not safe'.

388. *Her* (Q 2) F. 'My'; Q 1 omits the speech.

393. *sir,* (Q.) F. omits.

395. *and will* (A.W. after Pope) F. 'and I will'; Q. 'I will'. F.'s 'and' might easily have been interpolated in anticipation of Iago's 'And may', but it adds something to the sense (=not only ... but also) as well as to the dramatic effect of Iago's reply if we

take 'and' as a genuine correction but intended to replace Q.'s 'I'; cf. the echo of Othello's words at ll. 441–2: 'If it be that...' (and elsewhere). Cf. also *1 H. IV*, 5. 2. 35, 'Marry, and shall', and Abbott, §98.

397. *supervisor* (Q.) F. 'super-vision'.

gape on— (Dyce) Q. 'gape on,'; F. 'gape on?'.

408. *imputation...circumstance* A hendiadys = the implication of circumstantial evidence.

circumstance (A.W.) Q. F. 'circumstances'.

410. *might* (F.) Q. 'may', which is grammatically more logical, but F. seems more in character in view of 'I do not like the office' (l. 412).

424. *and* (Q.) F. omits.

426. *then* (Q.) F. omits.

427–8. *Over...sighed...kissed...Cried* (Q.) F. 'ore ...sigh...kisse...cry'. The F. verbs suggest tinkering with a view to carrying on the construction of ll. 423–4 ('would he gripe...'), but the ravelling may be due to the compositor's being distracted by the muddle he was making of the verse lining, which is here very confused.

430. *foregone conclusion* = past experience.

431. *'Tis...dream* Q. (+Al.) gives this to Iago.

434. *Nay, but* (Q.) F. 'Nay yet'.

yet...done 'This is an oblique and secret mock at Othello's saying "Give me the ocular proof" ' (Warb.).

436–7. *a handkerchief...strawberries* = a handkerchief 'embroidered with a strawberry pattern' (On.); see G. 'spot'. The handkerchief was 'one of the costly accessories necessary to every fashionable man and woman of this period and usually carried in the hand to show their richness. Some were of cutwork...some edged with gold and tassels...some 'spotted' with embroidery as was Othello's' (Linthicum, p. 270).

442. *any that* (Mal.) Q. F. 'any, it'. The emendation is clearly wanted, since both the iteration and the

element of doubt are in character and the Q. F.
assertion is not.

444. *the slave* i.e. Cassio.

446. Q. F. 'Looke heere *Iago*,'.

449. *thy…cell* (Q.) F. 'the…hell'. In either case,
hell, the abode of Ate is meant, but F.'s reading is too
obvious and loses the effectiveness of the triple invoca-
tion by substituting 'the' for 'thy'; 'hell' for 'cell' may
be merely due to assimilation to 'hollow' (cf. 'Revenge's
cave', *Tit.* 3. 1. 271, and 'Rouse up revenge from ebon
den', *2 H. IV*, 5. 5. 37).

450. *hearted throne* 'the heart on which thou wast
enthroned' (J.); cf. *Tw.N.* 1. 1. 37–9.

454. *perhaps* (Q.) F. omits.

455–8. *like to the Pontic sea…Hellespont* A recollection of Pliny: 'out of Pontus the sea alwaies floweth
and never ebbeth againe' (Holland's *Pliny*, iv. 13,
cited Hart). 'The rush of imaginative reminiscence…
here is of *precisely the same character* as the reminiscences
of the Arabian trees and the base Indian in Othello's
final speech' (Bradley, p. 431).

457. *feels* (Q2) F. 'keepes'; Q1 omits ll. 455–62
('Iago…heaven'). Clearly one of F.'s errors of anticipation and Q2's emendation has custom in its favour;
'knows' (Southern MS. in Camb.) is attractive.

463. S.D. Q. '*he kneeles*' (after l. 452) F. omits.

464. S.D. Q. '*Iago kneeles*' (after l. 466) F. omits.

470. *without remorse* (J.D.W. after anon. in Camb.)
Q. 'remorce'; F. 'in me remorse'. Presumably a
corrupt line, since it is difficult to see how 'remorse'
could mean 'solemn obligation' (On.'s gloss). The
emendation shores up the sense. J. C. Maxwell
compares Iago's with Sinon's speech, *Aen.* ii. 154–9:
'vos aeterni ignes…teneor patriae nec legibus ullis'.

471. S.D. (Camb. after Cap.) Q. F. omit.

475–7. *My friend…her!* As in Q. F. (spinning

out the matter so that the scene end corresponded with the page end) divides after 'dead;' and 'request'.

477. *damn her, damn her* (F.) Q. 'dam her'. Capell's rearrangement, reading 'My...request.' as one line, combined with Q.'s 'damn her' (once only), may be correct. On the other hand, F.'s 'damn her' should perhaps have been repeated again, thus restoring the metre.

3.4

S.D. *Loc.* (See 3.3. *Loc.*) *Entry* (F.) Q. '*Enter Desdemonia Emilla and the Clowne.*'

5. *one* (Q.) F. 'me'.

6. *is* (Q.) F. ''tis'.

stabbing Hart compares Dekker, *Seven Deadly Sins*, 'He that gives a soldier the Lye, lookes to receaue the stab'.

13. *lie...throat*=be guilty of a deliberate lie. The gradations of a lie were from the teeth to the lungs and heart (cf. 5. 2. 159), or even to the entrails.

16–7. *catechize...answer* The Clown picks up the religious association of 'edify', promising to ask the given questions and return the correct answers.

21–2. *To do...it* The lines are usually printed as prose (as in Q. and F.) but two rhyming lines ('...wit ...it') were perhaps intended. Q.'s 'I'le' (for 'I will') and 'of it' (for 'it') do not, however, restore the metre of the second line.

22. S.D. F. '*Exit Clo.*'

23. *that* (Q.) F. 'the'. Cf. Introduction, p. xlii n.

24. *I know not* She obeys her husband (3. 3. 321).

25. *lose* (Q.) F. 'haue lost'. Q. is more idiomatic.

29. *Is...jealous?* To the wife of Iago all husbands must be jealous.

33. S.D. As in Dyce. Q. places after 'him' in l. 31; F. after l. 31.

34. S.D. Aside first in Hanmer.

36. *moist*. A moist palm was taken to signify an amorous nature; cf. *Ven.* 25–6, 'his sweating palm, The precedent of pith and livelihood'.

37. *yet* (Q.) F. omits.

hath (F.) Q. 'has' (perhaps preferable for euphony).

age ...sorrow Both were supposed to dry up the blood; cf. *Ado*, 2. 1. 107, 4. 1. 192; *Ant* 4. 9. 17; and *Rom*. 3. 5. 59 n. What Othello means is not caught by Desdemona.

42. *there's* (Daniel conj.) Q. F. 'heere's'. The Q. F. reading may be an anticipation of 'here' later in the line or a misreading, since 'th' is easily misread 'h' in the secretary hand.

43. *rebels* Often used by Shakespeare with specific allusion to unrestrained natural impulses.

47. *our new heraldry* The thought passes from 'liberal' (see G.), implying gentle birth, to 'heraldry' (associated with the symbols of honour) and 'hands' and 'hearts' (as the symbols of good faith and affection). The meaning is 'marriage used to be a guarantee of affection, but it is now a mark of honour for marriage to be no assurance of love'. Possibly Othello has in mind the 'best conscience' of the Venetians (see 3. 3. 203–6). His riddling words are again lost on Desdemona. There is no need to force a topical allusion into the speech.

58. *That handkerchief* See 3. 3. 436–7 n.

59. *Egyptian* Probably a true Egyptian (not, as frequently at this time, a gipsy).

67. *wive* (Q.) F. 'Wiu'd'.

70. *lose't* (F.) Q. 'loose', perhaps rightly, as more idiomatic and euphonious; F. suggests sophistication.

73–5. *A sibyl ...work* Her longevity was plainly suggested by the Sibyl of Cumae (cf. *M.V.* 1. 2. 101; *Shr*. 1. 2. 69 and G.), whose prophetic fury was well-

known from Virgil. For the possible source of the lines, see Introduction, pp. xv–xvii.

80. *God* (Q.) F. 'Heauen'.

83. *is it* (Q.) F. 'is't'.

84. *Heaven* (Q.) F. omits, perhaps rightly.

87. *How* (F.) Q. 'Ha', which may be the correct interpretation of the ejaculation.

90. *sir,* (Q.) F. omits.

96–7. Desdemona. *I...handerchief!* (Q.) F. omits.

102. S.D. F. '*Exit Othello.*'

103. *Is...jealous?* She reverts to l. 29, having followed Othello's tantrums all this while. Critics are puzzled by her silence about the handkerchief: but her mind is busy not with handkerchiefs but with husbands. See ll. 162–6 below and J.D.W.'s discussion of Bridges on this point in *Aspects of Shakespeare* (British Academy Lectures, 1933), pp. 206–8.

108. *but*=merely; see Abbott, §128.

109. *hungerly* Also in *Shr.* 3. 2. 173 and *Tim.* 1. 1. 262; cf. 'angerly' (*Gent.* 1. 2. 63; *Macb.* 3. 5. 1).

110. S.D. Q. F. '*Enter Iago, and Cassio*' (Q. after l. 106, F. after 'belch us').

112. *the happiness!*=what luck!

117. *office*=devoted service (with allusion to the offices of the Church); cf. *Ant.* 1. 1. 5, 'office and devotion'. Q.'s 'duty' was a bad blunder.

120. *sorrow* (A.W. after S. Walker conj.) Q. F. 'Sorrowes'.

124. *clothe ...content*=perforce appear resigned.

141. *is he* (F.) Q. 'can he be'. Although the F. reading is metrically defective, it is probably nearer the truth than Q., which looks like an echo of l. 138. The reading should perhaps be 'is he now angry'.

144. S.D. F. '*Exit*' (after l. 143) Q. omits.

145. *unhatched* A frequent image with Shakespeare.

147. *puddled* 'Troubled' water was another

favourite image; cf. *Wint.* 1. 2. 325, 'Dost think I am so muddy, so unsettled'.

150–2. *For...pain* Refers to the sympathy between the body's members, often figuratively applied to the mental state of man or the body politic.

151. *members* (J.D.W. after Pope) Q. F. 'members, euen'. It looks as if 'euen' had been caught from l. 149.

155. *unhandsome* The word carries three meanings: (i) lack of fairness in appearance (recalling 2. 1. 179, 'O my fair warrior!'), (ii) unfairness in judgment, and (iii) unskilfulness in one's profession (since the word was primarily associated with 'hand'=skill). The last two meanings are here uppermost, and with painful truth Desdemona finds her grasp of the situation inept.

156. *Arraigning...soul*=charging him with unkindness to me.

165. *'tis* (Q.) F. 'It is'.

167. *that* (Q.) F. 'the' (full line).

169. *hereabout* (F 3) Q. F. 'heere about'.

172. S.D.¹ (after Q., placing opposite ll. 170–1); F. '*Exit*' (after l. 171).

S.D.² Q. after 'Cassio', l. 173.

173. *'Save* The apostrophe indicates (as in many F. texts) the colloquial omission of 'God'.

174. *is it* (Q.) F. 'is't'.

175. *In faith* (Q.) F. 'Indeed'.

182–3. *in...absence* i.e. make up for this neglect when I have more leisure; see G. 'continuate', 'score'.

183. S.D. (after Rowe) Q. F. omit.

191. *by my faith* (Q.) F. 'in good troth'.

192. *neither* An emphatic double negative.

194. *I'ld* (Q. 'I'de') F. 'I would'.

4. 1

S.D. *Loc.* (See 3. 3. *Loc.*) *Entry* (F.) Q. '*Enter Iago and* Othello,'.

9. *So* (Q.) F. 'If'.

17. *They…not* i.e. they are credited with what they have lost—a reminder of the Venetian pranks of 3. 3. 204–6 ('not to leave't undone, but keep't unknown').

21. *raven* Commonly believed to be a bird of ill omen (cf. *Macb.* 1. 5. 37–9), and this superstitition, rather than the belief that it carried infection on its wings (cf. *Tp.* 1. 2. 322–4 and *Jew of Malta*, 2. 1. 1–4) is alluded to here: the reminder spells death to hope of Desdemona's innocence.

infected (Q.) F. 'infectious'.

28. *Convinced…supplied* See G. The former word looks back to 'by their own importunate suit', the latter to 'voluntary dotage'.

32. *Faith* (Q.) F. 'Why'.

36. *'Zounds,* (Q.) F. omits.

38. *confess and be hanged* A proverbial phrase of obscure origin (O.E.D. 'confess' 10)=to tell a gross lie (connected therefore with the quibble on 'lie on' and 'belie' in ll. 35–6). Othello is also thinking of Cassio's confession of guilt and the penalty to be paid.

38–9. *first…to confess* i.e. he must die with no shriving time allowed.

39–41. *Nature…instruction* 'A blackness suddenly intervenes between his eyes and the world; he takes it for the shuddering testimony of nature to the horror he has just heard, and he falls senseless to the ground' (Bradley, p. 196).

40. *shadowing*=both the darkness of eclipse and its symbolic and sympathetic significance; cf. 5. 2. 102–4.

42. *Noses...lips* Cf. *Wint.* 1. 2. 284–6, but perhaps also to be associated with 4. 2. 78–81.

43. S.D. (F.) Q. 'He *fals downe*.' F. has undoubtedly the more Shakespearian touch; see G. 'trance'.

45. *My medicine, work* (Q.) F. 'My Medicine workes'.

45–7. *Thus...reproach* Cf. this address to the audience with that of Leontes in *Wint.* 1. 2. 190 ff. and note there to 192–3.

48. S.D. (Q. F.; Q. after the line).

52. *Rub...temples* 'Stroake it on the temples for the Lytargie' (Langham, *Garden of Health*, cited O.E.D. 'lethargy' 1).

No, forbear; (Q.) F. omits.

53. *lethargy*=coma (characteristic of catalepsy).

his=its.

56. *while.* (Al. 'while;') Q. F. 'while,'. The imperative implied by Al.'s punctuation is better than the Q. F. comma, making 'Do...while' conditional.

58. S.D. (after Q 2 and Rowe) Q 1, F. omit.

59. *your head* Alluding to the cuckold's horns.

60. *you! no* (Q.) F. 'you not'.

63–4. *There's...monster* Cf. *Wint.* 1. 2. 206–7.

66. *yoked*=married (with insulting allusion to horned draught-oxen).

68. *unproper* See G. Onions questions Schmidt's gloss 'improper', but cf. *Lr.* 5. 3. 221.

71. *secure* Here stressed on the first syllable.

73. *know what shall be* (A.W.) Q. F. 'I know what she shall be'; Steev. conj. om. 'she'. The Q. F. reading seems nonsense: if he knows he is a cuckold, he knows what she is and has been. What the words should mean is 'knowing I am cuckolded, know what follows' (i.e. what measures to take), thus adding point to Othello's 'O, thou art wise'.

75. *in a patient list* = 'within the bounds of patience' (Collins, cited Furness).

77. *unsuiting* (Q. corr.) Q. (uncorr.) 'vnfitting'; F. 'resulting'.

79. *scuse upon* (Q.) F. 'scuses vpon'. Emendation of F. is wanted for metre and Q. seems more likely to be right than F 2's 'scuses on'.

80. *and* (A.W.) Q. F. 'and heere'. After 'return', 'here' is redundant, as well as extra-metrical; it was presumably a stop-gap in Q., which has 'retire' for F.'s 'returne'.

87. *gestures* (A.W.) Q. F. 'gesture'. Cf. l. 102 and the plurals in l. 82.

88. *a spleen* (J.D.W. after J. conj.) Q. F. 'in Spleene'. Probably an error of repetition in Q.; 'a spleen' is wanted in antithesis to 'a man'. The spleen was thought to prompt all irrational impulses, and what distinguished man was reason.

92. S.D. (Camb.) Q. F. omit.

94. *hussy* (A.W.) Q. F. 'Huswife'; see 2. 1. 112 n.

95. *clothes* (Q.) F. 'Cloath'.

98. *refrain* (Q.) F. 'restraine'. The Q. reading is in accordance with Eliz. idiom and F.'s very probably the compositor's perversion.

99. S.D. (after Q. F.; Q. placing after l. 97).

101. *unbookish* An important word dramatically = unlearned in the ways of the world; cf. Othello's opinion of Iago—'wise' (l. 74) and 'knows all qualities, with a learnéd spirit, of human dealings' (3. 3. 261–2).

construe (Rowe) F. 'conserue'; Q. 'conster'. Possibly a sophistication in F.

102. *behaviours* The plural was frequently used where modern idiom requires the singular.

103. *now* (Q.) F. omits.

107. *power* (Q.) F. 'dowre', which is irrelevant; 'power' to grant the suit is wanted.

109 etc. S.D. Asides first in Theob.

110. *a* (Q.) F. omits.

111. *in faith* (Q.) F. 'indeed'.

119. *you ... you* (Q.) F. 'ye ... you'.

Roman 'Ironically' (J.); with reference to a Roman triumph, but also spoken with the consciousness of the difference between himself, the barbarian African, and a super-civilized Italian.

120. *her* (Q.) F. omits.

I prithee (Q.) F. 'prythee'. It looks as if this pronoun, like the earlier 'her', has been suppressed in the interests of F.'s verse arrangement of ll. 120–2.

120–1. *bear ... wit* = give me credit for some sense.

123. *win* (F4) Q. F. 'winnes'.

124. *Faith* (Q.) F. 'Why'.

that you (F.) Q. 'you shall'. A.W. prefers Q. or 'that you shall' (F3).

127. *scored* To 'score' meant originally 'cut', 'notch', and is used in this sense in *Ant.* 4. 7. 12. It was also generally used in connection with reckoning (cf. 3. 4. 183) and 'made my reckoning' is how the word is usually explained here. But Othello's last remark ('they laugh that win' = he laughs best who laughs last) suggests F. may be an error for 'scorned'. Cassio's ridicule and the proverbial fate of the scorner (see Prov. xix. 29) make error seem likely.

129–30. *her own love and flattery* = amour propre and conceit.

131. *beckons* (Q.) F. 'becomes', suggesting the collator's misreading of 'becons'.

134. *the bauble* (F. full line) Q. 'this bauble'.

135. *by this hand* (Q.) F. omits.

falls (F.) Q. (+editors) 'she fals'. The Q. pronoun breaks the metaphor of the bauble (see G.), hanging and dangling ('lolling') round Cassio's neck.

139. *shakes* (F.) Q. (+most editors) 'hales'.

'Hales' and 'pulls' amount to the same thing; 'shakes' and 'pulls' suggest both pulling about and plucking on.

145. *such another fitchew* 'Such another' was a good natured but often contemptuous expression for 'no better than another'; hence 'a regular polecat'. The 'fitchew' was associated with lechery (cf. *Lr.* 4.6.124–5) and used (fig.) for 'prostitute'.

145–6. *a perfumed one* Perfumes were associated with prostitutes (cf. *Tim.* 4. 3. 207, 'diseased perfumes') from classical times (cf. Lat. *schoeniculae*).

146. S.D. As in Dyce. F. places after l. 144; Q. after l. 143.

152. *not know* (Q.) F. 'know not'. Q. carries on the construction.

159–60. *An...an* (Q.) F. 'If...if'. Q.'s colloquialisms give speed to Bianca's flouncing exit.

160. S.D. Q. F. '*Exit*'.

162. *Faith,* (Q.) F. omits.
street (Q.) F. 'streets'.

164. *Faith* (Q.) F. 'Yes'.

168. S.D. Q. '*Exit* Cassio.' F. omits.

169. S.D. (after Cap.) Q. F. omit.

174. *by this hand* (F.) An impudently appropriate asseveration, which the F. expurgator overlooked. Q. omits the speech.

191. *a thousand, thousand* (Q.) F. 'a thousand, a thousand'.

192–3. *gentle...gentle* Used by Othello = 'well born', by Iago = 'lavish in favours'.

196. *be* (Q.) F. 'are'; cf. 3. 3. 248 n.

206. *Do...poison* An echo of the *novella*, where the possibility of poisoning Desdemona is discussed but dismissed as risky. Iago will not be implicated.

212. S.D. Q. '*A Trumpet.*' (after l. 211) F. omits.

213. S.D. Q. F. place after l. 211.

213–4. *I warrant...with him* (J.D.W., A.W.)

Neither text seems satisfactory. Q. reads

> Something from *Venice* sure, tis *Lodouico*,
> Come from the Duke, and see your wife is with him.

F. has

> I warrant something from Venice,
> 'Tis *Lodouico*, this, comes from the Duke.
> See, your wife's with him.

F.'s first line apparently corrects a memorial error in Q., but from this point F.'s splitting of the first line led to disorder, best remedied by conflation. Editors have generally followed Q. substantially, but there can be little doubt that Q.'s 'sure, tis *Lodouico*' was an anticipation of Iago's words at 5. 1. 190, the more explicable because of the mention, in both contexts, of Venice.

214. *and see* (Q.) F. 'See'.
wife is (Q.) F. 'wife's'.
215. *God* (Q.) F. omits.
With all my heart Used in the exchange of compliments (= I thank you); cf. *Shr.* Ind. i. 81–2, *Lr.* 4. 6. 32.
216. *senators* (Q.) F. 'the Senators'.
S.D. (Rowe). Q. F. omit.
217. S.D. (after Cap.) Q. F. omit.
225. S.D. Aside first in Theob.
227. S.D. (Theob.) Q. F. omit.
232, 234, 238 S.D. Aside (J.D.W.).
234. S.N. Oth. (Q. F.) After Othello's preceding outburst, the tone suggests some other speaker—either Iago (Fechter conj., cited Camb.), remonstrating aside to Othello, or more likely (since Desdemona asks him for an explanation) Lodovico, rebuking Desdemona for a second interruption of Othello's reading (A.W.) J.D.W. endorses the O.E.D. gloss of 'wise' (= sane) and believes the Q. F. speech prefix to be correct.
235. *the letter* (Q.) F. 'thLetter'.
238. *By my troth* (Q.) F. 'Trust me'.

239. *mad* (Q. F.) 'A puzzle to modern editors
though none in the 18th century seemed to find it so.
Till now Othello has ignored her; his comments on
her unhappily ambiguous remarks, being asides, she
only half hears. But when she actually says she is
"glad" her lover is to supplant Othello, and to be left in
Cyprus, presumably with her, he assumes she is really
beside herself with illicit passion and confronts her
with this savage irony. Shocked at the fury she at last
sees in his face, she exclaims "Why sweet Othello!"
At this he loses all control of himself and strikes her,
since he interprets the affection in her voice and
expression as devilish hypocrisy' (J.D.W.). A.W. thinks
'madam' (Nicholson conj. in Camb.) is the true
reading. It is then the unwonted formality of Othello's
greeting that startles Desdemona. What precipitates
this crisis should be conveyed in the dialogue and the
dramatic point of Othello's style of address and
Desdemona's reply would have been taken immediately
in the seventeenth century.

240. S.D. (Theob.) Q. F. omit.

243. *'Tis very much*=it is a shocking business; cf.
M.V. 3. 5. 37, *1 H. VI*, 4. 1. 192.

245. *teem* See G. An allusion to the doctrine of
spontaneous generation, according to which the sun
bred maggots in a dead dog (*Ham.* 2. 2. 181) or
quickened the fat and slimy mud of Nile to produce
crocodiles (cf. *Ant.* 1. 3. 68–9, 2. 7. 26–7); cf.
Golding's Ovid, i. 495–522.

247. S.D. (Rowe) Q. F. omit.

248. *an* (Q.) F. omits.

254. *turn and turn* See G. Cf. *1 H. VI*, 3. 3. 85,
'Done like a Frenchman: turn, and turn again!', and,
for the sexual sense, *M.V.* 1. 3. 78, 3. 4. 78.

261. *avaunt* Cf. 3. 4. 102 ('Away') and 4. 1. 247
('Out of my sight'), and see G.

S.D. (after Rowe) Q. F. omit.

264. *Goats and monkeys* Proverbially lecherous: Iago's words (3. 3. 405) 'still ring in the ears of Othello' (Mal.).

S.D. Q. F. '*Exit.*'

268–9. *The shot...pierce* i.e. was impervious to the slings and arrows of Fortune.

271. *censure* (Jennens) Q. 'censure,'; F. 'censure.' Jennens's pointing gives better sense; i.e. 'I should not like to say whether he is out of his mind or not; if he is not, he is the worse for that' (i.e. only madness could excuse his actions).

276. *work...blood*=anger him.

277. *new-create* (hyphen Pope).

this (Q.) F. 'his'.

4. 2

S.D. *Loc.* (after Mal. and Al.) *Entry* (Q. F.).

3. *Yes* 'Used to correct a negative statement' (On.)=but. J.D.W. conj. 'Yet'.

she Cf. Abbott, §211.

16. *the serpent's curse* i.e. God's curse for beguiling Eve.

19. S.D. Q. F. '*Exit Æmilia.*' (Q. placing after 'slander.').

21. *This...whore* Refers to Desdemona, not Emilia, who is a 'bawd'.

22. *A closet...key* i.e. one who keeps the key of all her secrets; see G. 'closet', and cf. *H.V.* 2. 2. 96 and *Ham.* 1. 3. 86.

24. *Pray* (Q.) F. 'Pray you'.

27. S.D. (Hanmer) Q. F. omit.

27–8. *Some...alone* i.e. Come, about your business, Mistress Bawd! Leave us alone. Othello addresses Emilia as if she kept a brothel; a 'door-keeper' was a bawd (cf. *Per.* 4. 6. 120).

30. S.D. Q. F. '*Exit Æmi.*'

31. *knees* (Q.) F. 'knee' (full line).

33. *But…words* (Q.) F. omits.

45. *haply* (Q.) F. 'happely'.

48. *Why*, (Q.) F. omits.

48–54. *Had it…patience* i.e. Had God tried him as Job was tried, he might have shown Job's patience.

49. *had they* (F.) Q. 'had he'. For the change in number, cf. *R. II*, 1. 2. 6–7, *Ham.* 3. 4. 173–5.

55. *A* (Q.) F. 'The'.

for the time of scorn A.W. takes this in the temporal sense (as in the biblical 'time of tribulation'), comparing Brabantio's 'And what's to come of my despiséd time Is nought but bitterness' (1. 1. 162–3); J.D.W explains (with Schmidt) as = 'for the scornful world', citing *Ham.* 3. 1. 70, 'the scorns of time'.

56. *slow unmoving* (Q.) F. 'slow, and mouing'. 'Slow' refers to the slow passage of time, 'unmoving' to Time's finger, unwaveringly fixed on Othello. Cf. *R. II*, 1. 3. 150–51, 'The sly slow hours shall not determinate The dateless limit of thy dear exile'.

60–3. *The fountain…gender in* Reflects Prov. v. 15–8 and note in Genevan version (Noble, pp. 67–8), which (exhorting to refrain from whoredom) speaks of a wife as a man's 'own cistern' and 'well', and of children born in wedlock as 'rivers' therefrom.

63–5. *Turn…hell!* A difficult passage. The general sense seems to be that Patience, conceived as one of God's cherubim looking down from heaven, turns grim as hell at the sight of Desdemona's adultery. For cherubs as the eyes of heaven, cf. *Ham.* 4. 3. 47 n. and *Il Penseroso*, 54, 'The Cherub Contemplation'. But there is probably some corruption, possibly an omission, as the transition is so abrupt.

65. *Ay, there* (Theob.) Q. F. 'I heere'.

70. *ne'er* (Q.) F. 'neuer'.

79. *The bawdy wind* Cf. *M.V.* 2. 6. 16, 'Hugged and embracéd by the strumpet wind'.

80. *the hollow mine of earth* The cave of the winds (*Aen.* 1. 50–63).

81. *hear it* (Steev.) Q. F. 'hear't'.

82. *Impudent strumpet!* (Q.) F. omits. *Impudent*=shameless (not 'saucy').

84. *this vessel* 'Echoes 1 Thess. iv. 4' (Mal.).

85. *other* (F.) J.D.W. conj., 'other's'.

foul Adverbial. The words are elliptical = 'not to preserve my chastity from the heinously wicked (i.e. sacrilegious) touch of another'.

91. S.D. (Globe) Q. F. omit.

93. *keep* (Rowe) Q. F. 'keepes'.

S.D. As in Dyce. Q. F. '*Enter Æmilia*' (Q. after 'saved', l. 87; F. after l. 91).

94. *We've* (Dyce ii, 'We ha' Q.) F. 'We haue'.

95. S.D. Q. F. '*Exit.*'

105. *by water*=(i) as tears, (ii) uselessly; to write in or on water was proverbially unavailing.

107. S.D. Q. F. '*Exit.*' R. M. Alden suggested (*M.L.R.* x (1915), p. 376) that Emilia's exit should be delayed until after 'meet' in l. 108 on the grounds that l. 108 is at odds with ll. 109–10, but it seems more natural to assume that the whole speech is one of self-reproach for not knowing what offence she has given unawares. Cf. her self-criticism at 3. 4. 155.

109–10. *How…least misuse* (F.) Q. 'How… greatest abuse'. F. implies more than it says; Q. says more than is implied. The meaning of F. is 'how enormous my smallest fault must have been that the least significance could be attached to it'. Onions glosses 'opinion' as='censure', but the word was usually neutral in sense.

110. S.D. Q. F. '*Enter Iago, and Æmilia.*' (Q. opposite l. 111).

115. *What's* (F4) Q. F. 'What is'.

118. *As...bear* (Q.) F. 'That...beare it' (suggesting sophistication).

heart (F. uncorrected, Oxford facsimile) Q. F. (corrected) 'hearts'. Editors have preferred the plural, but the reference is surely to Desdemona. Emilia is explaining the cause of Desdemona's dejection.

120. *said* (F.) Q. (+most editors) 'sayes'. She refers to 'bewhored' in l. 116.

129. *It is my wretched fortune* Probably alluding to her ill-starred name (δυσδαίμων), about the significance of which nothing is said in the *novella*; but in the discussion at the beginning of the following tale the company blamed Desdemona's parents for having given her a name of ill omen ('nome d'infelice augurio'). Cf. 5. 2. 275.

131. *eternal* Bradley (O.E.D. 7) quotes Schmidt ('used to express extreme abhorrence'), but it means simply 'everlasting' and whether in a good sense (as in *Macb.* 3. 1. 67, where the 'eternal jewel'=the immortal soul) or a bad sense (=inveterate), as here, depends on the word it qualifies (cf. the use of 'precious', 5. 2. 238, and 'excellent', *Ant.* 1. 1. 40).

134. *I'll* (Q.) F. 'I will'.

142. *heaven* (Q.) F. 'Heauens'.

147. *turned...without* i.e. made a fool of you.

149. *Alas* (F.) Q. 'O Good'. F. seems more in keeping with Desdemona's dejection than Q. (a backwash probably from 'Good friend' in l. 151, though it has been taken as a misprint for 'O God').

156. *them in* (Q2) F. 'them: or'; Q1 omits ll. 152–65 ('Here I kneel...make me').

168. *And...you* (Q.) F. omits.

169. *'Tis* (Q.) F. 'It is'.

S.D. (after Rowe) Q. F. omit.

171. *stay* (Q. in a garbled version) F. 'staies'.

172. S.D.¹ F. '*Exeunt Desdemona and Æmilia.*'
Q. '*Exit women.*'

S.D.² Q. places after 'Roderigo!'.

176. *daff'st* (Dyce) F. 'dafts'; Q. 'dofftst'. To
'daff' (a variant of 'doff') was to put off one's clothes;
hence (fig.) to cast off someone one had no use for.
O.E.D. and On. here gloss 'to put off with an excuse',
but 'with some device' = 'with an excuse', and the word
simply means 'fob off' (cf. *Ado*, 5. 1. 78, 'Canst thou
so daff me').

183. *Faith,* (Q.) F. omits.

183–4. *I have ...together* F.'s uncorrected forme
(exemplified in the Oxford facsimile, head of vv3,
p. 333) has here one of the strangest errors in the
Folio; see Hinman in *Library*, xxiii (1942), pp. 101–7.
With the exception noted above (l. 183) and below
we follow the corrected state.

183. *for* (Q.) F. 'and'.

188. *to Desdemona* (Q.) F. omits 'to'.

190–1. *expectations ...respect*=hopes and encour-
agement of immediate favour.

194. *By this hand* (Q.) F. 'Nay'.
think (F.) Q. 'say', which editors prefer; but there
seems no incongruity in Roderigo's swearing to his
thoughts and 'begin to find myself fopped in it' suggests a sequel to cogitation ('think') rather than speech.

'tis very (Q.) F. 'it is' (om. 'very'). Q.'s elision
has the support of what precedes and what follows,
and 'very scurvy' is wanted in reply to the preceding
'very well'.

200. *solicitation*=suit. On.'s gloss 'illicit courtship'
includes the qualifying 'unlawful'.

225. *takes* (Q.) F. 'taketh' (to justify the line),
a bad sequel to 'goes'.

229. *of him* (Q.) F. omits 'of'.

242. *supper-time* Usually about 5.30 p.m. in Shakespeare's day (*Sh. Eng.* ii, 134).

243. *grows to waste* O.E.D. (citing as the only instance of the expression, 'waste' 10c) explains as = approaching its end. But this is not so (see l. 242 n.), and the words probably mean (as Hart suggested) 'we are wasting the night hours'. Iago has a harvest of mischief to reap in the coming night.

245. S.D. F. '*Exeunt.*' Q. '*Ex.* Iag. *and* Rod.'

4. 3

S.D. *Loc.* (after Mal. and Al.) *Entry* (F.) Q. 'Enter *Othello, Desdemona, Lodouico ...*' (after 4. 2. 243). See p. 140.

10. S.D. (after Cap.) Q. '*Exeunt.*' F. '*Exit.*' (both after l. 9).

13. *He hath* (Q.) F. 'And hath'.

14. *bade* (Q. 'bad') F. 'bid'.

16. *nightly wearing* i.e. a smock (see 5. 2. 276), and probably a kind of light cape called night-rail; cf. Linthicum, pp. 215, 166.

21. *in them* (Q.) F. omits.

23. *faith* (Q.) F. 'Father'—a curious error, suggesting the collator's misreading (cf., for the same error, Q2 *Rom.* 4. 4. 20).

24. *thee* (Q.) F. omits.

25. *those* (Q.) F. 'these'.

talk sc., at random, idly; cf. *Macb.* 4. 2. 63, 'Poor prattler, how thou talk'st'.

26. *Barbara* (F2) Q. '*Barbary*'; F. '*Barbarie*'. The pronunciation suggested by Q. F. was customary.

32. *But* = not to; see Abbott, §122.

33. *Barbara* (F2) F. '*Brabarie*'; Q. omits ll. 31–52 ('I have ...next.') and 54–6.

40. S.D. (after Q2) F. omits.

The poor soul... Shakespeare apparently adapted a current song, intended for a man. A longer version is preserved, with accompaniment for the lute, in a contemporary MS. (B.M. Add. 15117) and a longer version still was printed by Percy. See Noble, *Shakespeare's Use of Song*, 1923, pp. 152–4. The willow was emblematic of disappointed love; cf. Linthicum, p. 34.

sighing (Q2) F. (uncorrected) '*sining*'; (corrected) '*singing*'.

sycamore tree = the biblical sycamore (*Ficus sycomorus*), the fig mulberry—not our sycamore (a type of maple). Hart cites Folkard's statement that in Sicily it is emblematic of a wife's infidelity and a husband's patience.

43, 55. *willow...willow* (Q2) F. '*Willough, &c.*'

47–8. *Lay...willow* (Cap.) F. prints as follows:

Sing Willough, &c. (Lay by these)
Willough, Willough. (Prythee high thee: he'le come anon)

54. S.D. (after Camb.) F. omits.

58. *Does that* (Q.) F. 'Doth that'. The juxtaposition of final and initial 'th' is awkward and the tendency seems to have been to avoid it, as at 1. 1. 67 ('do's the' F.) and 4. 2. 96 ('do's this', F.).

69. *prize* Q. F. 'price' (an obsolescent form).

73. *done't* (A.W., Q. 'done it') F. 'done'.

75. *exhibition* See G. O.E.D. and On. gloss 'gift', 'present', perhaps unnecessarily.

76. *ud's pity* (Q.) F. 'why'.

105. S.D. (after R. M. Alden) Q. F. omit. 'Heaven...mend' is a prayer (see *M.L.R.* x (1915), pp. 376–7).

105–6. *Heaven...mend* i.e. Heaven give me grace to learn good, not evil, from the evil that has befallen me.

106. S.D. (after R. M. Alden) Q. F. '*Exeunt*'.

5. 1

S.D. *Loc.* (Camb.) *Entry* (Q. F.)

1. *bulk* (Q.) F. 'Barke'.

7. S.D. (Camb. after Cap.) Q. F. omit.

14. *gain* (F.+most editors) Q. 'game', which Barker (p. 107 n.) supports, as suggesting gambling; but this would make Iago's situation less serious than it is.

22. *Be't* (Q.) F. 'But'.

hear (Q.) F. 'heard'.

23. S.D. (Camb. after Cap.) Q. F. omit.

25. *coat* Hart and Fortescue (*Sh. Eng.* i, 128) take as = a brigandine or 'privy coat' (a flexible steelplated protection used for interlining, or worn under the outer clothing). The knee-length coat was, however, a substantial garment (see Linthicum, pp. 196–7).

think'st (Q.) F. 'know'st', which looks like a recollection of 'know' in l. 23; Q. gives better sense.

26. S.D.[1] (Cap.) Q. F. omit.

S.D.[2] (after Cap.) Q. F. omit. 'He does not waste time thrusting at Cassio's padded doublet. Iago's aim would be better and the stroke a fairly fatal one had he not to keep his face hidden' (Barker, p. 109, n. 1).

27. S.D.[1] (Camb. after Cap.) Q. F. omit.

S.D.[2] (Q. F.) Rowe reads 'Enter Othello, above at a Window'. Cf. Barker (p. 109), 'the noise brings Othello out upon the balcony above'.

29. *It...so* 'Could be read—the voice mistaken for Cassio's—as a savagely sarcastic comment' (Barker, p. 109, n. 2).

35. *Forth* (Q.) F. 'For' (full line).

36. S.D.[1] F. '*Exit Othello.*'

42. *It is a* (Q.) F. ''Tis'. The *novella* supports Q. ('essendo la notte buia').

44. *in to* (Cap.) Q. F. 'into'. The meaning must be

'approach', 'intervene' ('come in') in response to the outcry.

S.D. (J.D.W.) Q. F. omit. They are dim shadows which Iago catches sight of at l. 59.

46. S.D. (after Q., placing after l. 45) F. '*Enter Iago.*' (after l. 45).

49. *Did* (Q.) F. 'Do'.

50. *heaven*'s (Q.) F. 'heauen'.

59. S.D. (after Theob.) Q. F. omit.

60. *here* (Q.) F. 'there'. Roderigo draws attention to his whereabouts.

61. S.D. (Camb. after Q2) Q1, F. omit.

64. S.D. (J.D.W.) Q. F. omit.

89. *my dear countryman* Cf. 1. 1. 20 n. and 3. 3. 203–5.

90. '*tis* (A.W.) F. 'Yes, 'tis'; Q. 'O heauen'. The surprise of 'O heaven' would be out of place after 'yes, sure'. A.W. thinks F.'s 'tis' a genuine correction and the preceding extrametrical 'yes' an accidental repetition of the compositor's. J.D.W. accepts F. but asks why Iago should not say 'yes' twice in his pretended excitement.

98. S.D. (after Mal.) Q. F. omit.

100. S.D. (J.) Q. F. omit.

101. *Save...labour* She is fussing over Cassio. Iago pushes her roughly aside so as to have a word with Cassio to make sure that he has no clue to his assailants (Barker, p. 112).

104. S.D.¹ (J.) Q. F. omit.

out (Q.) F. omits (full line).

out o'th'air Fresh air was thought bad for the sick and wounded; cf. Tilley, A93; *Ham.* 2. 2. 208; *3 H. VI*, 2. 6. 27.

S.D.² (J.D.W.) Q. F. omit. Camb. 'Cassio and Roderigo are borne off' suggests a chair for each, which is absurd.

110. S.D. (Q.) F. omits.

111. 'Las (Q.) F. 'Alas'.

what's ...what's (Q.) F. 'what is ... What is'.

114. *dead* (Q.) F. 'quite dead'—an interpolation possibly suggested by 'almost', but anyhow ludicrous.

116. *fruits* (F.) Q. 'fruite'. The construction is in accordance with Shakespearian idiom.

121. *O, fie* (F.) Q. 'Fie, fie'. Either readings might be due to accidental repetition.

123. *foh!* (Q.) F. omits.

124. *let's* (A.W. after Pope) Q. F. 'Let's go'. The Q. F. reading seems only possible if 'gentlemen' is dissyllabic, but as it is trisyllabic elsewhere in this scene it seems more likely that 'go' was a Q. interpolation.

128. S.D. Aside first in Steev.

5. 2

S.D. *Loc.* (after Cap. and Al.) *Entry* (J.D.W. combining Q. F. and Collier MS. 'Oth. lockes the doore'; cf. 5. 2. 108) Q. '*Enter* Othello *with a light.*'; F. '*Enter Othello, and Desdemona in her bed.*' Steev., followed by Camb. and most modern editors, has 'a light burning' in the room. But Barker notes (p. 116, n. 1) the intention of Q. 'plainly is that Othello shall enter with the light illuminating his face; and the steadiness with which he carries the (presumably) naked candle does something to emphasize the abnormal calm which gives dramatic distinction to his appearance'. Locking the door was already the stage practice early in the 19th c., while it is an old tradition, dating perhaps from the 17th c., that the bed should be at the back of the stage, centre (see Sprague, pp. 209–13, 401).

1. *cause*=offence; cf. *Lr.* 4. 6. 111, 'I pardon that

man's life. What was thy cause? Adultery?' The punishment was death (see Lev. xx. 10; John viii. 5). Othello has become the minister of justice. Like Lear, he thinks of himself as a judge, but unlike Lear he must grant no pardon: she must die for adultery and he will nerve himself to do the deed by keeping the sin rather than the sinner before his eyes (see l. 7, n.).

2. *Let...stars* Cf. *Macb.* 1. 4. 50, 'Stars, hide your fires' and *Aen.* iv. 519–20, 'conscia sidera'.

chaste Evil and corruption in the universe were sublunary only.

4. *whiter skin...than snow* For the word order, see Abbott, § 419a.

6. *else...men* This puzzles some. To put her away is not enough. He is more than the wronged husband: as the minister of justice he must protect mankind in general and save her from herself, as Bradley notes (p. 197).

7. *Put out...light* At this point, Theob. explains, he intends to kill her in the darkness, not trusting himself to look upon her as he does it. But he looks first, and so the flaming minister is never put out.

13. S.D. (Theob.) Q. F. omit.

the rose (Q.) F. 'thy Rose'. Furness, defending F., saw here a reference to 'beauty's rose' (*Son.* 1. 2). This complicates and distracts. The impersonal reading of Q. is similarly better in l. 15.

15. *smell it* (Q.) F. 'smell thee'.

S.D. (Q. '*He kisses her*') F. omits.

21. *this sorrow's heavenly* 'For whom the Lord loveth he chasteneth' (Heb. xii. 6). J.'s note (wishing 'these two lines could be honestly ejected') misses the point of 'heavenly', as his paraphrase shows. Barker, seeing the point, found the words blasphemy (see Introduction, p. xlix). But the associations of these lines have been so skilfully insinuated by the 'monumental

alabaster' and 'flaming minister' that it is sacrilegious
to take exception to them.

26. *Desdemona* (Q.) F. '*Desdemon*', which would
be in accordance with F. usage were it not that
'Desdemona' immediately above makes it look like the
compositor's slip.

32–3. *I would…soul* Steev. observes that Shakespeare has bestowed on Othello a piety which he had
refused to Hamlet. The difference stresses the difference
of mood—Hamlet thirsting to drink hot blood, Othello
the minister of justice.

33. *heaven* (Q.) F. 'Heauens'.

38. *so* (Q.) F. omits.

39. *Hum* Hart compares *Cor.* 5. 1. 48–50,
remarking that 'these outward displays of passion
would appear to have been usual in the time of
Shakespeare. A tragic scene almost required them.
Expressions such as "gnaw the lip", or "bite the
thumb"…were so common that they must have
reference to actual practices.' A.W. is sceptical and
suspects that, on the contrary, they were stock verbal
expressions used to compensate for facial expressions
which the audience as a whole could not see.

43. *They…you* Cf. Col. iii. 2, 'Set your affection
on things above, not on things on the earth'.

46. *gnaw…lip* See l. 39 n.

49. *point on*=signalise, presage (cf. 'portents', l. 48).
For similar astrological associations, cf. *J.C.* 1. 3. 32
and *Son.* 26, 9–10, 'Till whatsoever star that guides my
moving Points on me graciously with fair aspect';
Barnes, *Devil's Charter*, ll. 279–80, associates, as here,
with 'malignant aspect' of the stars.

53. *Sweet soul* Echoes her 'by my life and soul'.

55. *Yes,* (Q.) F. omits.

60. *Lord* (Q.) F. 'Heauen'. Q.'s 'Then Lord' has
greater solemnity (J.D.W.).

67–8. *And mak'st ... sacrifice* i.e. turn what seemed a sacred duty to a vulgar crime: 'sacrifice' defines the mood of his entry ('It is the cause ...').

67. *mak'st* (Q.) F. 'makes'.

73. *hath used* (F.) Q. 'hath —vds death'; Al. 'hath —ud's death!— used thee'. J.D.W. favours Al.'s conflation, supposing expurgation in F. A.W. finds the unmetrical oath out of harmony with the dignity of this dialogue and supposes vulgarization in Q.

86. *Being done* 'Now that it is being done' (Hart), but perhaps 'all that need be said, has been said'. Othello has taken Desdemona's unfortunate words of l. 80 as a confession of guilt.

87. *late.* (F.) Q. 'late./*Des.* O Lord, Lord, Lord.' In view of Emilia's following cry to Othello ('What, ho! my lord, my lord'), A.W. thinks Q. interpolated; J.D.W. (like Barker, p. 122 n.) defends it: 'it is her prayer, brief but enough for devout Elizabethan hearers, and despite his words not "too late". It lends point also to "Not dead" etc.'

S.D. ('*Smothers her*' F.) Q. '*he stifles her*'.

88. S.D. F. '*Æmilia at the doore.*'; Q. 'Emillia *calls within.*'

90. *that am* (F. corrected) F. (uncorrected) 'am that'.

92. *So, so* In some 18th century productions (but not Garrick's) Othello here stabbed her and certain critics (e.g. Steev.) approved, it being supposed that after smothering the victim would either recover altogether or not at all; cf. Sprague, pp. 214–16, and note in Furness (pp. 302–7) which prove that 'so, so' implies not a dagger but further use of the pillow.

S.D. (after F. '*Æmil within.*' as S.N.) Q. omits.

93, 104. S.D. (after Mal.) Q. F. omit.

93. *I'ld* ('I'de' Q.) F. 'I would'.

96. *high* Referring to the commotion caused by the attack on Cassio.

104. *Should* (Q.) F. 'Did'. The meaning is 'a change such as this should be accompanied by eclipse and chaos' (cf. 3. 3. 91–3); Nature should invest herself in some shadowing passion (cf. 4. 1.39–41).

I do beseech (J.D.W.) Q. F. 'I do beseech you'. Pope omitted 'do', but 'you' seems the more suspect word, as intrusion after 'beseech' would be natural, especially with 'you' in the next line. The Q. F. reading lacks urgency.

107. *the curtains* The bed is therefore on the inner stage, and the smothering performed by the player with his back to the audience—an important point; see 5. 2. S.D. n.

108. S.D.¹ (Theob.) Q. F. omit, but it is clearly necessary, though no editor but Collier has, it seems, provided for an earlier 'locking'. Cf. Sprague, p. 401, n. 92.

S.D.² F. after l. 108; Q. after l. 107.

109. *murder* (A.W. after Theob.) Q. F. 'Murthers'. Emilia's plural in l. 173 is idiomatic but less so here where it looks like a case of assimilation to 'yonder's'.

112. *error* Superstition associated the moon with lunacy, and the nearer it was to the earth, the greater the danger. Cf. 2. 3. 178 n.

115. *hath* (F.) Q. 'has', perhaps rightly.

122. S.D. (J.D.W.) Q. F. omit. Clearly the cries in l. 123 follow the discovery of the dying mistress.

128. S.D. (Q. '*she dies*.') F. omits.

130. *heard* (Q.) F. 'heare'.

132. *She's like … hell* See Introduction, p. xlvii, n. 2.

135. *She …whore* Noble compares Deut. xxii. 21, 'because she hath wrought folly in Israel, to play the whore'. See G. 'folly'.

146. *Nay,* (Q.) F. omits.

146–9. *had she …for it* Cf. below, ll. 349–50.

150. *on her* (F.) Q. (+most editors) omit, perhaps rightly.

151–2. *hates...deeds* Emilia knows Iago well enough to know that this cap did not fit.

155. *that* (Q2) F. omits. Q1 omits ll. 154–7.

165–6. *Thou...hurt* i.e. 'I can bear more than twice the pain you can inflict' (=I am not afraid).

170. *hath* (F.) Q. 'has'; cf. l. 115 n.

S.D. (Q.) F. '*Enter Montano, Gratiano, and Iago.*'

194. *I think upon't*=I remember.

smell't She suspects villainy of some kind (though not Iago's). Full realization, involving him, only comes at l. 221. J.D.W. questions whether F. 'smel't' was not an error for 'smelt't', and conj. 'I think I smelt't'.

195. *I thought so then* Cf. Emilia's suspicions at 3. 3. 311–21, 4. 2. 131–48.

201. S.D. (Q. 'Oth. *fals on the bed*.') F. omits.

203. S.D. (Theob.) Q. F. omit.

212. *reprobance* (F.) Q. 'reprobation'; cf. 'iterance' (l. 153).

221. *God...heavenly God* (Q.) F. 'Heauen... heauenly Powres'.

222. *'Zounds* (Q.) F. 'Come'.

222–3. '*Twill out...the north* (F.) Q. 'Twill out, 'twill: I hold my peace sir, no,/I'le be in speaking, liberall as the ayre'. Greg (*Sh.F.F.* p. 368) finds merits evenly matched, but there is certainly interpolation in Q. when Emilia addresses Iago as 'sir', and to speak as liberally as the air is too feeble for a Shakespearian first shot. For comparison with the gale of Emilia's passion, the wind is wanted. The air may move freely, but it does not 'speak aloud' (cf. 2. 1. 5) like the storm.

223. *the north*=(poet.) the north wind. Cf. O.E.D., 'north', sb. B. 4; 'south', sb. B. 5. The allusion is, of course, to its 'churlish chiding' (as in *A.Y.L.* 2. 1. 7).

226. S.D. (after Rowe) Q. F. omit.

232. *steal it* (Q.) F. 'steale't'.

234. *Filth* A term of abuse from the 14th century.

238. *serve* (F4) Q. F. 'serues'.

S.D. (J.D.W. after Dyce) Q. '*The Moore runnes at* Iago. Iago *kils his wife.*' (after 'wife?' in l. 237) and (at l. 240) '*Exit* Iago.' F. omits.

243. *here* (Q.) F. omits.

246. S.D. (after Camb.) Q. '*Exit* Mont. *and* Gratiano.'; F. '*Exit.*'

247–8. *But...But* (Q. F.) The repetition suggests a common error; 'For' in l. 247 or 'Yet' in l. 248 might, for instance, have been lost through anticipation or recollection.

248. *why should honour...honesty* i.e. why should reputation outlive honour.

251. S.D. (Dyce) F. omits. Q. omits ll. 249–51 ('What...willow.').

254. S.D. ('*she dies*' Q.) F. omits.

256. *It was* (F.) Q. 'It is'. The personal note of 'was' (implying acquired in Spain) is more characteristic. Othello's thoughts from now on range over his travels' history.

the ice brook's temper See G. 'temper'. 'They have a great advauntage in Spayne, to temper their blades well, bycause of the nature of their ryvers' (Palsgrave, 1530, cited O.E.D. 'temper', verb 14). Hart cites Holland's *Pliny*, xxxiv. 14, to the same effect. The advantage lay in the fact that the rivers were fed by melting snow. Toledo on the Tagus was especially famous for its steel. Fortescue's conj. 'Innsbruck temper' (*Sh. Eng.* i, 132–3) is inept.

258. S.D. (after Q. S.D. 'Gra. *within.*') F. omits.

261. S.D. (Theob.) Q. F. omit.

273. *Man* A.W. accepts 'man but a rush' as an oxymoron, taking 'man' = 'provide men for' (as in 'manning a gun', 'a ship' etc.); i.e. at one time, it would have needed more than twenty Gratianos with

swords to subdue Othello, but all now needed is men enough to handle a rush, the feeblest of weapons.

275. S.D. (J.D.W.) Q. F. omit.

ill-starred See 4. 2. 129 n.

280. *slave* Both Booth (see Furness) and Barker (p. 141) take this to mean Iago. Furness, much more plausibly, thinks it refers to Othello himself. Othello's thoughts are on Desdemona, and self-recrimination (as in 'Whip me...') seems more likely.

284. S.D. (Mal. after Cap.) Q. '*Enter* Lodouico, Montano, Iago, *and Officers* Cassio *in a Chaire.*' F. '*Enter Lodouico, Cassio, Montano, and Iago, with Officers.*'

288. *fable* i.e. that the devil has cloven feet.

289. S.D. (after Rowe) Q. F. omit.

293. *wert* (Q.) F. 'was' (perhaps for 'wast').

294. *damnèd slave* (Q.) F. 'cursed Slaue'. If the 'cursed slave' of l. 280 is Othello, F.'s reading is here unconvincing; that the F. compositor substituted the one word for the other is very probable.

297. *did I* (Q.) F. 'I did'.

in honour = in defence of honour and chastity.

304. *my soul* (Q. F.) J.D.W. thinks 'me, soul' (anon. seventeenth-century conj. in Camb.) worth record.

305–6. *Demand...word* Cf. Introduction, p. xxvi.

319. *nick* (Q.) F. 'interim' (a sophistication).

320. *the* (Q.) F. 'thou'.

323. *but even* (Cap.) Q. 'it euen'; F. 'it but euen'.

340 ff. *Soft you...* See Introduction, pp. l–lv.

349. *Indian* (Q.) F. 'Iudean', which some prefer and take as referring to Judas. But he was the archetype of treachery, of which Othello, an 'honourable murderer', never accuses himself. The (American) Indian's ignorance of the value of gold and precious stones was

notorious and, through ignorance, Othello has thrown away his perfect chrysolite (cf. ll. 147–9).

352. *Drop* (Q2) Q. F. 'Drops'.

Arabian trees The phrase is evocative of something more than Othello's travels' history, like the whole of this speech. The 'medicinable gum' of Arabia was myrrh, associated with incense, and therefore atonement and sacrifice.

358. S.D. (Q.) F. omits.

359. *that's* (Q.) F. 'that is'.

361. S.D. (Camb.) Q. '*He dies.*' F. '*Dyes*'.

363. S.D. (Theob.) Q. F. omit.

Spartan dog 'a kind of bloodhound' (O.E.D.). Iago is so called not only because of his relentless inhumanity but also because of his silence (ll. 305–6). Madden (p. 20) notes that 'the pure-bred bloodhound …was all nose and no cry, being used to hunt absolutely mute' (J.D.W.)

367. S.D. (J.D.W.) Q. F. omit.

373. S.D. F. '*Exeunt.*' Q. '*Exeunt omnes.*'

GLOSSARY

Note. Where there is equivocation, the meanings are distinguished as (*a*) and (*b*)

ABHOR, disgust, horrify; 4. 2. 163

ABILITY, capacity or power to act, (i) equipment (see note); 1. 3. 25; (ii) 'do... abilities' = exert all my powers; 3. 3. 1–2

ABODE, temporary stay, sojourn; 4. 2. 226

ABROAD, by the world, commonly; 1. 3. 385

ABUSE, corrupt, deceive, slander, revile; 1. 1. 174; 1. 2. 74; 1. 3. 60, 393; 2. 1. 229, 300; 3. 3. 202, 269, 338; 4. 2. 14, 140; 4. 3. 61; 5. 1. 123

ABUSER, deceiver, corrupter; 1. 2. 78

ACCENT, tone of voice; 1. 1. 76

ACCIDENT, (i) occurrence, event; 1. 1. 143; 1. 3. 135; 4. 2. 227; 5. 1. 94; (ii) 'of accident' = fortuitous; 4. 1. 268

ACCOMMODATION, suitable provision, (hence) comfort; 1..3. 238

ACHIEVE, win; 2. 1. 61

ACKNOW, acknowledge; 'be not acknown' = feign ignorance; 3. 3. 321

ACT, action; 1. 1. 63; 3. 3. 330

ADDICTION, inclination; 2. 2. 6

ADDITION, distinction, title; 3. 4. 198; 4. 1. 104; 4. 2. 164

ADVANTAGE, (i) opportunity; 1. 3. 297; 2. 1. 240 (see note); 3. 1. 52; 4. 2. 179; (ii) 'to the advantage' = opportunely; 3. 3. 314

ADVISED, 'be advised' = be cautious, take care; 1. 2. 55

ADVOCATION, advocacy; 3. 4. 127

AFFECT (sb.), desire; 1. 3. 263

AFFECT (vb.), desire; 3. 3. 231

AFFECTION, inclination; 1. 1. 36; 2. 1. 237; 4. 3. 99, 101

AFFINED, bound, constrained; 1. 1. 39; 2. 3. 214

AFFINITY, family connections; 3. 1. 46

AGAIN, moreover; 1. 3. 21

AGNIZE, acknowledge; 1. 3. 231

AIM, guess (see note); 1. 3. 6

ALARUM, (lit.) call to arms, (fig.) incitement; 2. 3. 25

ALLOWANCE, approval, commendation; 1. 1. 128; 2. 1. 49

ALLOWED, approved; 1. 3. 224

ALMAIN, German; 2. 3. 81

ALMOST, 'not almost' (= for the most part not), hardly; 3. 3. 67

AMAZED, dumbfounded; 3. 3. 373; 4. 2. 239

AMIABLE, loveable; 3. 4. 62

ANCIENT, ensign; 1. 1. 33 etc.

ANGRY, (*a*) irritable, (*b*) inflamed (as a sore); 5. 1. 12

ANSWER, (i) reply to a legal charge; I. I. 120, 121; I. 2. 87; (ii) face the consequences of, 3. 3. 365

ANSWERABLE, corresponding; I. 3. 344

ANTHROPOPHAGI, man-eaters, cannibals (word from Herodotus in Pliny, *Nat. Hist.* VII, ii); I. 3. 144

ANTRE, cavern; I. 3. 140

APPREHEND, arrest; I. I. 178; I. 2. 77

APPREHENSION, idea; 3. 3. 142

APPROVE, (i) endorse; I. 3. 11; 2. 3. 60; 4. 3. 51; (ii) esteem; 2. 1. 44; 4. 3. 19; (iii) prove, attest; 2. 3. 207 (see note), 305

APPROVED, esteemed; I. 3. 77; 2. 1. 49

APT, (i) congruous, likely; 2. 1. 281; 5. 2. 180; (ii) willing; 2. 3. 313

ARRIVANCE, arrival, (here abst. for concr.) landings; 2. 1. 42

ARTICLE, item; I. 3. 11; 3. 3. 22; 5. 2. 57

ARTS INHIBITED, prohibited (i.e. magic) practices; I. 2. 79

ASPIC, asp; 3. 3. 452

ASSAY (sb.), test; I. 3. 18

ASSAY (vb.), essay, try; 2. 1. 120; 2. 3. 203

ATONE, set at one, reconcile; 4. 1. 231

ATTACH, arrest; I. 2. 77

ATTEND, await; 3. 3. 283; 3. 4. 197, 204

AULD (*Sc.*), old; 2. 3. 95

AVAUNT!, begone! (a cry of abhorrence, usually addressed to a devil or witch); 3. 3. 337; 4. 1. 261

BATTLE, army (also = battalion, one of the main divisions); I. I. 23

BAUBLE, trinket; (fig.) 4. 1. 134

BEAM, the horizontal bar of a balance from the ends of which the scales are suspended; I. 3. 326

BEAR (sb.), used for both the Great Bear and Lesser Bear; 2. 1. 14

BEAR (vb.), (i) 'bear up to' = sail towards (lit. in the direction of the wind); I. 3. 8; (ii) carry (by force of arms), subdue; I. 3. 23; (iii) 'bear...out' = survive; 2. 1. 19

BEFORE ME! (asseveration), upon my soul!; 4. 1. 144

BEGUILE, (i) rob (usually by trickery); I. 3. 66, 156 (see note), 210; (ii) disguise; 2. 1. 122

BELEE'D, intercepted (by having the wind taken out of one's sails); I. 1. 30

BELIE, calumniate; 4. 1. 36; 5. 2. 136

BENEFICIAL, favourable; 2. 2. 6

BESHREW (a very mild imprecation), plague on; 3. 4. 154; 4. 2. 129

BESORT (sb.), company (cf. the vb. *Lr.* 1. 4. 272); I. 3. 238

BETRAY, entrap; 5. 2. 6; (*a*) entrap, (*b*) expose, unmask; 5. 2. 80

BEWHORE, call whore; 4. 2. 116

BLACK, (*a*) dark-complexioned, (*b*) wicked; 2. 1. 131, 132

BLACKNESS, (*a*) dark complexion, (*b*) wickedness; 2. 1. 133

BLANK, (lit.) the white spot in the centre of the target, (hence) range of fire; 3. 4. 132

BLAZON, (lit.) describe or paint armorial bearings, (hence) set forth in fine terms, eulogise (see note); 2. 1. 63

BLOOD, (i) consanguinity; 1. 1. 170; (ii) natural impulses, passion; 1. 3. 104, 123, 327, 334; 2. 1. 224; 2. 3. 201; 4. 1. 276

BLOWING, depositing of (flies') eggs; 4. 2. 68

BLOWN, inflated; 3. 3. 184

BOB, defraud; 5. 1. 16

BODING, ominous; 4. 1. 22

BOLSTER, lie (together) on a bolster; 3. 3. 401

BOMBAST (ppl.a), (fig.) turgid (cf. vb. = pad, stuff, and sb. = cotton wool for padding); 1. 1. 13

BOOKISH, learned, erudite (disparagingly, cf. *2 H. VI*, 1. 1. 257); 1. 1. 24

BOUND, under obligation, obliged; 1. 3. 182; 3. 1. 55; 3. 3. 215

BRACE, portion of suit of armour for the arms, (hence fig.) state of defence (see note); 1. 3. 24

BRAVE, defy; 5. 2. 328

BREACH, gap in fortifications (esp. made by a battery); 1. 3. 136

BREEDING, upbringing; 1. 3. 239

BRING IN, establish (in an office); 3. 1. 50; 3. 3. 75

BROW, 'brow of the sea' = sea-edge, shore; 2. 1. 53

BRUISED, broken; 1. 3. 219

BULK, framework of shop projecting into the street; 5. 1. 1

BURNING, shining; 2. 1. 14; 'ever-burning', 3. 3. 465

BUT, see notes to 1. 1. 65, 126; 3. 3. 92, 142, 227; 3. 4. 108; 4. 3. 32

BUTT, terminal point, boundary mark (O.E.D., citing this and (c. 1475) 'We be come for our synnys to the butte & terme or marke of vniuersale kynde of man'); 5. 2. 270

BY, (prep.) concerning; 1. 3. 17; (ii) (adv.) aside; 5. 2. 31

CABLE, (fig.) scope (cf. mod. 'give him rope'); 1. 2. 17

CAITIFF, wretch, (in contemptuous pity) 4. 1. 108; (in abuse) 5. 2. 320

CALLET, trull, drab; 4. 2. 122

CALMED, becalmed, (fig.) frustrated; 1. 1. 30

CANAKIN, small drinking-can; 2. 3. 67, 68

CAPABLE, comprehensive; 3. 3. 461

CARACK, large merchant ship (esp. associated with rich cargoes from the E. and W. Indies); 1. 2. 50

CARRY'T, 'get away with it'; 1. 1. 68

CARVE FOR, (a) strike in accordance with, (b) indulge, gratify (cf. *Ham.* 1. 3. 20 and G.); 2. 3. 169

CAST, dismiss, discard (esp. in a mil. sense); 1. 1. 150; 2. 3. 14, 268; 5. 2. 329

CAUSE, (a legal term) offence for which one is charged O.E.D. 9); 5. 2. 1, 3

CENSURE, (i) judgement, opinion; 2. 3. 189; 4. 1. 271; (ii) judicial sentence; 5. 2. 370

CERTES, assuredly; 1. 1. 16

CHAIR, chair or litter carried on poles by two men (cf. O.E.D. 10); 5. 1. 82, 96, 98

CHALLENGE, claim; 1. 3. 188; 2. 1. 209

CHAMBERER, (a) city-dweller (see note), (b) 'one who frequents ladies' chambers; a gallant' (O.E.D. 4; cf. Rom. xiii, 13, 'chambering and wantonness'); 3. 3. 267

CHANGE, exchange; 1. 3. 316, 349; 2. 1. 155; 4. 3. 98

CHARM (sb.), magic spell (not as now restricted to protective magic); 1. 1. 172; 1. 2. 73; 1. 3. 91; 5. 1. 35

CHARM (vb.), lay a spell on, (hence fig.) 'charm... tongue'=hold one's tongue; 5. 2. 186, 187

CHARMER, enchantress; 3. 4. 60

CHARTER, official privilege; 1. 3. 245

CHECK, rebuke; 1. 1. 149 (see note); 3. 3. 68; 4. 3. 20

CHERUBIN, for 'cherub' sing. (fr. Heb. plur. 'cherubim'); 4. 2. 64

CHIDE, quarrel; 4. 2. 168

CHRYSOLITE, name of various golden coloured gems (by derivation=golden stone), here prob.=the topaz, the largest and most costly of all precious stones; 5. 2. 148

CHUCK, term of endearment; 3. 4. 49; 4. 2. 24

CIRCUMSCRIPTION, restriction; 1. 2. 27

CIRCUMSTANCE, (i) long-winded tale; 1. 1. 13; (ii) accident, contingency (cf. 2 H. VI, 5. 2. 39); 3. 3. 16; (iii) ceremony; 3. 3. 356; (iv) adjuncts of a fact constituting circumstantial evidence (cf. Wint. 5. 2. 30–1, Ham. 2. 2. 157); 3. 3. 408

CIRCUMSTANCED, 'governed by circumstances' (O.E.D.); 3. 4. 205

CIVIL, well-mannered, urbane; 2. 1. 236; 2. 3. 186; (a) urbane, (b) urban; 4. 1. 64

CLIMATE, CLIME, region, country; 1. 1. 71; 3. 3. 232

CLIP, embrace, enfold; 3. 3. 466

CLOG, block of wood tied to the leg or neck to prevent escape; 1. 3. 198

CLOSE, secret, reserved; 3. 3. 126

CLOSET (adj.), belonging to a 'closet', i.e. a repository for private papers (cf. Macb. 5. 1. 6); 4. 2. 22

CLYSTER-PIPE, tube for injecting an enema; 2. 1. 176

COAT, (see note) 5. 1. 25

COD'S HEAD, (a) literal sense, (b) blockhead, fool; 2. 1. 155

COGGING, cheating; 4. 2. 133

COLLY, darken; 2. 3. 202

COLOQUINTIDA, colocynth or 'bitter apple', which furnished an intensely bitter purgative drug; 1. 3. 348

COME, (i) 'come on, come on', phrase of remonstrance (cf.

COME (i) (*cont*.):
mod. 'come, come'); 2. 1. 109; (ii) 'come near'= affect closely; 4. 1. 197; (iii) 'come in'=intervene (esp. in a fight, Schmidt); 5. 1. 44; 5. 2. 320

COMFORT, satisfaction, joy; 1. 3. 213; 2. 1. 31, 82, 189, 191, 205; 4. 2. 160, 190

COMMISSION, mandate; 1. 3. 281; 2. 1. 29; 4. 2. 221

COMMIT, i.e. commit adultery (cf. 'commit not', *Lr*. 3. 4. 83–4); 4. 2. 73, 74, 77, 81

COMMON, open to all (cf. *All's*, 5. 3. 187; 2 *H. IV*, 2. 2. 166); 3. 3. 304

COMMONER, prostitute; 4. 2. 74

COMPANION, (contemptuous) fellow; 4. 2. 142

COMPASS, revolution; 3. 4. 74

COMPLEXION, (mod. sense) colour of skin, esp. of face; 3. 3. 232; 4. 2. 63

COMPLIMENT, obsequiousness (often contemptuous with Sh.; cf. *A.Y.L.* 2. 5. 24–5; 'that they call compliment is like th' encounter of two dog-apes'); 1. 1. 64

COMPLY WITH, act in accordance with (see note to l. 264); 1. 3. 263

COMPOSITION, congruity, consistency; 1. 3. 1

COMPT, 'at compt'=at the day of reckoning, i.e. Day of Judgement; 5. 2. 276

COMPULSIVE, coercive; 3. 3. 456

CONCEIT (sb.), idea, fancy (O.E.D. 1); 3. 3. 118, 328

CONCEIT (vb.), form an idea or notion, imagine; 3. 3. 152

CONCEPTION, (i) fancy; 3. 4. 160; (ii) purpose, design (with ref. to the primary sense; cf. *Troil*. 1. 3. 312); 5. 2. 58

CONCLUSION, final result; 1. 1. 15 (see note); 1. 3. 329; 3. 3. 430

CONDITION, disposition; 2. 1. 246; 4. 1. 192

CONFINE, confinement, restriction; 1. 2. 27

CONJUNCTIVE, united, confederate; 1. 3. 365

CONJURATION, incantation; 1. 3. 92

CONJURE, (i) influence by magic; 1. 3. 105; (ii) adjure; 3. 3. 296

CONSCIONABLE, conscientious, scrupulous; 2. 1. 235

CONSENT IN, agree to, 'agree in planning' (On.); 5. 2. 299

CONSERVE, make into a conserve; 3. 4. 78

CONSTRUE, interpret; 4. 1. 101

CONSUL, senator; 1. 1. 25; 1. 2. 43

CONTENT, (i) 'content you'= don't worry; 1. 1. 41; (ii) remunerate; 3. 1. 1

CONTINUATE, uninterrupted; 3. 4. 182

CONVENIENCE, 'agreement, correspondence' (O.E.D. 1 *b*, citing), compatibility (see note); 2. 1. 228

CONVENIENCY, opportunity; 4. 2. 178

CONVERSATION, behaviour; 3. 3. 266

CONVERSE, conversation (cf. *Ham*. 2. 1. 41); 3. 1. 37

CONVEYANCE, escort; 1. 3. 285

CONVINCE, overcome; 4. 1. 28

Cope, have to do with; 4. 1. 86

Corrigible, corrective; 1. 3. 325

Couch, lie; 4. 3. 56

Counter-caster, one who casts or reckons with counters, 'a word of contempt for an arithmetician' (J.), a book-keeper (see note); 1. 1. 31

Course (sb.), procedure, proceeding; 1. 2. 86; 1. 3. 111; 4. 1. 280; 4. 2. 94

Course (vb.), pursue its appointed planetary course; 3. 4. 74

Court and guard, a perversion of 'court of guard'? (q.v. and see note); 2. 3. 212

Court of guard, perversion of *corps de garde*, guard-house, guard-room; 2. 1. 215

Courtship, courtesy; 2. 1. 170

Cousin, (i) grandchild; 1. 1. 114; (ii) kinsman; 4. 1. 223

Cover, copulate (of a stallion and mare); 1. 1. 112

Coxcomb, fool (alluding to the professional fool's cap); 5. 2. 236

Cozening, cheating; 4. 2. 133

Credit, (i) reputation; 1. 3. 97; (ii) credibility; 2. 1. 281

Creditor, see Debitor-and-creditor; 1. 1. 31

Critical, censorious; 2. 1. 119

Crusado, Portuguese coin, orig. of gold, stamped with a cross; 3. 4. 26

Cry (sb.), (i) pack of hounds; 2. 3. 357; (ii) report, rumour; 4. 1. 124

Cry (vb.), (i) call for, demand; 1. 3. 276; (ii) 'cry on'=

call out, exclaim (cf. *Ham.* 5. 2. 362, 'cries on havoc'); 5. 1. 48; (iii) 'cry mercy', see Mercy; 4. 2. 89; 5. 1. 69

Cunning, knowledge; 'in cunning'=knowingly; 3. 3. 50

Cure, 'stand in bold cure'= 'are in a healthy state' (On.), are sanguine (cf. *Lr.* 3. 6. 107, 'stand in hard cure'); 2. 1. 51

Curlèd, lit. having artificially curled hair, (hence, by metonymy) elegant; 1. 2. 68

Customer, one who invites custom (J.), prostitute (cf. *All's*, 5. 3. 285); 4. 1. 120

Daff, fob off (see note); 4. 2. 176

Daw, jackdaw (type of foolishness); 1. 1. 66

Dear, (i) heartfelt, zealous; 1. 3. 85; (ii) dire (etymol. a diff. word), grievous; 1. 3. 259; (iii) loving; 2. 1. 285

Debitor-and-creditor. Generally = book-keeping, the system of double entry, incoming payments being entered in a column headed 'Debitor' and outgoing in one headed 'Creditor', but here contemptuously for a book-keeper, office worker; 1. 1. 31

Defeat, orig.=unmake, hence (i) disfigure (see note); 1. 3. 340; (ii) destroy; 4. 2. 161

Defend, 'heaven defend'= God forbid; 1. 3. 266

Delicate, pleasant; 1. 3. 352

Delighted, possessing delight, delightful; 1. 3. 289

15

DELIVER, (i) relate; 1. 3. 90; 2. 3. 215; (ii) bring to birth; 1. 3. 368

DEMERIT, merit (O.E.D. 1); 1. 2. 22

DEMONSTRABLE, evident, apparent (O.E.D. 1); 3. 4. 146

DENOTEMENT, indication, designation; 2. 3. 310

DESERT, any uninhabited and uncultivated region, including forest land (not necessarily arid); 1. 3. 140

DESERVE, requite; 1. 1. 184

DESIGNMENT, design, project; 2. 1. 22

DESPITE, (i) insult; 4. 2. 117; (ii) 'in despite'=out of spite; 4. 3. 92

DETERMINATE, decisive; 4. 2. 228

DIABLO (Span.), devil; 2. 3. 157

DIAL, clock; 3. 4. 179

DIAN, Diana, goddess of chastity; 3. 3. 389

DIET, feed; 2. 1. 288

DILATE, relate at length; 1. 3. 153

DILATION, (a) expansion (of a bodily organ), (b) delay (see note); 3. 3. 126

DIRECT, straightforward, immediate; 1. 2. 86

DIRECTLY, (i) undoubtedly, plainly; 2. 1. 216; (ii) straightforwardly; 2. 3. 343; 3. 3. 409; 4. 2. 209

DISCONTENTED, full of discontent, reproachful; 5. 2. 316

DISCOURSE, 'discourse of thought' = process of thought, meditation (cf. Ham. G.); 4. 2. 154

DISCRETION, 'do your discretion'=act as you think fit; 3. 3. 34

DISLIKE, displease; 2. 3. 45

DISPLANTING, uprooting, removal; 2. 1. 270

DISPLEASURE, 'your displeasure'=the disfavour you have fallen into; 3. 1. 42

DISPORT, sport, pleasure; 1. 3. 271

DISPOSE, external manner; 'smooth dispose'=easy way with him (see SMOOTH); 1. 3. 395

DISPOSITION, arrangement; 1. 3. 236

DISPROPORTIONED, inconsistent; 1. 3. 2

DISPUTE ON, argue (contextually=in a court of law); 1. 2. 75

DISTASTE, offend the taste, disgust; 3. 3. 329

DISTEMPERING, intoxicating; 1. 1. 100

DISTINCT, individual; 1. 3. 264

DISTINCTLY, specifically; 3. 3. 237

DISTRACT, (i) divide (see note); 1. 3. 323; (ii) alarm, frighten; 2. 3. 251

DIVISION, arrangement of parts, disposition (O.E.D. 1d); 1. 1. 23

DOOR, 'speak within door'= don't talk so loud ('in Warwickshire "speak within the house" was current till recently in the same sense', On.); 4. 2. 145

DOTAGE, infatuation; 4. 1. 27

DOTE, talk (or act) foolishly; 2. 1. 204

DOUBLE, of double strength (cf. *2 H. VI*, 2. 3. 64, 'double beer'=strong beer); 1. 2. 14

DOUBT (sb.), apprehension, fear; 3. 3. 190, 431

DOUBT (vb.), fear, suspect; 3. 3. 19, 172, 192

DOWN THE WIND, with the wind behind (see note); 3. 3. 264

DRAW, (lit.) pull a vehicle, (hence) 'draw with'=(fig.) be in like case with (quibbling on lit. meaning); 4. 1. 67

DRESS, (i) 'dress in'=equip with; 1. 3. 26; (ii) treat a wounded man or his wounds; 5. 1. 124

DROWSY, soporific; 3. 3. 333

DUE, straight (with ref. to the points of the compass), 'due course', a nautical phrase (cf. *H.V*, 3 Chor. 17); 1. 3. 34

DULL, sluggish, unresponsive; 2. 1. 224

DUTY, respect; 1. 1. 50; 'do my duties'=pay my respects; 3. 2. 2

ECSTASY, 'applied ... to all morbid states characterized by unconsciousness, as swoon, trance, catalepsy...' (O.E.D. 2); 4. 1. 79

EFFECT, result; 1. 3. 225

ELSE, besides (see note); 2. 3. 53

EMBARKED, (fig.) engaged; 1. 1. 150

ENCAVE, (fig.) conceal; 4. 1. 81

ENCHAFÉD, enraged, raging; 2. 1. 17

ENGINE, orig. mother wit (Lat. 'ingenium'), hence ingenuity or a product of it, (i) instrument of war, cannon; 3. 3. 357; (ii) plot; 4. 2. 218

ENGLUT, swallow up; 1. 3. 57

ENTERTAINMENT, taking a person into service, hence (contextually) = reinstatement; 3. 3. 252

ENWHEEL, encircle; 2. 1. 87

EPITHET, term; 1. 1. 14

ERR, stray; 1. 3. 62, etc.

ERRING, errant, vagrant; 1. 3. 354

ERROR, deviation from a normal course; 5. 2. 112

ESTIMATION, repute, reputation; 1. 3. 274

ETERNAL, (see note); 4. 2. 131

EVEN, settle accounts; 2. 1. 293

EXECUTE, 'to bring (a weapon) into operation' (O.E.D. 1 *b*, citing *York. Trag.* 1. 3. 81, 'I will execute the point [of a dagger] on thee'); 2. 3. 224

EXECUTION, operation; 3. 3. 468

EXERCISE, religious observance; 3. 4. 41

EXHIBITION, allowance for support; 1. 3. 237; 4. 3. 75 (see note)

EXPECTANCY, expectation; 2. 1. 41

EXPERT, 'tried, proved by experience' (O.E.D. 3, citing); 2. 1. 49

EXSUFFLICATE, 'inflated, windy' (O.E.D., the only ex.); 3. 3. 184

EXTEND, show in condescension (cf. *Ham.* G. 'extent'); 2. 1. 98

EXTINCTED, extinguished; 2. 1.
81

EXTRAVAGANT, vagrant
(O.E.D. 1); 1. 1. 137

EXTREMITY, extreme; 5. 2. 142

FAITH, (i) 'faith', 'good faith',
'in faith' (asseverations);
(ii) fidelity; 1. 3. 294

FALL (sb.), letting fall, down-
ward stroke (cf. 'fall' of
weapons, *R. III*, 5. 3. 111,
Lr. 1. 1. 146); 2. 3. 230

FALL (vb.), (i) 'fall in'=pass
into a state of mind
(O.E.D. 38), hence 'fall in
fright'=become alarmed; 2.
3. 228; (ii) come, chance,
begin (O.E.D. 47); 3. 3.
239; (iii) let fall (O.E.D.
49); 4. 1. 246

FAME, report, rumour; 2. 1. 62

FAMILIAR, friendly (with allusion to the familiar spirit
of sorcery); 2. 3. 302

FANTASY, whim, caprice; 3. 3.
301

FASHION, shape; 'out of
fashion'=incoherently (see
note); 2. 1. 204

FAST (adj.), firm, staunch; 1.
3. 360

FAST (adv.), securely; 1. 2. 11

FATHOM, (fig.) compass, capability, grasp (see note);
1. 1. 153

FAVOUR, (i) face, countenance;
1. 3. 340; 2. 1. 226; 3. 4.
129; (ii) attraction, charm;
4. 3. 21

FEAR, terrify; 1. 2. 71

FEARFUL, causing apprehension, alarming; 1. 3. 12;
3. 3. 84

FELL, cruel; 5. 2. 364

FIELD, (i) battlefield; 1. 1. 22;
1. 3. 85; (ii) land in general;
1. 3. 135

FIG, 'type of anything...
valueless or contemptible'
(O.E.D.), 'fig's end'=mere
rubbish; 2. 1. 247

FIGURE, shape, design; 1. 1. 63

FILTH, slut, drab, whore;
5. 2. 234

FIND, 'see through' (Schmidt);
2. 1. 244

FINELESS, unbounded, infinite;
3. 3. 175

FITCHEW, polecat, (fig.) prostitute (see note); 4. 1. 145

FLATTERY, 'her own flattery'
=self-conceit; 4. 1. 129–30

FLEER, sneer; 4. 1. 82

FLOOD, sea; 1. 3. 135; 2. 1.
2, 17

FLOOD-GATE, torrential (see
note); 1. 3. 56

FLUSTER, make half tipsy;
2. 3. 56

FOH! an exclamation of abhorrence or disgust; 3. 3.
234; 5. 1. 123

FOLLY, (i) (*a*) foolishness,
(*b*) wantonness; 2. 1. 137;
(ii) wantonness; 2. 1. 243;
5. 2. 135

FOND, (i) doting, loving to excess; 1. 3. 318; 3. 3. 447;
4. 1. 196; 5. 2. 160;
(ii) foolish; 2. 1. 138

FONDLY, dotingly; 3. 3. 172

FOOTING, setting foot on land,
landing (cf. 'foot' vb. *H. V*,
2. 4. 143); 2. 1. 76

FOP, fool, dupe; 4. 2. 195

FOR, (i) ready for, prepared for;
1. 2. 58; (ii) in favour of;
2. 3. 85; (iii) for why=
wherefore; 1. 3. 257

FORBEAR, spare, let alone; 1. 2. 10

FORDO, ruin, destroy; 5. 1. 129

FOREGONE, past, previous; 3. 3. 430

FORFEND, forbid; 5. 2. 33, 189

FORGET, (abs.) forget oneself; 2. 3. 184, 237

FORKÈD, horned (esp. of deer), (hence) cuckolded; 3. 3. 278

FORM, (i) manner, way, fashion; 1. 1. 50; 2. 1. 236; 4. 2. 139; (ii) style of beauty, good looks; 3. 3. 239 (see note); 4. 2. 156

FORSWEAR, lit. renounce on oath, abandon; 4. 2. 160

FORTITUDE, material strength (see note); 1. 3. 222

FOUL, (i) wicked; 1. 3. 65, 117; (ii) exceedingly stormy; 2. 1. 34; (iii) (a) ugly, (b) wicked; 2. 1. 140, 141, 142

FRANK, (a) liberal, open, (b) unrestrained (O.E.D. 1 c) or bounteous in a bad sense (O.E.D. 2, citing Pope, *Ep. Lady* 71, 'Chaste to her husband, frank to all beside'; cf. 'liberal', q.v.); 3. 4. 44

FRAUGHT, freight; 3. 3. 451

FREE, (i) willing; 1. 3. 41; 2. 3. 312; 3. 3. 187; (ii) generous; 1. 3. 265, 397; (iii) guiltless; 3. 3. 257

FREELY, unreservedly; 2. 3. 322; 5. 2. 56

FRIEZE, a kind of woollen cloth with a heavy nap on it of which soldiers' jerkins were made (see Linthicum, p. 76) 2. 1. 126

FROM, contrary to; 1. 1. 132

FRONT, forehead; (i) 'head and front', see HEAD; 1. 3. 80; (ii) 'by the front'=by the forelock (see note); 3. 1. 49

FRUITFUL, bountiful, beneficent; 2. 3. 334

FRUITFULNESS, (a) liberality, (b) amorousness (cf. *Ant.* 1. 2. 51); 3. 4. 38

FULL, perfect; 2. 1. 36

FULSOME, filthy, obscene; 4. 1. 37

FUNCTION, (i) operation of the faculties; 2. 3. 341; (ii) office, business; 4. 2. 27

FURY, inspired frenzy; 3. 4. 75

FUSTIAN, (lit.) coarse cloth of cotton and flax, (fig.) ranting nonsense; 2. 3. 275

GALL (sb.), bile, supposed seat of bitterness and rancour of spirit; 4. 3. 93

GALL (vb.), chafe, fret; 1. 1. 149; 2. 1. 97

GALLEY, low, one-decked vessel, propelled by sails and oars, used in the Mediterranean, esp. for war; 1. 2. 40; 1. 3. 3, 13

GAME, amorous play; 2. 3. 19

GARB, manner, fashion (never 'dress' in Sh.); 2. 1. 300

GASTNESS, terror; 5. 1. 106

GENDER (sb.), sort, kind; 1. 3. 323

GENDER (vb.), engender, breed; 4. 2. 63

GENEROUS, high-born, noble (Lat. *generosus*); 3. 3. 282

GERMAN, near relative; 1. 1. 114

GET, beget; 1. 3. 191

Go to, phrase expressing remonstrance or derisive incredulity; 3. 4. 187 etc.

God bu'y, God bu'y you, God be with you, farewell; 1. 3. 189; 3. 3. 377

Gown, (i) worn over the doublet by old men, who were not fully dressed without it; 1. 1. 87; (ii) for women; 4. 3. 74

Gradation, 'the process of advancing step by step' (O.E.D. 1); 1. 1. 37

Grange, country (or farm) house; 1. 1. 107

Gratify, reward (O.E.D. 1); 5. 2. 216

Green, immature, (fig.) inexperienced; 2. 1. 243

Grief, (a) affliction, (b) legal complaint; 1. 3. 215

Grievance, injury; 1. 2. 15

Grim, savage, unmerciful; 4. 2. 65; 5. 2. 206

Gripe, grip; 3. 3. 423

Grise(or'grece'), step; 1. 3. 200

Gross, palpable, evident; 1. 2. 72; (with quibble on 'gross' =coarse) 3. 3. 221

Grossly, (a) stupidly, (b) indecently; 3. 3. 397

Grow, used (freq.) of the passage of time; 2. 1. 192; 'grows to waste'=passes unprofitably (see note); 4. 2. 243

Guardage, guardianship, guardian; 1. 2. 70

Guards, two stars, β and γ, of the Lesser Bear (Ursa Minor), pointing to the pole-star; 2. 1. 15

Guinea-hen, (fig.) strumpet; 1. 3. 315

Gull, fool, dupe; 5. 2. 166

Guttered, furrowed, gullied; 2. 1. 69

Gyve, fetter; 2. 1. 170

Habit, mode of dress (O.E.D. 1) (see note); 1. 3. 108

Haggard, adult female hawk caught wild, which if tamed and trained made the best kind of falcon, but was otherwise worthless (see Madden, 142–3); 3. 3. 262

Happily, haply, perhaps; 3. 3. 240

Hard (adv.), hardly; 'full hard'=with very great difficulty; 1. 2. 10

Hardness, (i) hardship (see note); 1. 3. 233; (ii) difficulty; 3. 4. 34

Harlotry, harlot (contemptuous); 4. 2. 234

Harsh, discordant; 5. 2. 119

Haste-post-haste, with the utmost speed (words often written on urgent dispatches, see O.E.D. 'posthaste'); 1. 2. 37

Haunt, frequent; 'haunt about'=hang about; 1. 1. 97

Have with you, a stock reply of assent to 'will you go?'= Coming! I'm ready! (see O.E.D. have 19–20); 1. 2. 53

Having, 'allowance for expenses' (J.), but gen. in Sh.=possessions, property; 4. 3. 92

Head, (i) 'head and front' = height and breadth (Schmidt); 1. 3. 80; (ii)

'make head'=raise troops, muster; (fig.) 1. 3. 274

HEART-STRINGS, 'In old notions of anatomy, the tendons or nerves supposed to brace and sustain the heart' (O.E.D.); 3. 3. 263

HEARTED, from, or in, the heart; 1. 3. 364; 3. 3. 450

HEAT, (i) (fig.) urgency; 1. 2. 40; (ii) ardour, eagerness (see note to l. 264); 1. 3. 263

HEAVY, (i) burdensome, distressing; 1. 3. 258; 4. 2. 43, 117; (ii) dark; 5. 1. 42

HELLESPONT, the Dardanelles; 3. 3. 458

HELM, helmet; 1. 3. 272

HIE, hasten; 4. 3. 49; 5. 1. 34

HIGH (adv.), fully (cf. mod. 'it's high time'); 4. 2. 242

HIGH-WROUGHT, highly agitated, stormy; 2. 1. 2

HINT, (i) opportunity (O.E.D. 1); 1. 3. 142; (ii) suggestion; 1. 3. 166

HIP, 'have on the hip'=have at an advantage (a wrestling phrase= to get a grip round one's opponent's hips; cf. Tilley, H 474); 2. 1. 299

HISTORY, story; 2. 1. 253

HOBBY-HORSE, (fig.) prostitute (cf. *Wint.* 1. 2. 276); 4. 1. 154

HOLLA!, stop!; 1. 2. 56

HOLLANDER, Dutchman; 2. 3. 82

HOME (adv.), (i) 'to the point aimed at' (O.E.D. 4); 5. 1. 2; (ii) (fig.) 'to the very heart of the matter' (O.E.D. 5), plainly; 2. 1. 165

HONEST, a wide term of praise; (i) honourable; 1. 1. 49, etc.;

(ii) sexually moral (usu. of women), chaste; 3. 3. 386, etc.

HONESTY, honour; 5. 2. 248

HONOUR, (i) creditable action; 1. 2. 20; (ii) reputation; 2. 3. 54; 5. 2. 248; (iii) chastity; 4. 1. 14, 16, etc. (iv) 'in honour'=as a moral duty (O.E.D.9 *b*); 5. 2. 297

HOROLOGE, clock; 2. 3. 130

HOTLY, (fig.) urgently; 1. 2. 44

How!, what!; 1. 2. 93, etc.

HUMANE, civil, courteous (O.E.D. 1 *a*); 2. 1. 236

HUMOUR, (i) one of the four fluids in the body (blood, phlegm, choler, melancholy) supposed, acc. to Eliz. physiology, to determine a person's physical and mental qualities; 3. 4. 31; (ii) disposition, temperament; 3. 4. 129; (iii) whim, caprice; 4. 2. 166

HUNGERLY, hungrily; 3. 4. 109

HYDRA, the many-headed snake slain by Hercules as one of his twelve labours; 2. 3. 297

HYSSOP, aromatic herb, formerly much used medicinally; 1. 3. 322

IDLE, (i) void of worth, trifling; 1. 2. 95; 2. 3. 263; (ii) either=unprofitable, or =void of people, unfrequented (see note); 1. 3. 140

ILL-STARRED (1st instance O.E.D.), ill-fated (see 4. 2. 129 n); 5. 2. 275

IMMEDIATE, directly touching, personal; 3. 3. 159

IMPATIENT, angry (cf. *Ant.* 2. 2. 68); 1. 3. 242

IMPERIOUS, imperial (the lion being the king of animals); 2. 3. 270

IMPORT, concern; 1. 3. 283

IMPORTANCY, importance; 1. 3. 20.

IMPOSITION, a name or attribute bestowed, attribution (cf. O.E.D. 2 and see note); 2. 3. 264

IMPUTATION, implication (esp. of guilt); 3. 3. 408

INCLINING (ppl.a.), favourably bent, gracious; 2. 3. 333

INCLINING (sb.), side, party; 1. 2. 82

INCONTINENT, INCONTINENTLY, forthwith, immediately; 1. 3. 305; 4. 3. 12

INCORPORATE, united in body; 2. 1. 257

INDEX, (lit.) a pointer, (hence) prefatory table of contents; 2. 1. 252

INDIGN, unworthy, shameful; 1. 3. 273

INDIRECT, crooked, corrupt; 1. 3. 111

INDUE, lead on, induce; 3. 4. 150

INFERENCE, what is alleged, allegation; 3. 3. 185

INGENER (or 'enginer'), inventor (see note); 2. 1. 65

INGRAFT, implanted, constitutional; 2. 3. 140

INGREDIENCE, composition of a mixture; 2. 3. 301

INJOINT, unite; 1. 3. 35

INNOVATION, breach with custom, disorder, confusion; 2. 3. 38

INORDINATE, immoderate; 2. 3. 300

INSTEEPED, submerged; 2. 1. 70

INSTRUCTION, intimation; 4. 1. 41

INSTRUMENT, agent, means; (i) written mandate; 4. 1. 217; (ii) instigator; 4. 2. 46

INTENTIVELY, intently, attentively; 1. 3. 155

INVENTION (a term in rhetoric), 'the finding out or selection of topics to be treated, or arguments to be used' (O.E.D. 1 *d*), often=imagination; 2. 1. 125; 4. 1. 189

ITERANCE, iteration, repetition; 5. 2. 153

JANUS, the Roman god with two faces; 1. 2. 33

JEALOUS, suspicious in general (but passes into mod. sense); 3. 3. 185, etc.

JEALOUSY, suspicion (again passing into the specific sexual meaning, from 3. 3. 167 on); 3. 3. 150, etc.

JENNET, small Spanish horse; 1. 1. 114

JERK, strike, thrust (see note); 1. 2. 5

JESSES, narrow strips of soft leather, silk or other material, fastened round the legs of a trained hawk, with small silver rings through which passed the line that held it to the falconer's wrist; 3. 3. 263

JOINT-RING, finger-ring made in two separate parts; 4. 3. 74

JUMP (adv.), exactly; 2. 3. 378

JUMP (vb.), tally; 1. 3. 5

JUST, exact; 1. 3. 5; 2. 3. 124

JUSTICE, 'do...justice'=pledge in drinking (O.E.D. 11 *b*; cf. *2 H. IV*, 5. 3. 74, 'done me right'); 2. 3. 85–6

KEEP, (i) hold, conduct, preside over; 3. 3. 143; (ii) 'keep up'=sheathe; 1. 2. 59; (iii) 'keep up'=restrain, curb; 3. 1. 23

KNAVE, (i) servant; 1. 1. 45, 126; (ii) (*a*) servant, (*b*) rascal; 1. 1. 49

KNEE-CROOKING, obsequious; 1. 1. 45

KNOT, copulate (Schmidt); 4. 2. 63

LARGER, (*a*) greater, (*b*) grosser; 3. 3. 221

'LAS, alas; 5. 1. 111

LAW-DAY, meeting day for a court of law, esp. the sheriff's court; 3. 3. 143

LAY (sb.), stake in a wager; 2. 3. 316

LAY (vb.), 'lay upon'=give (an office, duty, etc.) to; 2. 1. 260

LEADEN, heavy, depressing; 3. 4. 181

LEARN, teach; 1. 3. 183

LEARNÉD, expert; 3. 3. 261

LEET, court of record held by the lord of the manor, yearly or half yearly; 3. 3. 143

LETHARGY, coma; 4. 1. 53

LETTER, letter (of recommendation); 1. 1. 36

LEVEL, be on a par, match; 1. 3. 239

LIBERAL (adj.), (i) licentious; 2. 1. 164; (ii) (*a*) generous, (*b*) licentious; 3. 4. 38, 46

LIBERAL (adv.), frankly, without restraint; 5. 2. 223

LIE, (i) dwell, lodge (with quibbles); 3. 4. 2, etc.; (ii) 'lie on'=calumniate (with quibble); 4. 1. 35

LIEUTENANTRY, office of lieutenant; 2. 1. 172

LIGHT, worthless and unstable, irresponsible; 2. 3. 273

LIGHT OF BRAIN, deranged; 4. 1. 270

LINE, provide a lining; 'line their coats'=feather their nests; 1. 1. 53

LIP, kiss; 4. 1. 71

LIST, (i) desire, inclination; 2. 1. 104; (ii) (a different word) limit, bounds; 4. 1. 75

LIVING, real (cf. *A.Y.L.* 3. 2. 408); 3. 3. 411

LOCUST, locust bean, fruit of the carob (see note); 1. 3. 347

LOOK AFTER, look for, demand (O.E.D. 12 *d*); 2. 1. 243

LOOSE, (i) immoral; 2. 1. 237; (ii) (*a*) loose in morals, (*b*) loose of tongue, indiscreet; 3. 3. 418

LOST, (lit.) wasted, (hence) groundless; 5. 2. 272

LOUD, clamorous, (hence) urgent; 1. 1. 151

LOWN (or LOON), rogue, scamp; 2. 3. 91

LUSTY, lustful; 2. 1. 289

MAGNIFICO, title of magnates of Venice; 1. 2. 12

MAIDHOOD, maidenhood; 1. 1. 173

MAIN, (ellipt.) main sea, open sea; 2. 1. 3, 39

MAKE, (i) 'make after'=go after; 1. 1. 69; (ii) interrogatively=do; 'what makes he'=what is he doing (a common idiom); 1. 2. 49; 3. 4. 173; (iii) 'make away' =get away; 5. 1. 58; (iv) 'make mocks with', see MOCK; 5. 2. 154

MALIGNANT, rebellious (esp. against God, O.E.D. 1), infidel; 5. 2. 355

MAMMER, stammer, mutter, (hence) hesitate, waver; 3. 3. 71

MAN, provide men (see note); 5. 2. 273

MANAGE, carry on; 2. 3. 211

MANDRAGORA, mandrake, a poisonous plant which gives a powerful narcotic; 3. 3. 332

MANE, crest of hair, (fig.) crest of wave; 2. 1. 13

MARBLE, (a) shining like marble (cf. Aen. vi. 729, aequor marmoreum), (b) hard as marble, inexorable; 3. 3. 462

MARK, 'God bless the mark'= God help me (prob. orig. a formula to avert an evil omen), here derisive; 1. 1. 33

MASTER, a polite form of address; 2. 3. 119 etc.

MAZARD, (lit.) drinking cup or bowl, (jocularly) head (cf. Ham. 5. 1. 87); 2. 3. 150

MEASURE OF LAWN, a 'plight' (O.E.D. sb.² 3), acc. to Linthicum (p. 98), 1¼ yds.

MEAT, food, meal; 3. 3. 169; 4. 2. 171

MEDICINE, (included drugs for both remedial and hurtful ends) poison, philtre; 1. 3. 61; 4. 1. 45

MERCY, 'cry mercy'=beg pardon; 4. 2. 89; 5. 1. 69

MERE, absolute, utter; 2. 2. 3

MESS (lit.) portion of food, (hence) piece, gobbet; 4. 1. 199

MINCE, make light of; 2. 3. 243

MINERAL, mineral medicine or poison; 1. 2. 74; 2. 1. 291

MINION, hussy; 5. 1. 33

MISCHIEF, misfortune; 1. 3. 204, 205

MISUSE, misconduct; 4. 2. 110

MOCK, 'make mocks with'= make game of (O.E.D. sb. 1 b); 5. 2. 154

MODERN, 'ordinary, commonplace' (On.) (see note); 1. 3. 109

MOE, more; 4. 3. 56

MOOD, anger; 2. 3. 268

MORALLER, moralist (the only O.E.D. ex.); 2. 3. 292

MORTAL, deadly, fatal; 2. 1. 72; 3. 3. 357; 3. 4. 119; 5. 2. 208

MOTION, (i) impulse (of mind); 1. 2. 75 (see note); 1. 3. 95, 330; (ii) movement (of body); 2. 3. 170

MOUNTEBANK, itinerant quack; 1. 3. 61

MOVE, stir; (i) plead (a cause or suit), supplicate; 2. 3. 375; 3. 4. 19, 170; (ii) perturb, upset; 3. 3. 219, 226; 4. 1. 235

MUCH (predicative use) 'it is much'=it is a serious matter; 4. 1. 243

MUMMY, preparation from dead bodies (see *Macb.* G.) credited with preservative and restorative powers, a kind of elixir; 3. 4. 77

MUTINY, fall to strife; 2. 1. 268

MUTUALITY, reciprocation (O.E.D. 1); 2. 1. 256

MYSTERY, trade, craft; 4. 2. 30

NAKED, without weapons, unarmed; 5. 2. 261

NAPKIN, handkerchief (the usual sense in Sh.); 3. 3. 289, 292, 323

NATIVE, natural; 1. 1. 63; 2. 1. 214

NECK, 'on your neck'=(laying) a charge upon a person (freq. in 16th c.); 5. 2. 173

NEPHEW, grandson; 1. 1. 113

NEW-CREATE, create for the first time; 4. 1. 277

NEXT, nearest, quickest; 1. 3. 205

NICE, slender, thin; 3. 3. 15

NICK, 'in the nick'=at the right moment; 5. 2. 319

NIGHT-GOWN, dressing-gown; 4. 3. 34

NONSUIT, (a legal term) bring about the voluntary withdrawal of the plaintiff; 1. 1. 16

NORTH, (poet.) the north wind (O.E.D. B 4); 5. 2. 223

NOTHING (adv.), not at all; 2. 3. 220, 283

NOTORIOUS, egregious; 4. 2. 141; 5. 2. 242

OBJECT, spectacle; 5. 2. 366

OBSERVANCE, observation; 3. 3. 154

OCCASION, (i) opportunity; 2. 1. 239, 261; 3. 1. 49; (ii) 'on great occasion'=for an important reason; 4. 1. 58

ODD, fortuitous; 2. 3. 127

ODD-EVEN (adj.) 'odd-even... time of night'='midnight or thereabouts' (On.); 1. 1. 124

ODDS, strife; 2. 3. 181

OFF-CAP, doff the cap (a sign of respect); 1. 1. 10

OFFENCE, deliberate harm; 2. 3. 48, 218

OFFEND, (i) pain, grieve (physically); 2. 3. 195; 3. 4. 51; (ii) wrong, sin against; 5. 2. 62

OFFICE, pl. parts of building for household work, esp. kitchen, buttery, cellars, etc.; 2. 2. 8

OFFICED, on duty; 1. 3. 270

OLD, customary; 1. 1. 37

OPEN, guileless; 1. 3. 397

OPINION, (i) public opinion (O.E.D. 1c); 1. 3. 224; (ii) reputation; 2. 3. 191; (iii) significance (see note); 4. 2. 110

OPPOSITE, opposed; 1. 2. 67

OPPOSITION, combat; 2. 3. 180

ORDER, 'take order'=make arrangements; 5. 2. 76

OTHER, anything else, otherwise; 4. 2. 13

OTTOMITES, Ottoman Turks; 1. 3. 33, 234; 2. 3. 167

OUT OF THE WAY, see WAY; 1. 3. 357; 3. 4. 83

OWE, own; 1. 1. 67; 3. 3. 335

PADDLE WITH, stroke or finger fondly (cf. *Ham.* 3. 4. 185, *Wint.* 1. 2. 115); 2. 1. 250

PARAGON, match in perfection (see note); 2. 1. 62

PARALLEL, running even with, in conformity with; 2. 3. 342

PARCEL, part, portion; 'by parcels'=piecemeal (O.E.D. 1); 1. 3. 154

PARROT, 'speak parrot'=talk nonsense, utter words without understanding their meaning; 2. 3. 274

PART, (i) personal quality; 1. 2. 31; 1. 3. 253; 3. 3. 266; (ii) 'in your own part'=on your own behalf; 1. 3. 74

PARTIALLY, by partiality, with undue favour (O.E.D. 1); 2. 3. 214

PARTICULAR, personal, private; 1. 3. 55

PASS (sb.), thrust (of a weapon); 5. 1. 23 S.D.

PASS (vb.) (i) pass through, experience; 1. 3. 131, 167; (ii) let pass, disregard; 2. 3. 242

PASSAGE, (i) 'passage free'=free course; 1. 2. 98; (ii) people passing by (O.E.D. 1 b); 5. 1. 37

PASSING (adv.), surpassing, exceedingly; 1. 3. 160

PATTERN, model, example; 5. 2. 11

PECULIAR, private, personal; 1. 1. 61; 3. 3. 80; 4. 1. 69

PEEVISH, senseless (O.E.D. 1); 2. 3. 181; 4. 3. 90

PEG, 'set down the pegs'=(lit.) slacken the string of a musical instrument, (fig.) lower in esteem, mortify (O.E.D. 3; cf. Tilley, P 181); 2. 1. 198

PERDURABLE, lasting; 1. 3. 338

PERFECT, 'perfect soul'=clear conscience; 1. 2. 31

PERIOD, conclusion, end; 5. 2. 359

PERPLEXED, bewildered (O.E.D. 1); 5. 2. 348

PICK, cull, select; 4. 3. 106

PIECE, mend; 1. 3. 219

PIONEER, a soldier armed not with weapons but with spade or pickaxe to dig trenches, etc.; the lowest of the camp; 3. 3. 348

PITH, strength; 1. 3. 83

PLACE, lodging; 1. 3. 237

PLATFORM, level place for mounting guns; 2. 3. 119

PLEASANCE, pleasure, delight (O.E.D. 1); 2. 3. 285

PLIANT, what lends itself to the purpose, (hence) suitable; 1. 3. 151

PLUCK, pull; 4. 1. 140

PLUME UP, set a crest on (see note); 1. 3. 391

POINT ON, point to, presage (see note); 5. 2. 49

POISE (sb.), weight (O.E.D. 1); 3. 3. 83

POISE (vb.), to weigh in a balance; 1. 3. 327

POLE, pole star (in the Lesser Bear); 2. 1. 15

POLICY, prudent conduct of public affairs; 2. 3. 268; 3. 3. 14

PONTIC SEA, Black Sea; 3. 3. 455

POPPY, the opium poppy; 3. 3. 332

PORTANCE, bearing, behaviour; 1. 3. 139

POSITION, proposition, assertion (O.E.D. 2); 2. 1. 233;

'in position distinctly'=
categorically; 3. 3. 236

POST-POST-HASTE, with the
utmost speed (cf. HASTE-
POST-HASTE); 1. 3. 46

POTENTIAL, powerful (O.E.D.
1); 1. 2. 13

POTTING, tippling (O.E.D. 1);
2. 3. 75

POTTLE, two-quart pot; 2. 3.
82

POTTLE-DEEP, to the bottom
of the 2 quart tankard; 2. 3.
52

Pox, 'a pox of'=a plague on,
hang; 1. 3. 356

PRACTICE, plot, trickery; 1. 3.
102; 3. 4. 145; 5. 2. 294

PRACTISE ON, UPON, plot
against, use trickery against;
1. 2. 73; 2. 1. 304

PRANK, wanton act; 2. 1. 142;
3. 3. 204

PRATE, speak insolently; 1. 2.
6; 2. 3. 148

PRECIOUS, (used intensively)
egregious, arrant; 5. 2. 238

PREFER, (i) put forward, prof-
fer; 1. 3. 109; (ii) promote
(O.E.D. 1); 2. 1. 272

PREFERMENT, promotion; 1. 1.
36

PREGNANT, cogent, obvious
(from Fr. *preignant*=press-
ing, not Lat. *praegnans*=
full of meaning); 2. 1. 232

PREPARATION, (lit.) action of
preparing; hence (concr.)
hostile fleet (cf. *1 H IV*, 4.
1. 93; *Cor.* 1. 2. 15); 1. 3.
14, 221

PREPOSTEROUS, extraordinary;
1. 3. 328–9

PREPOSTEROUSLY, extraordin-
arily, unnaturally; 1. 3. 62

PREROGATIVED, privileged; 3.
3. 276

PRESCRIPTION, (a) immemorial
right; (b) medical prescription; 1. 3. 309

PRESENT, immediate; 1. 2. 90;
3. 3. 48

PRESENTLY, (i) at once (the
more usual meaning); 3. 1.
35; 5. 2. 55; (ii) very soon;
2. 1. 211; 2. 3. 299

PRICE, value, worth; 1. 1. 11

PRIDE, sexual desire; 3. 3. 406

PRIME, sexually excited
(O.E.D. adj. 5, the only ex.;
perhaps connected with dialect 'prime'=ready, eager,
see D.D.); 3. 3. 405

PRIZE, capture, seizure (esp.
of a ship at sea); 1. 2. 51

PROBABLE, demonstrable
(O.E.D. 1); 1. 2. 76

PROBAL (app. a nonce word),
probable; 2. 3. 331

PROBATION, proof; 3. 3. 367

PROCESS, proceeding (see note);
1. 3. 142

PROCLAIM, denounce; 1. 1. 70

PROCREANT, procreator; 4. 2.
28

PROFANE, indecent, unseemly;
1. 1. 115; 2. 1. 163

PROFIT, benefit (O.E.D. 1);
3. 3. 80, 381; 4. 2. 233

PROMETHEAN HEAT, celestial
fire. Acc. to Gk. myth,
Prometheus stole fire from
heaven to bring to men;
and acc. to medieval and
post-medieval 'philosophy'
(=science) life and the
spiritual side of human
nature are derived from the
celestial fire which lay
above the moon; 5. 2. 12

PROMULGATE, publish; 1. 2. 21

PROPER, (i) one's own; 1. 3. 69, 264; (ii) handsome; 1. 3. 390; 4. 3. 35

PROPERTY, natural characteristics; 1. 1. 173

PROPONTIC, Sea of Marmora; 3. 3. 458

PROPOSE, (a) propound a scheme, (b) hold forth in speech; 1. 1. 25

PROPRIETY, proper state or condition; 2. 3. 172

PROSPECT, view; 'to that prospect'= to present themselves thus; 3. 3. 400

PROSPEROUS, favourable; 1. 3. 244

PROTEST, affirm (O.E.D. 1); 4. 2. 209

PROVE, become (cf. *Tp.* 4. 1. 238–9); 4. 3. 27

PUBLIC, common, accessible to all; 4. 2. 74

PUDDING, (lit.) the stomach or entrail of pig stuffed with meat, etc. and boiled; (hence) stuff and nonsense; 2. 1. 249

PUDDLE, make muddy, (hence) trouble; 3. 4. 147

PURCHASE, acquisition; 2. 3. 9

PURE, sheer; 5. 2. 208

PUT, (i) 'put to it'= force one to do one's utmost; 2. 1. 118; 3. 3. 473; (ii) 'put on' = encourage, incite; 2. 1. 146; 2. 3. 344; (iii) 'put from'= divert from; 3. 4. 91; (iv) 'put up'= put up with, submit to; 4. 2. 180; (v) thrust; 5. 1. 2

PUTTING ON, incitement, goading on; 2. 1. 298

QUALIFICATION, dilution, (fig.) disaffection (see note); 2. 1. 269

QUALIFY, dilute; 2. 3. 38

QUALITY, (i) (a) character, disposition, (b) profession; 1. 3. 251, 282; (ii) attributes; 3. 3. 355

QUARTER, 'in quarter'= in relations with one another; 2. 3. 176

QUAT, pimple, (contemptuous of a person); 5. 1. 11

QUEST, search, (fig.) search party; 1. 2. 46

QUESTION, (lit.) judicial examination or trial; hence (fig.) trial by arms (see note); 1. 3. 23; (ii) discourse, conversation; 1. 3. 113

QUICKEN, (i) receive life; 3. 3. 279; (ii) give life; 4. 2. 68

QUIRK, clever turn, conceit, flourish; 2. 1. 63

QUILLET, quibble; 3. 1. 23

RAISE, arouse; 1. 1. 159, 168, 183; 1. 2. 29, 43; 2. 3. 246

RANK, lascivious; 2. 1. 300; 3. 3. 234

RASH (adj.) reckless and precipitate; 2. 1. 266; 5. 2. 137

RASH (adv.), excitedly; 3. 4. 82

RATHER, earlier, sooner; 2. 3. 229

REBEL, (with specialized sexual meaning; cf. *M.V.* 3. 1. 32; *Meas.* 3. 2. 112; *2 H. IV*, 2. 4. 347–8; *All's*, G. 'rebellion'); 3. 4. 43

RECOGNIZANCE, (lit.) bond formally entered into; (hence) solemn token; 5. 2. 217

RECOIL, (*a*) spring back in horror, (*b*) revert; 3. 3. 238

RECOMMEND, inform; 1. 3. 41

RECONCILIATION, 'take reconciliation', see TAKE; 3. 3. 48

RECOVER, (i) bring back to friendship, reconcile; 2. 3. 267; (ii) get hold of; 5. 2. 243

REFER (refl.), appeal; 1. 2. 64

REFERENCE, assignment; 1. 3. 237

REFUSE, reject; 3. 1. 47

REGARD, (i) respect, connexion; 1. 1. 154; (ii) view, prospect; 2. 1. 40

RELUME, rekindle; 5. 2. 13

REMEMBRANCE, keepsake; 3. 3. 293; 3. 4. 190

REMORSE, pity (see note); 3. 3. 470

REPEAL, call back (into favour); 2. 3. 350

REPROBANCE, state of reprobation; 5. 2. 212

RESERVE, keep; 3. 3. 297

RESOLVED, freed from uncertainty, settled; 3. 3. 182

RESPECT, (i) rank, standing; 1. 3. 282; (ii) regard, favour; 2. 1. 209; 4. 2. 191

RE-STEM (naut.), head in the opposite direction (cf. O.E.D. stem vb.³); 1. 3. 37

REVENGE, desire for revenge (O.E.D. 1 *b*); 4. 3. 94

REVEREND, revered, honoured; 1. 1. 94; 1. 3. 33, 76

REVOLT, mutinous act; but here prob. outburst or revulsion of sexual desire (cf. *Tw. N.* 2. 4. 99 and O.E.D. 'revolt', vb. 3); 1. 1. 135; 3. 3. 190

RHEUM, see SALT RHEUM; 3. 4. 51

RIGHT, privilege; 1. 3. 257

ROUND, plain, straightforward; 1. 3. 90

ROUSE, (prob. aphetic form of *carouse*), full draught of liquor, bumper; 2. 3. 62

ROUT, uproar, riot; 2. 3. 206

RUFFIAN, bluster, rage; 2. 1. 7

SADLY, gravely; 2. 1. 32

SAGITTARY (see note); 1. 1. 159; 1. 3. 115

SALT, salacious, lascivious; 2. 1. 237; 3. 3. 406

SALT RHEUM, running cold (cf. *Err.* 3. 2. 128); 3. 4. 51

SANS, without; 1. 3. 64

SATISFY, (*a*) liquidate (a debt), (*b*) content (cf. l. 316); (*c*) answer; 5. 2. 320

SAUCY, insolent; 1. 1. 129

'SBLOOD, an oath (= God's blood); 1. 1. 4

SCAN, consider; 3. 3. 247

SCANT, (i) neglect; 1. 3. 267; (ii) diminish, cut down; 4. 3. 92

SCAPE (sb. and vb.), aphetic variant of 'escape'; 1. 3. 136; 5. 1. 113

SCATTERING, random; 3. 3. 154

SCION, slip, sucker, etc. for grafting; 1. 3. 332

SCORE (sb.), record of a debt; 3. 4. 183

SCORE (vb.), see note; 4. 1. 127

SCURVY, contemptible; 1. 2. 7; 4. 2. 141, 194

SCUSE, aphetic variant of 'excuse'; 4. 1. 79

SEA-BANK, sea shore; 4. 1. 133

SEAL, token or symbol of a covenant; 2. 3. 337

SEA-MARK, object serving for the direction of mariners; such marks were set up by Trinity House acc. to an act of 1566 (O.E.D. 2); 5. 2. 271

SEARCH, investigation, (fig.) search party; 1. 1. 159

SEA-SIDE, sea shore; 2. 1. 36

SECURE (adj.), free from suspicion or care; 3. 3. 200; 4. 1. 71

SEEL (UP), (term of falconry) close a hawk's eyes by stitching the eyelids, (fig.) hoodwink, blind; 1. 3. 269; 3. 3. 212

SEEMING, external appearance (as distinguished from reality); 1. 3. 109; 2. 1. 236; 3. 3. 211

SEGREGATION, dispersal, scattering; 2. 1. 10

SELF-BOUNTY, personal goodness; 3. 3. 202

SELF-CHARITY, love for one's self; 2. 3. 198

SE'NNIGHT, week; 2. 1. 77

SENSE, (i) perception, understanding; 1. 1. 132; 1. 2. 64, 72; 1. 3. 12, 63, 69; 2. 1. 71; 3. 3. 340, 376; (ii) the five senses; 4. 3. 95; (iii) 'to the sense'=to the quick; 5. 1. 11; (iv) opinion; 5. 2. 292

SENTENCE, (a) maxim, aphorism; (b) judicial sentence; 1. 3. 199, 212, 214, 216

SEQUENT, consecutive; 1. 2. 41

SEQUESTER, sequestration (O.E.D. 1, only ex.); 3. 4. 40

SEQUESTRATION, separation; 1. 3. 344–5

SERVITOR, servant; 1. 3. 40

SESSION, sitting of a court of justice; 1. 2. 86; 3. 3. 143

SET (sb.), (i) slip, sucker; 1. 3. 331; (ii) round of the clock; 2. 3. 130

SET (vb.), (i) 'set down the pegs', see PEG; 2. 1. 197–8; (ii) 'set the watch'=mount guard; 2. 3. 119–20; (iii) 'set on'=instigate; 2. 3. 206, 376; 5. 2. 190, 331

SEVERAL, separate, different; 1. 2. 46

SHADOWING, (a) obscuring, darkening, (b) symbolising (see note); 4. 1. 40

SHAKE OFF, cast off, abandon; 4. 2. 158

SHAPE, frame (in imagination), imagine; 2. 1. 55; 3. 3. 151

SHIFT AWAY, contrive to get (a person) out of the way; 4. 1. 78

SHIPPED, 'well shipped'=provided with a good ship; 2. 1. 47

SHREWD, of evil import, ominous; 3. 3. 431

SHRIFT, confessional; 3. 3. 24

SHUT UP IN, confine to; 3. 4. 125

SIBYL, prophetess; 3. 4. 73

SIEGE, (lit.) seat of office, (fig.) rank, dignity (cf. *Ham.* 4. 7. 75); 1. 2. 22

SIGN, (i) ensign; 1. 1. 157; (ii) semblance; 1. 1. 158

SIGNIOR (Ital.), gentleman, sir; 1. 1. 85, etc.

SIGNIORY, governing body of Venice; 1. 2. 18

SIMPLE, silly; 4. 2. 20

SINK, fall, perish; 2. 3. 205

SIR, fine gentleman (sarcastic); 2. 1. 174

SIRRAH, form of address to inferiors; 3. 4. 1.

SITH, since; 3. 3. 382, 413

SKILLET, saucepan; 1. 3. 272

SLACK, be remiss in, neglect (O.E.D. 1); 4. 3. 88

SLAVE, villain; 3. 3. 444; 4. 2. 133, etc.

SLIPPER, slippery, shifty; 2. 1. 238

SLUBBER, sully; 1. 3. 226

SMALL BEER, (lit.) weak beer, (fig.) trivial occupations (O.E.D., citing as earliest ex.); 2. 1. 160

SMOCK, woman's under-garment or night-dress, a 'straight two-piece garment, 30 to 40 in. long with collar and sleeve-bands usually lace-trimmed' (Linthicum, p. 189); 5. 2. 276

SMOOTH, bland; 1. 3. 395

SNIPE, (type of foolishness) fool; 1. 3. 383

SNORT, snore ('common from Chaucer to 1650', O.E.D.); 1. 1. 91

SO, (sarcastic) all right, good!; 4. 1. 123

SOFT, gently, wait!; 5. 2. 340

SOLICITATION, suit (see note); 4. 2. 200

SOLICITOR, advocate; 3. 3. 27

SOMETHING, somewhat; 2. 3. 195

SOON AT NIGHT, (a common idiom) towards evening; 3. 4. 202

SORRY, painful, miserable; 3. 4. 51

SPEAK WITHIN DOOR, see DOOR; 4. 2. 145

16

SPECULATIVE, having the power of vision; 1. 3. 270

SPEED, succeed; 4. 1. 108

SPEND, (i) utter, say; 1. 2. 48; (ii) squander (see note to l. 190); 2. 3. 191

SPLEEN, the supposed seat of all ill humours; 4. 1. 88

SPLINTER, splint; 2. 3. 316

SPOIL, maim; 5. 1. 54

SPOT, work or stitch details of a pattern in embroidery or lace (see Linthicum, pp. 129–30; cf. *Cor.* 1. 3. 56); 3. 3. 437

SQUIRE,   (contemptuously) young fellow; 4. 2. 146

STAMP, coin (see note); 2. 1. 239

STAND (denoting state, condition=be), (i) 'stand in act' =be in progress; 1. 1. 152; (ii) 'stand in'=be the object of; 1. 3. 70; (iii) 'stand in bold cure', see CURE; 2. 1. 51

START, startle, disturb; 1. 1. 102

STARTINGLY, (lit.) jerkily ('start' = move suddenly), hence, 'abruptly' (Schmidt); 3. 4. 82

STAY, await; 4. 2. 171

STEAD, help, benefit; 1. 3. 338

STEEP-DOWN, precipitous (cf. Matt. viii. 32 (Genevan vers.) 'a stiepe downe place into the sea', and *Son.* 7. 5, 'the 'steep-up heavenly hill'); 5. 2. 283

STILL (adv.), constantly; 1. 3. 129, 147, etc.

STILLNESS, quietness of behaviour, steadiness; 2. 3. 187

STING, goad, impulse; 1. 3. 330

STOMACH, appetite, capacity; 5. 2. 79

STONE (sb.), thunderbolt; 5. 2. 237

STONE (vb.), turn to stone, harden; 5. 2. 66

STOP, (i) pause (in speaking), hesitation; 3. 3. 123; (ii) obstruction; 5. 2. 267

STOUP, drinking vessel (of varying measure); 2. 3. 28

STRAIGHT (adv.), straightway, immediately; 1. 1. 138; 1. 3. 48; 3. 3. 88, etc.

STRAIN, force, urge; 3. 3. 252

STRANGENESS, aloofness, estrangement; 3. 3. 12

STRANGER, foreigner (O.E.D. 1); 1. 1. 137

STREAM, current (of any kind; cf. Gulf Stream); 2. 3. 61

STUBBORN, (a) difficult (to work or manage), (b) fierce; 1. 3. 227

STUFF, substance; 'very stuff o'th'conscience'= 'absolute matter of conscience' (On.); 1. 2. 2

SUBDUE, overpower; 1. 2. 81

SUBDUED, (i) subjugated; 1. 3. 250; (ii) overcome (by grief); 5. 2. 350

SUBSTITUTE, deputy; 1. 3. 223

SUBTLE, crafty, cunning; 2. 1. 238; 4. 2. 21

SUCCESS, sequel, result; 3. 3. 224

SUDDEN, (i) hasty, impetuous; 2. 1. 266; (ii) immediate; 4. 2. 190

SUFFERANCE, suffering, damage; 2. 1. 23

SUFFICIENCY, ability, competence; 1. 3. 224

SUFFICIENT, able (esp. for a post or task); 3. 4. 95; 4. 1 266

SUGGEST, tempt; 2. 3. 345

SUPERVISOR, (a) looker-on, (b) director; 3. 3. 397

SUPPLY, (i) occupy by a substitute; 3. 3. 17; (ii) satisfy the desires of (cf. Meas. 5. 1. 208); 4. 1. 28

SUSTAIN ITSELF, 'find a place' (O.E.D.), hang; 5. 2. 263

SWAG-BELLIED, having a pendulous belly; 2. 3. 76

SWEETING, sweet; 2. 3. 248

SWELLING, 'noble swelling'= swelling with nobility, high-mettled (see note); 2. 3. 53

SYRUP, medicinal decoction (O.E.D. 1 a); 3. 3. 333

TAINT, (i) injure, impair; 1. 3. 271; 4. 2. 162; (ii) cast a slur on; 2. 1. 262

TAKE, (i) 'take up' (a quarrel) =settle, arrange amicably; 1. 3. 173; (ii) 'take reconciliation'=accept reconciliation (cf. K.J. 3. 1. 17 n. 'take a truce'); 3. 3. 48; (iii) 'take out'=take a copy of; 3. 3. 298; 3. 4. 184; 4. 1. 150, 153, 155; (iv) 'take off'=take away; 5. 2. 333; (v.) 'take order', see ORDER; 5. 2. 76

TALL, (conventional epithet for large ships, On.) fine, gallant; 2. 1. 79

TAPER, candle; 1. 1. 142, 167; 5. 2. 13 S.D.

TASK, put a strain on; 2. 3. 40

TEEM, conceive, become pregnant; 4. 1 245

TELL, (i) 'never tell me', an expression of incredulity or impatience,= fiddle-de-dee; 1. 1. 1; (ii) strike (of bell or clock); 2. 2. 10; (iii) count; 3. 3. 171

TEMPER, degree of hardness imparted to steel; 5. 2. 256

TENDERLY, gently (O.E.D. 1); 1. 3. 399

TENDERNESS, youthfulness (O.E.D. 1); 2. 1. 229

TENTED, covered with tents; 'tented field'= camp; 1. 3. 85

TERM, respect (O.E.D. 10, citing this and *M.V.* 2. 1. 13), 'in any just term'= in any way justly (On.) (see note); 1. 1. 39

TEST, evidence, testimony; 1. 3. 107

THEORIC, theory; 1. 1. 24

THING, pudendum (cf. Chaucer, *Wife of Bath*, Prol. 121); 3. 3. 304

THINK UPON, remember; 5. 2. 194

THRICE-DRIVEN, thrice-winnowed (technical term= with the lighter down separated from the heavier by currents of air driven three times through it); 1. 3. 231

THROW ON, UPON, (i) in a good sense, bestow on, impart to; 1. 1. 52; 1. 3. 225; (ii) in a bad sense, inflict on, lay on; 1. 1. 73; 4. 2. 117; 4. 3. 91

TIE IN, bind up with; 1. 1. 136

TILT, thrust; 2. 3. 179

TIMBERED, built of wood; 'stoutly timbered' = a strong one; 2. 1. 48

TIME, (i) 'in good time'= (iron.) forsooth; 1. 1. 32; (ii) present circumstances; 1. 3. 300; (iii) 'in happy time'= (ellipt.) you have come at the right time, well met; 3. 1. 29; (iv) musical measure; (fig.) 4. 1. 92; (v) 'the time of scorn'= the scornful world (Schmidt, On.) (see note); 4. 2. 55

TIMOROUS, terrifying; 1. 1. 76

TINE, wild vetch, tare (see note); 1. 3. 322

TIRE, exhaust; 2. 1. 65

TITTLE, legal right to possession; 1. 2. 31

TOGÈD, gowned (not an anachronism. *Togati* seems to have been an epithet for the Councillors; cf. 'togeman', cant term for cloak); 1. 1. 25

TOP, 'cover', copulate with (O.E.D. 11, citing *Oth.* and Ford, 1633, only); cf. 'tup' of different origin but related meaning); 3. 3. 398; 5. 2. 139

TOUCH, (i) 'touch near'= come near, touch to the quick; 2. 3. 216; (ii) test (as with a touchstone); 3. 3. 82; (iii) concern; 4. 1. 197

TOY, (i) trifling matter, trifle; 1. 3. 268; (ii) idle fancy, freak; 3. 4. 160

TRADE, occupation, profession; 1. 2. 1

TRANCE, swoon; 4. 1. 43 S.D.

TRASH, worthless person or stuff; 2. 1. 297; 3. 3. 160; 5. 1. 85

TRAVERSE,= (ellipt.) traverse one's ground, a military term, to march backwards

TRAVERSE (*cont.*):
and forwards (On.) (see note); 1. 3. 368

TRICK, caprice; 4. 2. 130

TRIMMED, decked out; 1. 1. 50

TRIUMPH (sb.), public rejoicing; 'put oneself into triumph'=make holiday; 2. 2. 4

TRIUMPH (vb.), celebrate victory (see note); 4. 1. 119

TRUMP, trumpet; 3. 3. 353

TUP (vb.) copulate with a ewe (from 'tup'=ram; cf. TOP); 1. 1. 90

TURK, (i) Sultan of Turkey; 1. 3. 20, 22, 27; (ii) infidel; 2. 1. 114

TURN (sb.) action (gen. with a qualifying word; cf. mod. 'a good turn'); 5. 2. 210

TURN (vb.), (*a*) return, (*b*) play false, (*c*) turn to men; 4. 1. 253, 254 (see note), 255

TWIGGEN, cased in wickerwork; 2. 3. 148

UD'S PITY, bless you! (an oath =God's pity); 4. 3. 76

UNBITTED, unbridled; 1. 3. 330

UNBLEST, (i) accursed; 2. 3. 300; (ii) miserable, wretched; 5. 1. 34

UNBONNETED, (see note); 1. 2. 23

UNBOOKISH, ignorant, artless; 4. 1. 101

UNCAPABLE, incapable; 4. 2. 230

UNDERTAKE, (abs.) take up a matter, take a matter in hand; 2. 3. 323

UNDERTAKER, 'be his undertaker'=settle his matters, dispose of him; 4. 1. 210

UNDO, annul; 4. 3. 72

UNDONE, (*a*) wrecked; (*b*) ruined by seduction; 5. 2. 80

UNFOLD, expose; 3. 3. 245; 4. 2. 142; 5. 1. 21

UNFOLDING, disclosing, explanation; 1. 3. 244

UNHANDSOME, (*a*) unfair in appearance; (*b*) unfair in mind; (*c*) unskilled, inept; 3. 4. 155

UNHATCHED, not yet brought to light (Schmidt); 3. 4. 145

UNHOUSÉD, homeless; 1. 2. 26

UNKIND, (*a*) unnatural, (*b*) cruel; 4. 1. 224

UNLACE, undo (see note); 2. 3. 190

UNPERFECTNESS, imperfection, vice; 2. 3. 290

UNPROPER, (*a*) not exclusively one's own, (*b*) improper, indecent (Schmidt) (see note); 4. 1. 68

UNPROVIDE, unsettle, make irresolute; 4. 1. 205

UNQUIETNESS, disquietude, perturbation; 3. 4. 137

UNSKILFUL, lacking in expert judgement, inept; 1. 3. 27

UNSURE, uncertain; 3. 3. 154

UNWHOLESOME, unsound; 4. 1. 121

UNWIT, deprive of wits; 2. 3. 178

USE (sb.), custom, habit; 4. 1. 275; 4. 3. 105

USE (vb.), have sexual intercourse with; 5. 2. 73

USURPED, (*a*) appropriated without right; (*b*) false (see note); 1. 3. 340

VAIN, useless; 3. 3. 472

VANTAGE, 'to th'vantage'=
to boot, in addition; 4. 3. 85

VESSEL, body (cf. 1 Thess. iv.
3–5); 4. 2. 84

VEXATION, torment (On.); 1.
1. 73

VICIOUS, (a) vicious in mod.
sense, (b) wrong, mistaken
(O.E.D. 6 d—the only ex.
of this precise use); 3. 3.
148

VIOLENCE, (i) violation, breach
of duty; 1. 3. 249; ve-
hemence; 2. 1. 219

VIRTUE, power; 1. 3. 318,
319, etc.

VIRTUOUS, efficacious; 3. 4.
115

VISAGE, assumed appearance
(O.E.D. 8); 1. 1. 50

VOICE, vote, approval; 1. 3.
225, 260

VOLUBLE, shifty, plausible,
glib; 2. 1. 235

VOTARIST, votary, person under
a vow; 4. 2. 189

VOUCH (sb.), testimony; 2. 1.
146

VOUCH (vb.); bear witness;
1. 3. 261

WAGE, hazard; 1. 3. 30

WARRANT, 'out of warrant'=
unlawful; 1. 2. 79

WARRANTY, authorization; 5.
2. 63

WASH, drown, drench; 5. 2.
283

WASTE, 'grow to waste',
see GROW; 4. 2. 243

WASTED, gone by, past; 1. 3.
84

WATCH, WATCHING (vb. and
vbl. sb.), (i) stay awake;
2. 3. 130; 3. 3. 287; (ii)

term in falconry=to pre-
vent a hawk from sleeping
in order to tame it; 3. 3. 23;
(iii) watch for; 4. 2. 236

WAY, 'out of the way'=(i) beside the mark; 1. 3. 357;
(ii) gone astray, missing;
3. 4. 83

WAYWARD, capriciously wilful;
3. 3. 294

WEED UP, eradicate; 1. 3. 322

WELL-PAINTED, well simu-
lated; 4. 1. 258

WELL SAID, well done, bravo!
2. 1. 167; 4. 1. 115; 5. 1.
98

WHAT, interr. (with ref. to
name, identity), who; 1. 1.
95, etc.

WHEELING, wandering about
(On.); 1. 1. 137

WHIP ME, (see note); 1. 1. 49

WHIPSTER, contemptible fellow; 5. 2. 247

WHISTLE OFF, (term of falconry) release a hawk from
the fist; 3. 3. 264

WHOLESOME, (i) healthy, salu-
tary; 1. 1. 146; 'wholesome
wisdom'=sound prudence;
3. 1. 46

WILD, (i) 'wild fame'=the
extravagances of hearsay;
2. 1. 62; (ii) in a disturbed
or lawless mood; 2. 3. 210

WILL, (i) desire, esp. carnal
desire; 1. 3. 346; 3. 3. 234,
238; 4. 2. 153; (ii) purpose;
1. 3. 391

WILLOW, emblem of disap-
pointed love; 4. 3. 28, 41
etc.

WIND, 'down the wind', see
DOWN; 3. 3. 264

WINK, close the eye; 4. 2. 78

WISE, in one's right mind, sane (O.E.D. 4, citing); 4. 1. 234

WIT, understanding, cleverness (=mother wit); 1. 1. 136; 2. 1. 129, 132; 2. 3. 361, 364, 365; 3. 3. 468; 3. 4. 21 etc.

WITTY, clever, wise; 2. 1. 131

WOMANED, accompanied by a woman; 3. 4. 199

WRANGLE, dispute angrily; 3. 4. 148

WRETCH, 'term of playful depreciation' (O.E.D.); 3. 3. 91

WRIT, 'Holy Writ'=Scripture; 3. 3. 326

WROUGHT, worked upon, moved; 5. 2. 347

YAWN, gape; 5. 2. 104

YOKED, (fig.) married (see note); 4. 1. 66

ZOUNDS, An oath (=God's wounds, i.e. Christ's wounds); 1. 1. 87, etc.